PEOPLE WITH DISABILITIES

To what extent are people with disabilities included in economic, political, and social life? People with disabilities have faced a long history of exclusion, stigma, and discrimination, but they have made impressive gains in the past several decades. These gains include the passage of major civil rights legislation and the adoption of the 2006 UN Convention on the Rights of Persons with Disabilities. This book provides an overview of the progress and continuing disparities faced by people with disabilities around the world, reviewing hundreds of studies and presenting new evidence from analyses of surveys and interviews with disability leaders. It shows the connections among economic, political, and social inclusion, and how the experience of disability can vary by gender, race, and ethnicity. It takes a multidisciplinary approach, drawing on theoretical models and research in economics, political science, psychology, disability studies, law, and sociology.

Lisa Schur is an Associate Professor in the School of Management and Labor Relations at Rutgers University. Her research focuses on disability, employment, corporate culture, and political participation, particularly nonstandard work arrangements among people with disabilities and the effects of disability and employment on their political participation. Dr. Schur is a leading expert on political participation among people with disabilities, having authored or co-authored many articles in this area.

Douglas Kruse is a Professor in the School of Management and Labor Relations at Rutgers University and a Research Associate at the National Bureau of Economic Research. His research has focused on the employment and earnings effects of disability, as well as the causes, consequences, and implications of employee ownership and profit sharing. He has authored, co-authored, or edited ten books. He served on the President's Committee on Employment of People with Disabilities and New Jersey's State Rehabilitation Council and is an editor of the *British Journal of Industrial Relations*.

Peter Blanck is a University Professor and Chairman of the Burton Blatt Institute at Syracuse University. He is Chairman of the Global Universal Design Commission and a founding member of Raising the Floor, U.S. Blanck's recent books include *Disability Civil Rights Law and Policy* (with E. Hill, C. Siegal, and M. Waterstone, 2009); *Race, Ethnicity, and Disability: Veterans and Benefits in Post–Civil War America* (with L. Logue, 2010); and *Legal Rights of Persons with Disabilities: An Analysis of Federal Law* (with B. Goldstein and W. Myhill, 2013).

CAMBRIDGE DISABILITY LAW AND POLICY SERIES

Edited by Peter Blanck and Robin Paul Malloy

The Disability Law and Policy series examines these topics in interdisciplinary and comparative terms. The books in the series reflect the diversity of definitions, causes, and consequences of discrimination against persons with disabilities while illuminating fundamental themes that unite countries in their pursuit of human rights laws and policies to improve the social and economic status of persons with disabilities. The series contains historical, contemporary, and comparative scholarship crucial to identifying individual, organizational, cultural, attitudinal, and legal themes necessary for the advancement of disability law and policy.

The book topics covered in the series also are reflective of the new moral and political commitment by countries throughout the world toward equal opportunity for persons with disabilities in such areas as employment, housing, transportation, rehabilitation, and individual human rights. The series will thus play a significant role in informing policy makers, researchers, and citizens of issues central to disability rights and disability antidiscrimination policies. The series grounds the future of disability law and policy as a vehicle for ensuring that those living with disabilities participate as equal citizens of the world.

Books in the Series:

Ruth Colker, *When Is Separate Unequal? A Disability Perspective*, 2009

Larry M. Logue and Peter Blanck, *Race, Ethnicity, and Disability: Veterans and Benefits in Post–Civil War America*, 2010

Lisa Vanhala, *Making Rights a Reality? Disability Rights Activists and Legal Mobilization*, 2010

Alicia Ouellette, *Bioethics and Disability: Toward a Disability-Conscious Bioethics*, 2011

Eilionoir Flynn, *From Rhetoric to Action: Implementing the UN Convention on the Rights of Persons with Disabilities*, 2011

Isabel Karpin and Kristin Savell, *Perfecting Pregnancy: Law, Disability, and the Future of Reproduction*, 2012

Arie Rimmerman, *Social Inclusion of People with Disabilities: National and International Perspectives*, 2012

Andrew Power, Janet E. Lord, and Allison S. deFranco, *Active Citizenship and Disability: Implementing the Personalisation of Support for Persons with Disabilities*, 2012

Lisa Schur, Douglas Kruse, and Peter Blanck, *People with Disabilities: Sidelined or Mainstreamed?*, 2013

Eliza Varney, *Disability and Information Technology: A Comparative Study in Media Regulation*, 2013

PEOPLE WITH DISABILITIES

Sidelined or Mainstreamed?

Lisa Schur

Rutgers University

Douglas Kruse

Rutgers University

Peter Blanck

Syracuse University

CAMBRIDGE
UNIVERSITY PRESS

32 Avenue of the Americas, New York NY 10013-2473, USA

Cambridge University Press is part of the University of Cambridge.

It furthers the University's mission by disseminating knowledge in the pursuit of
education, learning and research at the highest international levels of excellence.

www.cambridge.org
Information on this title: www.cambridge.org/9781107000476

© Lisa Schur, Douglas Kruse, and Peter Blanck 2013

First published 2013

A catalogue record for this publication is available from the British Library

Library of Congress Cataloguing in Publication data
Schur, Lisa, 1957–
   People with disabilities : sidelined or mainstreamed? / Lisa Schur, Rutgers University,
   Douglas Kruse, Rutgers University, Peter Blanck, Syracuse University.
      pages   cm. – (Cambridge disability law and policy series)
   Includes bibliographical references and index.
   ISBN 978-1-107-00047-6 (hardback)
   1. People with disabilities – Psychology.   2. Disabilities – Social aspects.
   3. Social medicine.   I. Kruse, Douglas.   II. Blanck, Peter David, 1957–   III. Title.
   RC451.4.H35S38   2013
   362.2–dc23   2012049893

ISBN 978-1-107-00047-6 Hardback

*Lisa and Doug dedicate this book to their parents: Janet Schur,
Ruth and Lowen Kruse, and the memory of Robert Schur.
Our parents have lived the values of inclusion and continue to teach
us those values.
As always for Peter, all roads lead to Wendy.*

Contents

Contents

Contents

Contents

Preface and Acknowledgments

People with disabilities must often contend with policy making and research based on ill-informed and paternalistic assumptions about their perspectives and needs. This has led to an important principle in the disability community: people with disabilities should be included in the design, implementation, and evaluation of all aspects of disability-related policy making and research. The shorthand phrase for this principle is "Nothing about us without us" (e.g., Charlton 1998). We support this perspective and want to briefly describe our own experience and history with disability issues that led to the writing of this book.

The specific concern of Lisa Schur and Doug Kruse with disability originated in 1990 when the car in which they were riding was struck by a drunk driver. As a result of the crash, Doug sustained a spinal cord injury and underwent months in a rehabilitation hospital, with Lisa, his wife and colleague, actively participating in the rehabilitation process. Their experiences in coping with disability-related problems, which coincidentally began in the year the Americans with Disabilities Act (ADA) was passed, opened their eyes to many of the social, political, economic, legal, and medical issues raised by disability. Lisa wrote her dissertation on disability and political participation, and went on to join the Rutgers faculty and conduct further research on the relationship of disability to political participation, ADA coverage, alternative work arrangements, corporate culture, and employment barriers.

Rutgers was very accommodating to Doug on his return to the faculty as a wheelchair user in 1990; there, he incorporated disability into his economic research by examining computer skills, return to work, employment trends, and employee attitudes and experiences.

Lisa and Doug have had a valued and productive collaboration with Peter Blanck for more than 15 years, and all have been fortunate to work with Meera Adya, Mason Ameri, Monroe Berkowitz, Joseph Blasi, David Braddock, Susanne Bruyere, Jim Dickson, Kyongji Han, Andrea Kim, Alan Krueger, Sophie Mitra, Michael Morris, William Myhill, Lisa Nishii, Arie Rimmerman, Kay Schriner, and Todd Shields, among others. This book summarizes and builds on our prior research, some of which was funded by the National Council on Disability, National Institute on Disability and Rehabilitation Research, Office of Disability Employment Policy, Social Security Administration, and New Jersey Developmental Disabilities Council (although none of these organizations bears any responsibility for the views and conclusions expressed here). The research has received valuable feedback from conference participants at the Society for Disability Studies, American Political Science Association, Labor and Employment Relations Association, National Bureau of Economic Research, and Society for Industrial and Organizational Psychology, and from journal reviewers and editors.

We greatly appreciate the disability leaders and scholars who were interviewed for this book. Their perspectives helped ground and enrich the findings and provided new insights. Our understanding of the issues was also enhanced by a discussion with United Kingdom disability lawyers and policy experts arranged by Robin Allen QC, Head of Chambers at Cloisters. Over the years we have met and learned from many people who have worked for the inclusion of people with disabilities. We would like to particularly acknowledge the contributions and memories of Justin Dart, Fred Fay, and Paul Steven Miller.

The work of Lisa and Doug was aided by sabbaticals and ongoing support from the Rutgers School of Management and Labor Relations, including Dean Sue Schurman; former deans John Burton, Barbara

Lee, and David Finegold; Associate Dean David Lepak; department chairs Adrienne Eaton and Patrick McKay; and librarians Donna Schulman and Eugene McElroy. Useful comments and indexing were provided by Mason Ameri. Peter's participation was supported in part by the funders mentioned earlier, in particular the National Institute on Disability and Rehabilitation Research, as well as Syracuse University. Additional information on grant support can be found at the Burton Blatt Institute Web site, bbi.syr.edu.

Lisa and Doug have received tremendous support and love from their families: Janet Schur; Lowen and Ruth Kruse; Michelle, Madison, and Rita Link; and Jorika, Barry, Lauren, and Kiera Stockwell. To our nieces, Madison, Lauren, and Kiera: we look forward to seeing where your curiosity and brilliance take you!

1

Introduction

A. CHANGING VIEWS OF DISABILITY

People with disabilities have a long history of exclusion. In Babylon and ancient Greece, for example, children born with disabilities were often considered portents of evil or signs that their parents had displeased the gods, and infanticide was practiced against babies with congenital impairments in ancient Athens and Sparta (Rimmerman 2013: 13). In Europe in the Middle Ages, disabilities were often viewed as caused by the devil or demons, or as a punishment from God – a belief shared by early Puritans in America (Braddock and Parish 2001: 15, 17, 25).

People with disabilities have also been considered sources of ridicule and entertainment. For example, people of short stature were used as court jesters in ancient China and in the palaces of pharaohs in ancient Egypt. Slaves of short stature and slaves with intellectual disabilities were "kept" as fools by the wealthy during the Roman Empire and in Europe during the Middle Ages, while people with obvious physical or intellectual disabilities were frequently displayed as "monsters" in markets for profit during the Middle Ages and later in "freak shows" during the nineteenth and early twentieth centuries (Braddock and Parish 2001: 16; Chemers 2006; Bogdan 2009).

Along with provoking fear and providing entertainment, people with disabilities have often been subjects of pity and charity; for example, while some passages in the Old Testament portray disability as caused by divine retribution, other passages contain admonitions to be kind to people with disabilities (Rimmerman 2013: 11–12), and in ancient Athens (despite the practice of infanticide against babies with congenital disabilities) food was provided to people who developed disabilities and demonstrated economic need and the inability to work (Braddock and Parish 2001: 14, 16). Charity helped motivate the construction of early residential institutions for people with disabilities in the Arab world and Europe in the Middle Ages, such as hospices and schools for blind and deaf people (Braddock and Parish 2001: 17, 19–20; Hudson 2006: 855). However, the tremendous growth of mental asylums and other residential institutions in Europe and the United States in the eighteenth and nineteenth centuries often resulted in abusive and overcrowded conditions, and was fed by a desire to avoid people with disabilities and segregate them from mainstream society. Exclusion increased with the eugenics movement in the late 1800s and early 1900s. During this period people with disabilities were often portrayed as social deviants and menaces to society; many were prohibited from getting married and were sterilized (Trent 2006: 1501; Carey 2009: 52–82; Rimmerman 2013:18–19). This movement reached its most extreme form in Nazi Germany in the 1930s and 1940s when more than seventy thousand people with disabilities were murdered (Shakespeare 2006: 1136).

Along with this medley of responses – fear, ridicule, pity, avoidance, and loathing – people with disabilities have sometimes been treated with great respect or even exalted. In some ancient Arab societies, mental disabilities were sometimes seen as divinely inspired, while some ancient Chinese texts claimed that people with disabilities were more likely than others to reach spiritual transcendence, and there are thousand-year-old records in Korea of blind people being viewed as having supernatural power (Braddock and Parish 2001: 16; Kim 2006: 859). Soldiers with disabilities caused by war injuries have been honored and given pensions in many societies, dating back to ancient Greece (D. Cohen 2006). Nevertheless, throughout history people with disabilities have been much more likely to experience stigma and exclusion.

Over the past forty years, there has been a widespread shift in attitudes and policies toward people with disabilities, driven by the rise of the disability rights movement (Shapiro 1993; Scotch 2001; Barnartt and Scotch 2001; Blanck 2004; Longmore 2009; Nielsen 2012). This movement has fought for equal rights and full access and inclusion of people with disabilities around the world. It has led to the development of the "social model" of disability (reviewed later in the chapter) and the idea that the obstacles faced by people with disabilities are caused largely by society, not by individual impairments.

This widespread shift has resulted in the adoption of important legislation and policy initiatives. A number of countries have enacted civil rights protections for people with disabilities, such as the 1990 Americans with Disabilities Act in the United States, the 1990 Law of the People's Republic of China on the Protection of Disabled Persons, the 1992 Disability Discrimination Act in Australia, the 1995 Disability Discrimination Act in the United Kingdom, the 1998 Employment Equity Act in South Africa, and the 1998 Equal Rights for People with Disabilities Law in Israel. An important initiative took place in 2006 when the United Nations adopted the UN Convention on the Rights of Persons with Disabilities, which has now been signed by 153 countries. Legislative protections and initiatives will be discussed in Chapter 4.

The growth of the disability rights movement, and the passage of civil rights laws and the UN Convention, promote a new approach to disability – one based on rights, dignity, respect, and participation, rather than fear, pity, and exclusion. The question remains, however, to what extent these efforts have resulted in the full inclusion of people with disabilities in mainstream society. What are the current trends and prospects for greater inclusion?

B. PLAN OF THE BOOK

The broad purpose of this book is to provide an overview of the economic, political, and social conditions of people with disabilities around
the world and to discuss the barriers to and opportunities for greater
inclusion that they face. We analyze a wide range of evidence from
across the social sciences, including economics, political science, psychology, disability studies, law, and sociology. The disability literature
has increased greatly in the past few decades – there are now literally
thousands of publications; clearly, we cannot provide a comprehensive
review of the entire vast literature. We have nonetheless searched widely
for the important publications and evidence in this area, and will also
present new findings from our analysis of U.S. datasets and interviews,
in order to make the assessment as full and up to date as possible.

In the remainder of Chapter 1 we consider how to conceptualize
disability by discussing the major models: "medical," "social," and
"universalist." We then review the thorny issues involved in measuring
disability, along with recent estimates indicating that about one-sixth
of the world's population have disabilities.

Chapter 2 assesses the economic status of people with disabilities,
focusing on their generally low income and employment levels and
high poverty rates. We discuss the reasons for their low employment
rates, distinguishing between factors that affect labor supply (the willingness of people to participate in the labor market) and those that
affect labor demand (employers' willingness to offer jobs to people
with disabilities). We end the chapter by looking at the bad news and
good news in current labor market trends that affect the prospects for
increased employment among people with disabilities.

Chapter 3 delves more deeply into the critical area of employment.
We first explore the issue of alternative work arrangements, including
the growing use of technology for telecommuting and work-related
online education and training, along with part-time, temporary, and
flexible schedules that better meet the needs of many people with

disabilities, but also have certain drawbacks. We then review evidence on pay, job characteristics, and worker attitudes, documenting a number of areas where workers with disabilities fare worse than do otherwise similar workers without disabilities. We discuss theories that help explain these disparities, including models of discrimination. This leads to a discussion of how corporate culture may shape policies and attitudes that affect experiences and opportunities for job applicants and employees with disabilities. The chapter concludes with a review of workplace accommodations and a discussion of policies that may promote better employment outcomes for people with disabilities.

In Chapter 4 we turn to political inclusion. We first examine the factors underlying disability activism, and then explore voter turnout and political participation in general among people with disabilities. We conclude by reviewing evidence on political interest and views of people with disabilities, providing insights into how their greater political participation might affect the formation of public policies.

Chapter 5 focuses on social inclusion among people with disabilities, starting with factors that are linked to isolation – stigma, institutionalization, low marriage rates, higher likelihoods of living alone, and transportation difficulties. We then review the value of computer and Internet access and the lower levels of access to these technologies among people with disabilities. Looking more broadly at technology and the physical environment, we discuss the value of universal design, which can increase the accessibility of buildings, products, and services for people of all abilities. Finally, we turn to the important topic of education, documenting the generally lower educational levels among people with disabilities, the strong benefits education can provide, and efforts to create more inclusive educational programs.

In Chapter 6 we explore how the experience of disability may differ by gender, race, and ethnicity. For example, disability status may combine with gender or minority status to create a "double handicap" or even "triple handicap," leading to especially negative outcomes for women and members of disadvantaged minority groups. This includes a discussion of how disability may interact with traditional gender expectations in many societies and how it may create greater obstacles for members of disadvantaged racial and ethnic minority groups, who already face barriers and disparities related to stigma and prejudice.

Finally, in Chapter 7 we provide an overview of the progress and prospects for the full inclusion of people with disabilities. We do so, first, by reviewing the key points from the evidence in Chapters 1–6 along with an overview of implementation of the UN Convention and, second, by providing views from the disability community with a focus on 21 original interviews with disability leaders and scholars from the United States and the United Kingdom. The results from the qualitative interviews complement the findings from other studies and provide valuable perspectives on how people with disabilities may gain greater inclusion in the coming decades.

A note on language: there is a debate in the disability community over whether it is preferable to use the term "disabled" or to use "person-first" language. An argument for "person-first" language (saying "persons with disabilities" instead of "disabled people") is that it makes it clear that disability may be an aspect of a person's identity without being the defining trait, characteristic, or status (e.g., Perske 1988; Blaska 1993; Kailes 1985; Lynch et al. 1994). In this view, using the word "disabled" or placing the name of the medical condition before the word "person" or "people" places undue weight on people's specific impairments and detracts from their humanity. As Joan Blaska writes:

> The philosophy of using person first language demonstrates respect for people with disabilities by referring to them first as individuals, and then referring to their disability when it is needed. This philosophy demonstrates respect by emphasizing what people can do by focusing on their ability rather than their disability and by distinguishing the person from the disability. (Blaska 1993: 27)

This approach was developed in the 1970s and adopted by the Association for Persons with Severe Handicaps (Manus 1975; Bailey

1991). Since that time, many disability groups and advocacy organizations have attempted to educate the public regarding person-first language, and some academic journals and organizations (such as the American Psychological Association) now require person-first language in their publications (Olkin 2002). The UN Convention on the Rights of Persons with Disabilities uses this approach.

An opposing view is that person-first language creates the impression that disability is an individual property of a person rather than the creation of external societal factors that "disable" a person: "The British civil rights movement has rejected the term 'people with disabilities', as it implies that the disabling effect rests within the individual person rather than from society" (Clark and Marsh 2002). This distinction between the individual property of impairment and the social property of disability is central to the social model. The term "disabled people" is also widely used by international organizations such as Disabled Peoples' International.

Some people and groups have rejected person-first language for deafness, blindness, and autism. Those who identify with Deaf culture, for example, largely reject person-first language, along with the terms "disabled" and "disability", since Deaf people (with a capital "D") see themselves as a linguistic minority and being Deaf as a source of identity and pride (Clark and Marsh 2002; Padden and Humphries 2006). Vaughn, a scholar and advocate for the blind, maintains that person-first language may call "attention to a person as having some type of 'marred identity'" (Vaughn 2009), while Sinclair argues that saying "person with autism" creates an overly negative view of autism and suggests that the person can be separated from the condition.[1]

---

[1] autismmythbusters.com/general-public/autistic-vs-people-with-autism/jim-sinclair-why-i-dislike-person-first-language/ (accessed May 3, 2012). The U.S. National Federation for the Blind passed a resolution in 1993 dismissing the idea that "person" must come before "blind," saying that it is "overly defensive" and "implies shame instead of true equality." nfb.org/images/nfb/publications/bm/bm09/bm0903/bm090308.htm (accessed May 3, 2012).

We recognize that person-first language is not universally accepted and agree with many of the points of those who question or reject it. In this book, we describe many ways in which people with impairments become "disabled" by inaccessible environments and negative attitudes. Nevertheless, we have to choose consistent terminology for use throughout this book, and as U.S. scholars we will follow the current and predominant convention in the U.S. disability community by using person-first language – emphasizing that disability is not the defining aspect but only part of an individual's identity. The language debate has been divisive in the past, which disability advocate Irving Zola has said may not only "damage the unity so necessary to the cause of disability rights but also fail to see the forest for the trees. Our struggle is necessary because we live in a society which devalues, discriminates against and disparages people with disabilities" (Zola 1993: 171). We hope that our use of person-first language will not distract anyone reading our presentation and analysis of evidence on ways to increase the societal inclusion of people with disabilities.

C. MODELS OF DISABILITY

What do we mean by "disability"? How do we understand the complex relationship between individual impairments and environments? Three basic models have addressed these questions.[2]

---

[2] While there are clear distinctions among these models, they are not necessarily mutually exclusive. As will be seen, the World Health Organization proposes a "bio-psycho-social" model that combines elements of the medical and social models. Different government policies can reflect different models; for example, determination of disability benefits may rely on the medical model, while antidiscrimination laws may reflect the social model. A single law or policy can also contain elements of several models; for example, a person can be considered to have a disability under the Americans with Disabilities Act based on a physical or mental impairment (the medical model) or on how one is regarded by others (the social model).

Introduction

1. Medical Model

The traditional view of disability is based on the medical model, which focuses on functional impairments and health conditions. According to the medical model, disability is located within individuals and has little or no relation to the environment. The emphasis is on cure, without explicit awareness that many problems faced by people with disabilities are caused by social factors such as discrimination. The medical model is consistent with the value of individualism – it is up to the individual with a disability to "overcome" disability through hard work, determination, and a "positive attitude." This is reflected in many books, news stories, movies, and television programs in which people with disabilities heroically overcome adversity and self-pity and eventually show the "triumph of the human spirit" over their disabilities (Shapiro 1993).

2. Social Model

The disability rights movement has developed, and been largely based on, the social model, which views disability as caused by society.[3] People with disabilities are considered a distinct minority group with a shared experience of oppression. A defining statement of this model was articulated in 1976 by a British group called the Union of the Physically Impaired Against Segregation (UPIAS):

> In our view it is society which disables physically impaired people. Disability is something imposed on top of our impairments by the way we are unnecessarily isolated and excluded from full participation in society. Disabled people are therefore an oppressed group in society. (Quoted in Barnes and Mercer 2010: 31)

[3] For a more detailed description of the social model, see Barnes and Mercer (2010: 29–36).

A key aspect of the social model is the distinction made between "impairment," which is an aspect of an individual, and "disability," which is caused by social arrangements and thus subject to change through political means. Disability is not located within the individual (as maintained by the medical model), but in the interaction between an individual and his or her environment. According to this model, impairment alone is not disabling. Society creates disabilities by isolating, excluding, and stigmatizing people who have physical or mental impairments. For example, not being able to enter a building or not being able to enter it through the main entrance (e.g., through a back door) sends the message that people with disabilities are second-class citizens.

For advocates of the social model, the distinction between impairment and disability is fundamental because it identifies the source of discrimination and stigma, and reveals the appropriate targets for political action. Two strengths of the social model are that it identifies a political strategy – barrier removal – and helps empower people with disabilities by replacing a traditional focus on individual deficits with an understanding of social oppression (Shakespeare 2006: 30). The social model has been central to the development of the disability rights movement and has motivated generations of activists around the world:

> It is about the victim refusing the label, and instead focusing attention on the structural causes of victimization. It is about the subversion of stigma: taking a negative appellation and converting it into a badge of pride. (Shakespeare 1993: 253).

Using the social model, stigmatized and powerless people can transform the negative identity attached to disability and claim it in a positive way to challenge traditional power relations:

> Self-organization and direct action challenge prevailing stereotypes of powerlessness and objectification. This is important in the formation of disabled people's own identity, just as it is in breaking

down patterns of prejudice and discrimination. In making 'personal troubles' into 'public issues', disabled people are affirming the validity and importance of their own identity, rejecting both the victimizing tendencies of society at large, and their own socialization. (Shakespeare 1993: 263)

Despite its crucial impact, the social model has been criticized for marginalizing the experiences of particular groups of people with disabilities, such as women, gay men and lesbians, and people from minority ethnic groups, and for failing to recognize the importance of impairments in the experiences of those living with a disability (Shakespeare 2006; Dowse 2001). More broadly, Shakespeare, who had been an advocate of the social model, later criticized it for being overly simplistic. He questioned the distinction the social model makes between impairment and disability, and pointed out that it is not just the environment that causes disability: many disabilities are inherently associated with pain, fatigue, or other physical or mental difficulties, irrespective of social arrangements and attitudes. Similarly, Scotch and Schriner state:

Disability is associated with problems beyond discrimination and stigma. There are real aspects of disability that require social responses, and these characteristics shift over time, but they are nonetheless real. Many people with disabilities have problems in functioning that will not disappear even if prejudice and discrimination are eliminated (Scotch and Schriner 1997).

In other words, critics of the social model argue that it fails to acknowledge the profound impact impairments can have on individuals. Furthermore, the social model may make a rather crude distinction between impairment, which is medical, and disability, which is social. In real life, it is difficult to distinguish the impact of physical or mental impairments from the impact of disabilities caused by social barriers. What is important is the interaction between physical and social factors – recognizing that it is often impossible to separate the two.

Shakespeare also criticizes the social model for assuming people with disabilities are by definition oppressed. He claims that it is more accurate and valuable to look at whether people with disabilities experience oppression in specific situations. Different groups (and individuals within groups) may experience disability in different ways and have different issues to contend with. For example, many people with impairments may not identify themselves as having disabilities. This may be particularly true for older people who gradually develop limitations, but they may nonetheless become politically involved on issues related to their conditions or impairments.

3. Universalist Model

An alternative model has been developed that, in contrast to the social model, views impairments as existing on a continuum and does not separate the population into people with and without disabilities. One of the originators was Zola (1989), who observed that disability is not "fixed and dichotomous" but "fluid and continuous." This view underlies the closely related "universalist," "human variation," and "relational" models of disability (Scotch and Schriner 1997; Shakespeare 2006). Here we will use the term "universalist" in describing common elements of these models.[4]

The universalist model recognizes that across the life span (and environmental conditions) everyone experiences limitations and impairments – those who do not currently have disabilities may be referred to as "temporarily able-bodied" (Cherney 2009). This model is inclusive and applies to people who do not currently experience disability, so that political involvement on disability issues may be seen as having broader societal benefits. Disability is seen not as a minority issue, but

---

[4] See Shakespeare (2006: 9) for a discussion of the "family of social-contextual approaches to disability."

as a universal experience of humanity. It is a normal part of human variation – we all exist on a continuum of ability and disability, and most of us will experience disability at some point in our lives (Barnartt 2010: 2–13). Rather than seeing people with disabilities as a separate group in need of special protections, the universalist model emphasizes, for instance, the benefits of accommodations, universal design, and anti-discrimination laws for everyone. According to Thomas, the universalist approach has the advantage of "connecting with those people with impairments or chronic illnesses 'old and young', who do not identify as 'disabled' and 'refuse to recognize disabled signifiers in their own lives" (quoted in Barnes and Mercer 2010: 96). A universal approach recognizes commonalities among people without trivializing "impairment or the experience of disabled people" and aims "for justice in the distribution of resources and opportunities" (Shakespeare 2006: 64, 65).

People are diverse and have a wide range of responses to disability issues and experiences. In addition, the situations facing people with disabilities vary widely at different points in history and in different countries and regions around the world. Thus, different frameworks for understanding disability may be appropriate in different situations and may need to evolve over time. For example, the social model, which shifts the focus from individual impairments to society, may be the most effective way to unite people across disabilities and help mobilize them to fight for antidiscrimination and equal rights legislation, while the universalist model may be more effective after disability legislation is established and may help people with disabilities form coalitions with other groups to achieve greater economic and social equality.

Models are simplified descriptions of complex entities and processes and always provide incomplete pictures of reality. Clearly, no model of disability can capture the complete picture. Rather than seeking the one "best" or "right" model, it may be more valuable to recognize the strengths and limitations of different models for understanding disability, framing public policy, and motivating political action on disability issues.

D. MEASURING DISABILITY

1. Issues in Measuring Disability

Given the different models of disability, as well as the tremendous variety within and across medical conditions and the ways they interact with environments, it is no surprise that as an empirical matter measuring disability is difficult and subject to controversy:

> Definitions and methods for measuring disability vary across countries based on assumptions about human difference and disability and the importance given to the different aspects of disability – impairments, activity limitations and participation restriction, related health conditions, and environmental factors. (WHO/World Bank 2011: 209)[5]

Disability definitions also vary within countries. For instance, in the United States, state workers' compensation definitions of impairments and disability are different from federal definitions in programs such as Medicaid that help support health care benefits, and both are different from definitions used in the Individuals with Disabilities Education Act (IDEA) or the ADA.

The different definitions and methods can make it hard to analyze data, draw comparisons across and even within countries, and reach firm conclusions. For empirical purposes, the difficulties in measuring disability include the following:

1. Some surveys, particularly those in developing countries, collect data focused on a narrow set of impairments, which results in a low estimate of disability prevalence (WHO/World Bank 2011: 22). In addition, as mentioned, some estimates are based on who

---

[5] For an in-depth discussion of disability models and measurement, see Altman (2001), and for a presentation of a method to measure disability for different types of data needs see Altman et al. (2006).

is eligible for disability policies or programs, which is dependent on the legal or program rules for eligibility and will understate the total number of people with disabilities in a country. Surveys in developed countries are more likely to measure disability in a broader way that reflects the role of environmental factors and limitations in activities and participation.[6]

2. Measured prevalence rates fluctuate according to changing conceptions of what conditions constitute impairments or disabilities. For example, the new, 2013 version of the *Diagnostic Statistical Manual* (DSM V) modifies the definition of autism.

3. Even when surveys attempt to measure the same concept, different wording can lead to different prevalence rates; moreover, even with the same question wording, the response options may affect results (Banks et al. 2004, 2005). Changes in survey wording and administration, for example, contributed to the apparent decline in disability in France in the 1990s (Cambois et al. 2007).

4. The stigma and hidden nature or visibility of disability may influence the likelihood of reporting a disability or serious medical condition (Blanck 2001; Logue and Blanck 2010). Historically, for instance, mental health conditions have been particularly stigmatized and underreported. This is particularly likely to be true when the word "disability" is used in a survey question, because people may not self-identify as having a disability, which is why many disability surveys do not use that word. The idea that social and cultural norms matter in reporting a disability is given support by a Dutch study which found that respondents' reference groups influenced their likelihood of reporting a work disability, helping account for the fact that the self-reporting of work disability is higher in the Netherlands than in the United States (van Soest et al. 2011).

---

[6] Variance in disability estimates is explored by Altman and Gulley (2009), who find disability prevalence ranging from 13% to 37% using four different question sets on the same sample in Canada and the United States.

5. Similarly, the stigma of nonemployment may also influence the reporting of a disability or serious medical condition. There may be "justification bias" in survey responses as some respondents report a disability to justify their lack of employment or their receipt of disability benefits (Banks et al. 2004, 2005). A Canadian study that matched administrative medical data to survey responses found that nonemployed people were more likely to overreport medical conditions (e.g., high blood pressure) than were employed people (Baker et al. 2001).[7] If people become less likely to report a disability as they gain jobs even with no change in their impairments or medical conditions, reported trends in the employment of people with disabilities may be misleading. Some research, however, indicates that justification bias may be a problem in the United States but not in Europe, suggesting differences in social norms concerning work (e.g., Europeans are less likely than Americans to perceive stigma from not having a job) (Kapteyn et al. 2009).[8]

---

[7] See similar results on overreporting of disability among nonemployed workers in Kreider (1999) and Kreider and Pepper (2007). The macro-level evidence is not as clear: evidence from the United States and United Kingdom shows mixed results on the effect of the unemployment rate on reported medical conditions, leading Benitez-Silva et al. (2010) to conclude that the relationship between the business cycle and reports of general disability is very weak (although the relationship to work disability is positive, as noted later in the text). Some results indicate that people are more likely to report serious conditions when the employment rate is high, perhaps because they are less fearful of losing their jobs.

[8] Social norms also appear to be at work in the finding that Dutch respondents have a lower threshold in reporting work disability than do U.S. respondents (Kapteyn et al. 2007). Other research in the United States suggests that in reporting their disability status, applicants for Social Security Disability Insurance benefits generally appear to apply the rules that the program uses to determine eligibility, so there is no general bias in their self-reported disability status (although the awards process is "noisy," since about 20% of applicants who are awarded benefits do not appear to have a disability, and 60% of those who are denied benefits appear to have a disability) (Benitez-Silva et al. 2004).

6. Reporting a disability, particularly a mild disability, may be influenced by the availability of assistive and other technologies that reduce the likelihood that one's impairment limits daily activities. This appears to help explain a decline in reported disability among U.S. senior citizens (Schoeni et al. 2008; Aranovich et al. 2009).[9] With advances in mobile technologies that support education, independent living, and work, we may see further declines in previously claimed impairments (Blanck 2012).

7. There are particular problems associated with reporting a work disability – that is, an impairment or condition that specifically limits one's ability to work for pay. Reports may be influenced by the types of jobs available and workplace accessibility and accommodations: "For if people with disabilities have better access to work and more of them actually hold jobs, especially *good* jobs, they would no longer answer that they are limited in or unable to work 'due to their condition/disability'" (Kirchner 1996: 83).[10] Greater workplace accessibility and accommodations may even result in an apparent worsening of measured employment rates, if accommodated workers no longer report a work disability and there is a higher concentration of nonemployed people among those reporting a work disability. Despite the possibility of a general upward or downward bias in levels of reported work disability, Burkhauser (2002) found that the U.S. trend in self-reported work disability over the 1990s appears to match the trend using other disability measures.

8. Reports of work disability appear to be especially sensitive to the economy and the availability of disability income. Reports of work

---

[9] Also, greater use of assistive technology by more highly educated seniors helps explain how they cope better with disability (Cutler et al. 2009).

[10] Similarly, Benitez-Silva et al. (2010: 488) note that "[w]ork disability is a socially evolving concept, related to how society and employers accommodate the needs of individuals with certain conditions, including availability of part-time work and possible incentives to employer hiring or re-hiring of individuals with a disability."

disability increase when the unemployment rate goes up, unlike reports of general disability (not necessarily work-limiting) which are influenced more by underlying health conditions (Benitez-Silva et al. 2010). In addition, the incentive to report a disability may be influenced by the rules governing eligibility for disability benefit programs.[11]

9. Finally, a number of technical issues create problems in surveying people with disabilities. These issues include not only the screener questions used to establish disability, but also the survey mode and degree of accessibility (e.g., a random-digit-dialed phone survey will underrepresent people who are deaf or otherwise have difficulty in using a telephone), whether proxies are needed and how responses may be affected (e.g., a person with a disability and the proxy responding for him or her may disagree on whether the person has a disability),[12] question wording (e.g., the questions and answer options must be easily understood by people of all education levels and different cognitive abilities), question context (e.g., people may be more willing to reveal impairments in a survey with many health questions), and interviewer training to ensure sensitivity and respect for all respondents (Kirchner 2003; Kroll et al. 2006; Ballou and Markesich 2009).

Despite these difficulties in measuring disability, it is critically important to do so, given the need to monitor the status of people with

---

[11] Autor (2011) found that the number of U.S. Social Security Disability Insurance participants increased over the past 30 years due to changes in program eligibility requirements and declining earnings and employment opportunities for workers with low levels of education, rather than to an increase in disabling conditions. Economic shifts and the availability of disability income may have increased self-reported disability.

[12] Todorov and Kirchner (2000) found that proxy respondents underreported disabilities for people aged 18–64 but overreported disabilities for those aged 65 or older, concluding that the use of proxies introduces systematic biases in disability estimates.

disabilities and the effects of disability legislation and policy initiatives.[13] The efforts to measure disability have become more sophisticated over the past two decades:

> Countries are increasingly switching to a continuum approach to measurement, where estimates of prevalence of disability – and functioning – are derived from assessing levels of disability in multiple domains. Estimates vary according to where the thresholds on the continuum of disability are set, and the way environmental influences are taken into account. (WHO/World Bank 2011: 22).

While a wide range of approaches have been used across countries, the World Health Organization (WHO) has attempted to standardize and improve disability statistics based on the International Classification of Functioning, Disability, and Health (ICF).[14] The WHO promotes a "bio-psycho-social model" that combines elements of the medical and social models, in which disability is conceptualized as an interaction between an individual's health conditions and contextual factors (environmental and personal). The ICF distinguishes among three areas of functioning: impairments (e.g., paralysis or blindness), activity limitations (e.g., difficulty in walking or eating), and participation restrictions (e.g., difficulty in employment or transportation) (WHO/World Bank 2011: 5). Disability is the umbrella term that covers difficulty in any or all of these three areas of functioning. This approach is not without controversy. Barnes and Mercer (2010: 36–41) argue that the ICF approach "ignores the extent to which identifying and labeling deviations as illness or impairment are social processes, liable to vary between social groups and societies and over time," and that it "lacks a coherent theory of social action as a new basis for understanding disability" (2010: 38–39). They also point out that one of the architects

---

[13] See Houtenville et al. (2009) on the value of disability statistics and 10 papers exploring data issues and options for improvement.

[14] See Rimmerman (2013: 24–31) for a discussion of the evolution of models of disability that led to the ICF.

of the ICF notes that it does not lead to a clear definition of disability and that "different prevalence rates flow from different decisions.... [T]hese decisions cannot be made conceptually or scientifically, they are political" (quoted in Barnes and Mercer 2010: 40).

At least five organizations are working to standardize disability statistics based on the ICF (WHO/World Bank 2011: 281–285). The most prominent is the United Nation's Washington Group on Disability Statistics, which created six questions for use on disability surveys, measuring difficulties in functioning in six domains (seeing, hearing, mobility, cognition, self-care, and communication) (Madans et al. 2011). The Washington Group has assisted developing countries in building the capacity for data collection on disability and has advised them on the use of surveys to monitor the UN Convention on the Rights of Persons with Disabilities (WHO/World Bank 2011: 281–285).[15]

2. Estimates of Disability

Two major efforts to measure disability across countries in a consistent way have been made by the World Health Organization, based on the World Health Survey and the Global Burden of Disease survey.[16] The World Health Survey, conducted in 2002–2004 in 59 countries, measures level of difficulty in eight domains of functioning – affect, cognition, interpersonal relationships, mobility, pain, sleep and energy,

---

[15] For a review of issues in measuring disability and proposals to improve the measurement, see Houtenville et al. (2009). For a review of the development of the disability questions used by the U.S. Census Bureau since 2008, see Hale (2008).

[16] The Organisation for Economic Co-operation and Development (OECD) provides estimates of disability prevalence among 27 member countries, using country-specific surveys that employ different definitions and measures of disability. The overall estimated prevalence of disability among working-age people (aged 20–64) across the 27 countries is 14%. The lowest rates are in Korea (6%) and Mexico (7%), and the highest rates are in Estonia (23%) and Hungary (22%) (OECD 2010: 22).

self-care, and vision – and the results are used to create a composite disability score.[17] As illustrated in Figure 1.1, across the 59 countries 15.6% of adults aged 18 or older were estimated to have disabilities based on significant difficulties with functioning in their daily lives. The figure was higher in low-income countries (18.0%) than in high-income countries (11.8%), and was higher among rural residents than urban residents and among poorer people than richer people (WHO/World Bank 2011: 28).[18] The disability rate was estimated to be highest in Swaziland (35.9%), Morocco (32.0%), and Bangladesh (31.9%) and lowest in Ireland (4.3%), Norway (4.3%), and Malaysia (4.5%) (WHO/World Bank 2011: 271–276). In addition, 2.2% of adults around the globe, or 92 million people, were estimated to have "very significant" difficulties with functioning.

The second survey used across a large number of countries – the Global Burden of Disease survey – gathered more detailed data on more than 130 health conditions and limitations in functioning, as well as measures of disability among children, so the estimated total number of people with disabilities is higher than that indicated by the World Health Survey. As also shown in Figure 1.1, the Global Burden of Disease survey estimates a 19.4% rate of disability for those aged 15 or older and 5.1% for those under age 15. Across all ages, the 2004 survey estimates that 15.3% of the world's population had a moderate

---

[17] Individuals were asked to report the degree of difficulty in each domain, ranging from "no difficulty" to "extreme difficulty," and the scores were combined to create a scale from 9 (no disability) to 100 (complete disability). To divide the individuals into those with and without disability, the threshold score of 40 was used, representing the average score of those who expressed "extreme difficulty" in at least one domain or had chronic diseases such as arthritis, angina, asthma, diabetes, and depression. The threshold for "very significant" disabilities was a score of 50, representing extreme difficulty with functioning in three or more of the domains.

[18] The higher rate of disability in rural areas relative to urban areas may be related to lower levels of economic and social services, such as in South Africa, where blacks were segregated in impoverished areas under apartheid (Emmett and Alant 2006: 456).

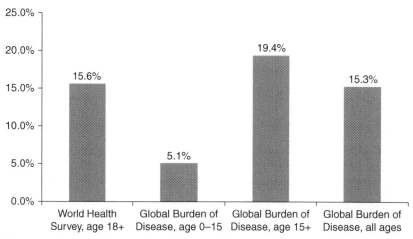

Figure 1.1. Disability prevalence from global surveys, 2004.

or severe disability, and 2.9% had a severe disability (WHO/World Bank 2011: 29).[19]

Therefore, on the basis of these surveys, the best estimates are that about one-sixth of people have disabilities around the world. Applying the survey estimates to the 2010 world population, somewhere between 785 and 975 million adults have disabilities, and including children brings the upper number to 1.056 billion (WHO/World Bank 2011: 29). As noted by the World Health Organization and World Bank, while these prevalence estimates "draw on the best available global data sets, they are not definitive estimates.... Disability prevalence is the result of a complex and dynamic relationship between health conditions and contextual factors, both personal and environmental" (2011: 31–32).

In the United States, the Census Bureau currently measures disability using six questions to capture four types of impairments (seeing, hearing, cognitive, and mobility) and two types of activity limitations

[19] Severe disability in this survey is measured by conditions: "the equivalent of disability inferred for conditions such as quadriplegia, severe depression, or blindness" (WHO/World Bank 2011: 29).

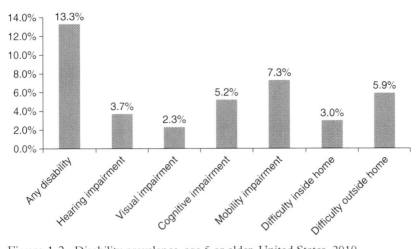

Figure 1.2. Disability prevalence, age 5 or older, United States, 2010.

(self-care inside the home and going outside the home alone). Across all Americans aged 5 or older in 2010, 13.3%, or 38.4 million have a disability as defined by one of these six impairments or activity limitations, based on the Census Bureau's American Community Survey.[20] As with the global data, the prevalence increases with age: the disability rate is 5.3% (2.8 million) among those aged 5–17, 10.2% (19.9 million) among those aged 18–64, and 38.6% (15.6 million) among those aged 65 or older.

Figure 1.2 shows the breakdown by question, indicating that mobility impairments are the most common type of disability (7.3% of the population), followed by disability in going outside the home alone (5.9%) and cognitive impairments (5.2%). Note that many people responded yes to more than one question, so there is overlap among these categories.

---

[20] These figures are based on analysis of the 2010 American Community Survey by the authors, with a representative sample of more than 3 million respondents. The figures include people living in the community and those living in institutional or noninstitutional group quarters.

These six questions may understate disability prevalence in the United States. They may not fully capture mental illnesses, such as bipolar disorder or depression, or conditions like diabetes or cancer. They also do not capture a significant number of people who report work disabilities (having a physical or mental condition that limits the kind or amount of work they can do) or who have qualified for government disability income (Burkhauser et al. 2011; Burkhauser, et al. forthcoming). A more expansive set of disability questions in the 2010 Survey of Income and Program Participation produces an estimate that 19%, or 57 million, of Americans have disabilities across all ages (Brault 2012), while findings from the 2001–2005 National Health Institute Survey indicate that 30%, or 62 million, of adult Americans have difficulty with basic actions (movement, sensory, cognitive, or emotional difficulties) (Altman and Bernstein 2008).

The prevalence of disability is likely to increase. One strong contributing factor is the aging population: "Despite differences between developing and developed nations, median ages are projected to increase markedly in all countries" (WHO/World Bank 2011: 35). Older people are more likely to have disabilities than younger people, as already noted; in addition, an increased lifespan leads to an increase in the expected number of years of living with a disability (Klijs et al. 2011).

For example, projections in Australia indicate a 70% increase in the number of older people with profound disability over the 2006–2031 period (Giles et al. 2003). While the overall rate of disability will be increased by the higher proportion of the population who are elderly, this may be mitigated somewhat by a declining rate of disability among senior citizens. A declining disability rate among senior citizens in the United States is tied in part to advances in medical care and to increased access to assistive technologies – such technologies can help compensate for physical and mental limitations and appear to lessen reports of disability among senior citizens (Schoeni et al. 2008; Martin et al. 2010).

The future rate of disability will also be strongly influenced by trends in medical conditions and illnesses. On a global basis, the continuing spread of HIV/AIDS is likely to be the leading cause of burden of disease by 2015 in middle- and low-income countries and a major contributor to disability and mortality by 2030 (Mathers and Loncar 2006). The risk of death for children under age 5 is expected to fall, so there will be a shift in the distribution of deaths from younger to older people (Mathers and Loncar 2006). The increasing rate of obesity in the United States is likely to increase the incidence of diabetes and other conditions that lead to disability (Sturm et al. 2004). The disability rate may be mitigated in the United States by a declining rate of smoking (Martin et al. 2010), although smoking-related disease and deaths are expected to rise globally (Mathers and Loncar 2006).

The prevalence of disability will also be influenced by trends in how work is performed. Industrial accidents are a major contributor to disability.[21] Declining rates of workplace injury within industries, along with declining employment in high-injury manufacturing industries, may lessen the disability rates in the United States and other developed countries, although a rise in manufacturing in developing countries may increase their disability rates through higher injury rates and pollution-related illnesses. An increase in work accommodations may decrease the likelihood that people will report work-limiting disabilities. Workplace organization may also matter: one study found that the growth of "lean production" – which puts greater responsibility on employees in a blend of craft and mass production – was associated with more stressful work and a rise in disability in the Netherlands in the 1980s and 1990s (Spithoven 2001).

To the extent that education levels rise, this should decrease the rate of disability. As will be discussed in Chapter 5, increased education

---

[21] For example, among people aged 51–61 reporting work disability in the United States, more than one-third (37%) said that the disability was the result of a work-related incident (Reville and Schoeni 2003).

can decrease the likelihood of developing a disability through safer work environments, better access to medical information and services, better ability to cope with stress and adversity, and increased access to technology and assistive devices (Cutler et al. 2009).

Finally, the prevalence of disability will be influenced by public policy. Policies help determine the built environment, access to medical care, assistive technologies, educational opportunities, workplace safety, and a host of other factors that determine the likelihood and consequences of disability.

While many variables will influence the future prevalence of disability, it is likely that it will increase as the population ages. The fact that about one-sixth of the world's population – close to 1 billion people – have disabilities is enough to provide a strong case for examining the economic, political, and social status of this substantial segment of the world's population. Even if people with disabilities constituted a much smaller share of the world's population, however, it would still be important to examine their status, given their history of marginalization and stigma and the importance of societal inclusion and human rights for all people, as stated in the UN Convention.

2

Economic Inclusion

A. INTRODUCTION

The importance of economic inclusion goes beyond the role of financial resources in supporting a fulfilling life. It also involves the social and psychological aspects of low economic resources. Employment, for example, not only increases incomes and helps lift people out of poverty, but also helps people overcome the social isolation that often accompanies disability (Schur 2003; A. Cohen 2006). Studies in Australia, Korea, the United Kingdom, and Switzerland that followed people over time show that leaving employment generally "leads to higher mental distress," while "finding a job results in improved mental health" (OECD 2010: 46–47). In addition, employment can lead to the development of civic skills and social connections that facilitate participation in community, recreational, and political activities outside the workplace, and otherwise increase the perceived social status and mainstream inclusion of people with disabilities (Schur 2003).

This chapter presents a broad view of the economic inclusion of people with disabilities, examining the relationship of disability to income, poverty rates, and employment levels and prospects. The next chapter examines the critical topic of employment among people with disabilities in greater detail.

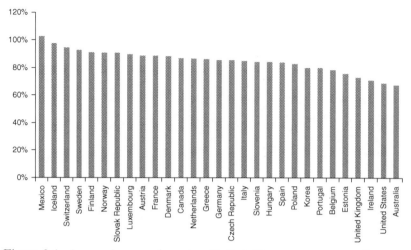

Figure 2.1. Average income of people with disabilities as a percentage of average income of working-age population, mid-2000s.
Source: Drawn from OECD 2010, Figure 2.5 Panel A.

B. ECONOMIC RESOURCES

1. Income and Poverty Levels

People with disabilities have lower income levels on average than people without disabilities. Figure 2.1 shows their average income as a percentage of the average income of working-age people without disabilities in 29 developed countries (OECD 2010: 54). The figures range from a high of 103% (Mexico) to a low of 68% (Australia), with most countries in the range of 80–90%.[1]

---

[1] Parish et al. (2010) found lower income among people with disabilities in the United States regardless of family structure (married couple, single women, or single men). People with disabilities in the United States were also found to be more likely than those without disabilities to say they are "struggling to get by" and less likely to say they are "financially comfortable" (Kessler/NOD/Harris 2010: 94). See Burkhauser et al. (2009) for evidence on the declining income of working-age men with disabilities relative to those without disabilities over the 1983–2004 period.

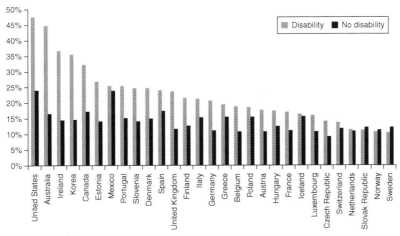

Figure 2.2. Poverty rates by disability status, mid-2000s.
Source: Drawn from OECD 2010, Figure 2.6.

Given that people with disabilities have lower average incomes than people without disabilities, it is not surprising that they are more likely to live in poverty. Figure 2.2 shows the poverty rates of people with and without disabilities in these 29 countries; it can be seen that the poverty rates of people with disabilities are especially high in the United States, Australia, and Ireland and that they are more likely than people without disabilities to be in poverty in all but three countries (Slovak Republic, Norway, and Sweden).[2] Consistent with this, a 2008 survey found that in each of the European Union countries, people with disabilities were more likely than those without to live in low-income households (with less than 60% of the median national income) (Grammenos 2010: 97–98).[3]

[2] A more recent study of 1984–2002 German data comparing otherwise similar people with and without disabilities found that disability appears to lower employment rates but not overall income, indicating "that the German social security systems appear to successfully mitigate or at least reduce the economic hardship that comes with the event of disability" (Lechner and Vazquez-Alvarez 2011).

[3] More recent data from the United Kingdom show that children are more likely to live in low-income households if there is a person with a disability in the household.

These patterns hold true not just among developed countries, but among developing nations. Poverty rates were found to be higher among people with disabilities in 13 of 15 developing countries, and people with disabilities had significantly lower mean assets in 11 of 15 countries (Mitra et al. 2011).[4] Overall, the economic status of people with disabilities is generally lower in both developed and developing countries.[5] As will be seen in the next section, these lower income levels and higher poverty rates are related to the lower employment levels among people with disabilities.

The poverty rate may not fully capture economic difficulties among people with disabilities. Both among those who live in poverty and those who do not, people with disabilities in the United States are more likely than those without disabilities to experience material hardship in food security (e.g., having to skip meals due to a lack of money) and inability to meet essential expenses (e.g., to pay rent, mortgage, or medical bills) (She and Livermore 2007; Parish et al. 2009).In the United Kingdom, people with disabilities are more likely to live in "fuel poverty" – needing to spend more than 10% of their income to pay for heating fuel.[6] In several developing countries, many people with disabilities have expressed unmet needs for health care, assistive devices, education, and vocational training and other services (Malawi, Namibia, Zambia, Zimbabwe, Morocco, Tonga, and China) (WHO/World Bank 2011: 41).

odi.dwp.gov.uk/roadmap-to-disability-equality/indicators.php, Table C1 (accessed May 22, 2012).

[4] See WHO/World Bank (2011: 40) for other studies finding lower asset levels among people with disabilities. Studies of U.S. data found that people with disabilities had poverty rates two to five times higher than among people without disabilities (She and Livermore 2009) and lower asset levels than among people without disabilities regardless of family structure (married couples, single women, or single men) (Parish et al. 2010).

[5] See WHO/World Bank (2011: 39–40) for further discussion. See Fremstad (2009) for a discussion of how disability must be taken into account in antipoverty policy.

[6] odi.dwp.gov.uk/roadmap-to-disability-equality/indicators.php, Table C4 (accessed May 22, 2012).

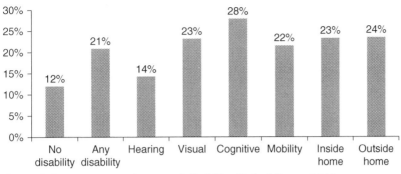

Figure 2.3. Poverty rates by type of disability, United States, 2010.

Do the poverty and income figures depend on type and severity of disability? The personal incomes of those with severe disabilities average about 85% of those with moderate disabilities in developed countries (OECD 2003: 29). Figure 2.3 provides a more detailed look at type of disability in the United States, showing that poverty rates are especially high for those with cognitive impairments, largely reflecting their low employment and earnings levels, as will be explored.[7]

The causal relationship between disability and poverty runs in both directions (Fremstad 2009). "People living in poverty are more at risk of having impairments and, at the same time, people who have impairments (which may not have been caused by poverty) are likely to be pushed into poverty by a multitude of disabling societal forces" (Lawson 2011: 49). The higher poverty rate among people with disabilities in the United Kingdom was found to reflect both a higher likelihood of developing disability among poverty households and a higher likelihood of entering poverty following the onset of disability (Burchardt 2003b). The higher development of disability among those who grew up in poverty households may occur due to lower access to

[7] Based on calculations from the 2010 American Community Survey, U.S. Census Bureau, for people not living in institutional group quarters. Earlier data from 2002 to 2004 show poverty rates of 19–29% among working-age people with disabilities, compared with 6–8% among those without disabilities (Burkhauser et al. 2009: 202).

preventive health care and to less safe environmental conditions (e.g., exposure to poor sanitation) (WHO/World Bank 2011: 36–37). The greater risk of entering poverty after the onset of disability may reflect the loss of income from employment and the extra expenses of living with a disability, as will be reviewed.

2. Costs of Disability

Economic resources of people with disabilities are limited not only by their lower average incomes and higher poverty rates, but also by the extra costs that are often associated with disability. Some are direct costs for disability-related items, such as hearing aids and wheelchair ramps, while others are increased costs for items or services also used by nondisabled people, such as housekeeping for people with mobility impairments. The costs of disability modifications are paid in some cases by government or insurance programs, but often are borne by people with disabilities and their families.

There are a variety of ways of estimating the extra costs associated with disability, some based on actual expenditure patterns and others based on judgments by people with disabilities and other experts about the resources needed for standards of living to be equivalent between people with and without disabilities (Zaidi and Burchardt 2005; Wilkinson-Meyers et al. 2010).[8] Studies have found extra costs of disability in the United Kingdom, Ireland, Australia, Vietnam, and Bosnia, averaging between 9% and 49% of average income.[9] This also

---

[8] Wilkinson-Meyers et al. (2010) advocate a mixed-methods approach using experts and people with disabilities.

[9] In the United Kingdom the extra costs were 18–30% of average income for a nonpensioner couple in which one person had a moderate disability and 41–49% of average income for a single nonpensioner with a moderate disability (Zaidi and Burchardt 2005: 105). In both Ireland and Australia the extra costs of disability were estimated as about 30% of average income for people who were somewhat limited by their

holds true in studies focused on expenses related to health care.[10] While people with disabilities may receive benefits to help cover such costs, the United Kingdom study found that more than 90% of people with disabilities still had extra costs they had to pay themselves (Zaidi and Burchardt 2005: 107), and a United States study found higher health care expenditures paid by people with disabilities (Mitra et al. 2009).

Taking these extra costs into account increases the number of people with disabilities who live in poverty. The study in Australia found that, after the extra costs of disability were accounted for, the poverty rate among people with disabilities jumped from 9% to more than 20%, compared with poverty rates of 5–7% among people without disabilities (Saunders 2007: 475). Similarly, poverty rates were found to increase in the developing countries of Bosnia and Vietnam after the extra costs associated with disability were accounted for (Braithwaite and Mont 2009).[11]

3. Disability Income

People with disabilities are often eligible for disability-related income and other types of benefits from either public or private programs.

disabilities and 33–48% for those who were severely limited (Cullinan et al. 2011; Saunders 2007). In the developing countries of Vietnam and Bosnia the extra costs of disability were found to average 9% and 14% of income, respectively (Braithwaite and Mont 2009). Focusing on a specific disability, the extra costs associated with spinal cord injury in the United States were estimated in 1998 to average about $244,000 in the first year and $25,000 in subsequent years (Berkowitz et al. 1998). See Stapleton et al. (2008) for a review of evidence on the costs of disability.

[10] The extra health care expenditures paid by people with disabilities in the United States were found to average about 10% of family income, compared with 2% for people without disabilities (Mitra et al. 2009). The same pattern was found in 10 of 14 countries (Mitra et al. 2011).

[11] The poverty rate for households with people with disabilities increased from 15.4% to 20.1% in Vietnam and from 21.1% to 30.8% in Bosnia after the costs of disability were accounted for (Braithwaite and Mont 2009: 230).

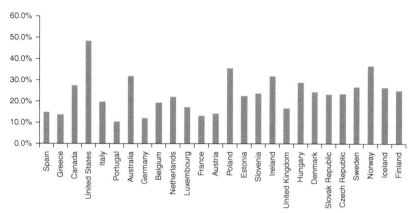

Figure 2.4. People with disabilities receiving public disability benefits.
Source: Drawn from OECD, 2010, Figure 2.7.

Disability income programs are part of the broader assistance and support that many countries provide to people with disabilities, including assistance tailored to specific needs such as housing, caregiving, education, transportation (e.g., subsidized rides or vehicle modifications), employment (e.g., workplace aides), assistive devices (e.g., wheelchairs), technology (e.g., computers), and communication (e.g., sign language interpreters) (for an overview, see chapter 5 of WHO/World Bank 2011). The assistance and support are often designed to go beyond ensuring a minimum standard of living by helping increase social and economic participation generally.

The percentage of people with disabilities receiving public disability benefits varies among industrialized countries, as shown in Figure 2.4, from a low of 10% in Portugal to more than 30% in Poland, Norway, and the United States. This percentage has increased since the 1990s for most countries, reflecting greater recipiency among older workers and those with mental impairments, though several countries have seen declines due to tighter limits on access to benefits (OECD 2010: 60–63).

The two main forms of public disability income in the United States are Social Security Disability Insurance (SSDI) and Supplemental

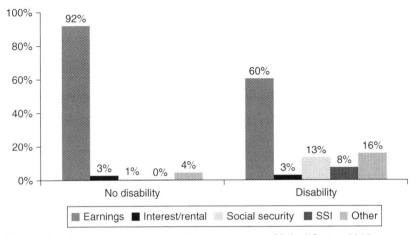

Figure 2.5. Type of income for working-age people, United States, 2010.

Security Income (SSI).[12] SSDI is based on pre-disability work earnings covered by the Social Security system, and SSI is a means-tested program available to those with low income and assets. As shown in Figure 2.5, these represent an average of 13% and 8%, respectively, of the total income of working-age people with disabilities.[13]

While each disability income program around the world is unique, they share basic features. Eligibility is generally based on establishing some type of permanent or long-term significant physical or mental impairment or medical condition. The assessment is often done by a medical practitioner, though some countries like Norway and the Netherlands have moved toward a direct assessment by rehabilitation specialists of a person's capacity for employment, and people may receive partial benefits depending on the degree to which their earnings capacity is restricted (OECD 2010: 105, 109; Mitra 2009).

---

[12] For an overview of these programs see Moulta-Ali (2012).

[13] Based on calculations from the 2010 American Community Survey, U.S. Census Bureau, for people not living in institutional group quarters. See Stapleton et al. (2009) for data and discussion on disability program participation in the United States.

In addition, a number of countries have moved toward providing temporary benefits with reassessments at regular intervals; these benefits are typically renewed and sometimes turned into permanent benefits (OECD 2010: 115). Once people receive disability benefits, there are often strong disincentives for employment, since becoming employed can result in the loss of some or all disability benefits. Across industrialized countries, it is estimated that becoming employed at the average wage results in the loss of 60% of one's earnings through benefit withdrawals and taxes (OECD 2010: 120).

For example, in the United States a person receiving SSDI can earn up to $1,000 per month and maintain full benefits, but all benefits are lost if one earns more than $1,000 per month for a sustained period. Due both to the availability of nonemployment income and to the lost earnings if one does become employed, few people relinquish disability benefits once they start receiving them (OECD 2010: 67). An international review found that economic conditions are important: higher unemployment levels help predict higher inflows into disability benefit receipt and lower outflows (Benitez-Silva et al. 2010). There have been a number of proposals to reform disability income programs due to their growing cost in many countries and a desire to reduce disincentives for employment (see the analyses of a number of European countries, Canada, and the United States in Wise, forthcoming). These proposals will be reviewed at the end of Chapter 3 along with other policies designed to increase employment among people with disabilities (OECD 2010, 70–124; WHO/World Bank 2011: 137–165).[14]

C. EMPLOYMENT LEVELS

Much of the lower average income of people with disabilities is tied to their lower levels of employment. In fact, the average income of

[14] For additional discussion see Benitez-Silva (2008).

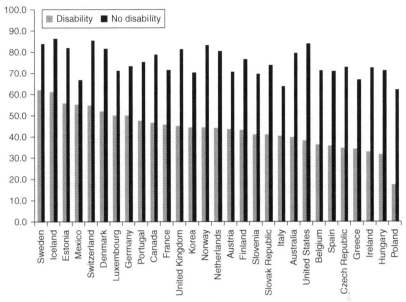

Figure 2.6. Employment rates by disability status, mid-2000s.
Source: Drawn from OECD, 2010, Figure 2.1.

employed people with disabilities is close to the average income of working-age people without disabilities in a large number of OECD countries (OECD 2010: 54); also, a country's employment gap between people with and without disabilities is a strong predictor of the country's average disability income gap.[15]

People with disabilities have lower employment rates than people without disabilities in all of the OECD countries. The rates for people with disabilities range from a high of 62% in Sweden to a low of 18% in Poland, as shown in Figure 2.6.

A broader survey of 51 countries showed average employment rates of 53% and 20% for men and women with disabilities, respectively, compared with 65% and 30% for men and women without disabilities

---

[15] The correlation between the income gap in Figure 2.1 and the employment gap in Figure 2.6 is .590.

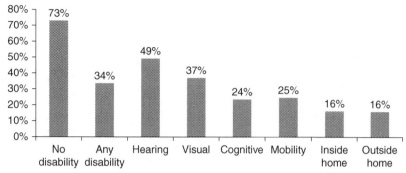

Figure 2.7: Employment rates by type of disability, 2010, United States.

(WHO/World Bank 2011: 237).[16] A serious concern is that the employment rates of people with disabilities, relative to those of people without disabilities, have not generally improved between the mid-1990s and the late 2000s, and in fact have declined in several countries (OECD 2010: 50–51; Burkhauser and Daly 2011). One country with a recent improvement in the employment rate of people with disabilities is the United Kingdom.[17]

The employment rate is low across all types of disability but does vary by type of disability, as shown in Figure 2.7 based on U.S. data.[18] Among working-age people with disabilities the employment rate is highest among those with hearing impairments (49%) and lowest among those who report difficulty carrying out daily activities inside or outside the home (16%). This is consistent with international data

[16] In addition to the countries shown in Figure 2.3, employment rates for people with disabilities were reported to be lower than average employment rates for the working-age population in India, Japan, Malawi, Peru, South Africa, and Zambia (WHO/World Bank 2011: 238).

[17] The employment rate improved from 45% to 48% over the 2002–2010 period for people with disabilities, while it declined from 81% to 78% for people without disabilities. odi.dwp.gov.uk/roadmap-to-disability-equality/indicators.php (accessed May 22, 2012).

[18] Based on calculations from the 2010 American Community Survey, U.S. Census Bureau, for people aged 18–64 who are not living in institutional group quarters.

showing lower employment rates among those with severe rather than moderate disabilities (OECD 2003: 35). In the United Kingdom, employment rates are lowest among people with depression, epilepsy, and impairments affecting the legs, feet, back, or neck.[19]

The negative effect of disability on the likelihood of employment is found not just in cross-sectional comparisons between people with and without disabilities, but also in longitudinal comparisons in the United States, United Kingdom, and Australia that follow workers before and after the onset of disability (e.g., Famulari 1992; Krueger and Kruse 1995; Reville and Schoeni, 2003; Butler et al. 2006; Campolieti and Krashinski 2006; Polidano and Hong 2012). The low employment rate of people with disabilities partly reflects that they are more likely than people without disabilities to lose their jobs when a recession occurs, as found in several U.S. studies (Stapleton et al. 2005; Kaye 2010; Mitra and Kruse 2011a, 2011b).

The unemployment rate provides an additional measure of employment status. This measures those who do not have a job but are actively searching for one, as a percentage of all those who are in the labor force due to either having a job or actively searching for one. In the United States, disability measures were introduced into the government's monthly employment survey in 2008, so that employment statistics are now reported for people with disabilities on a monthly basis.[20] The monthly unemployment rate in 2010 averaged 14.8% for people with disabilities compared with 9.4% for those without disabilities.[21] Likewise, unemployment rates in 2008 were higher in

---

[19] odi.dwp.gov.uk/roadmap-to-disability-equality/indicators.php, Table B2 (accessed May 22, 2012).

[20] The current employment statistics by disability status are reported at www.bls.gov/news.release/empsit.t06.htm.

[21] U.S. Bureau of Labor Statistics, "Persons with a Disability: Labor force Characteristics – 2010," USDL 11–9021, June 24, 2011. The official unemployment rate does not include "discouraged workers" and others who want a job but are not actively searching because they think no jobs are available or face other constraints.

all of the European Union countries for people with disabilities compared with those without disabilities (Grammenos 2010: 83). The higher unemployment rates point toward greater difficulties in finding and maintaining employment even among people with disabilities who have a strong attachment to the labor market.

1. Why the Lower Employment?

Most nonemployed working-age people with disabilities in the United States say they would prefer to be working (63% in a 2004 survey) or would like a paid job now or in the future (80% in a 2006 survey, similar to the 78% figure for people without disabilities) (NOD/Harris 2004; Ali et al. 2011).[22] However, people with disabilities express greater pessimism about finding a job: only 25% of nonemployed people with disabilities in the 2006 survey said they were "very likely" to get a job, compared with 51% of people without disabilities (Ali et al. 2011).[23]

The Bureau of Labor Statistics estimates that, in an average month in 2010, among people with disabilities 570,000 wanted a job but were not actively searching, which was about two-thirds of the number classified as officially unemployed (857,000), while among people without disabilities 5.5 million wanted a job but were not actively searching, which was about two-fifths of the number of officially unemployed (14.0 million). Therefore on a percentage basis, the official unemployment statistics may understate the unemployment problem more for people with disabilities than for people without disabilities.

[22] Among disability income beneficiaries in the United States, a 2004 survey found that 30% had personal goals of getting a job, moving up in a job, or learning new job skills; 26% saw themselves working for pay in the next five years; and 15% saw themselves working in the next five years and earning enough to stop receiving disability benefits (Livermore et al. 2007: 90).

[23] This helps account for the low rate of active job search among nonemployed people with disabilities. In a 2006 survey, only 20% of nonemployed people with disabilities were actively searching for a job, compared with 33% of people without disabilities (Ali et al. 2011), while data based on a different survey and definition of disability in 2010 showed that only 8% of nonemployed working-age people with disabilities

What accounts for the low employment levels of people with disabilities and their pessimism about finding jobs? The major reasons for low employment rates can be divided into those affecting labor supply (reflecting the ability and willingness of individuals to be employed) and labor demand (reflecting the willingness of employers to hire). On the labor supply side, the key factors are the following:

- *Extra costs of work*: People with disabilities may face extra time, energy, or financial costs in getting ready for work, transportation (e.g., the costs of modified vehicles or extra commuting time),[24] and medical care (e.g., medical equipment or attendant care to prepare for work or required at work). These costs can be substantially affected by the built environment and infrastructure – for example, the time and difficulty in getting to work can be greatly affected by the accessibility of one's home and workplace and the availability of accessible public transportation.
- *Extra need for flexibility*: Some disabilities require extra time for self-care, therapy, and medical appointments, and transportation problems can introduce an added level of uncertainty and difficulty in daily schedules. For these reasons, many people with disabilities are not able to accept traditional full-time jobs, and those

were actively searching for a job compared with 24% of people without disabilities (based on calculations from www.bls.gov/news.release/pdf/disabl.pdf) (accessed October 19, 2011). Among those who were not searching for employment in another 2010 survey, a large majority of nonemployed people with disabilities blamed their lack of employment on their disability (94%), while two-fifths (42%) said they did not believe they could get necessary accommodations to perform effectively at work, one-third (32%) said that additional income would make them ineligible for disability benefits, and one-fourth (24%) said there were no jobs available in their line of work (Kessler/NOD/Harris 2010: 55).

[24] See Berkowitz et al. (1998) regarding costs of vehicle modifications and the strong influence of having an accessible vehicle on the likelihood of employment for people with spinal cord injuries. For an exploration of the relationship between transportation and employment for Canadians with disabilities, see Farber and Paez (2010).

who want to be employed may be drawn to part-time and flexible work arrangements, as explored in the next chapter.

- *Education and training*: People with disabilities tend to have lower average levels of education and training, which reduce their earnings power (see Chapter 5). Educational level is a standard strong predictor of employment status and may be more important for people with disabilities than for those without disabilities. For example, among working-age people with disabilities in the United States in 2010, only one-fifth (20%) of those without a high school degree were employed, compared with one-half (51%) of those with a college degree. The increase in employment with education among people with disabilities was greater than among people without disabilities (62% for those without high school degrees compared with 82% for those with college degrees), although employment gaps still exist at all education levels.[25] Higher education levels not only increase the likelihood of employment, but also substantially raise earnings power among the employed. A study of U.S. data found that higher levels of education appear to narrow the pay gap between workers with and without disabilities, although a gap still remains (Hollenbeck and Kimmel 2008). The importance of education for employment is further indicated by the result that the income levels among people with disabilities with post-secondary education exceed the average income of the entire working-age population in 19 of 23 developed countries, while the income levels of people with disabilities with lower levels of education fall below the national average incomes (OECD 2010: 54).

- *Disability income and health care*: As discussed, many people with disabilities receive public or private disability income, which may

---

[25] Based on analysis of the 2010 American Community Survey, conducted by the U.S. Census Bureau, for working-age (18–64) people who are not living in institutional group quarters. Similarly, Kirchner and Smith (2005) found rising employment levels with higher levels of education among people with visual impairments in the United States.

decrease the likelihood of employment by providing a livable income and by providing disincentives to become employed. People with disabilities are often reluctant to become employed for fear of jeopardizing these benefits, and research shows that these benefits affect labor market exits and return to work (Mashaw et al. 1996; Bound and Burkhauser 1999).[26]

- *Attitudes and social barriers*: The stigma and prejudice associated with disability can dissuade some people from searching for and maintaining jobs that might expose them to negative attitudes from managers, co-workers, and customers.

Apart from factors affecting the labor supply of people with disabilities, there are several key issues that affect employer demand:

- *Employer discrimination and reluctance to hire*: Close to one-third of employers in the United States report that discomfort or unfamiliarity is a challenge in hiring people with disabilities (Domzal et al. 2008: 13). Surveys also find that about 20% of U.S. employers say the greatest barrier to the employment of people with disabilities is employers' discrimination, prejudice, or reluctance to hire them, and that attitudes and stereotypes are a barrier to the employment of people with disabilities in their own firms (Dixon et al. 2003; Bruyère 2000). These numbers may be understated by social desirability bias in surveys, in which respondents are reluctant to

---

[26] A study of the U.S. disability insurance system in the 1990s found that labor force participation of beneficiaries "would have been at most 20 percentage points higher had none received benefits" (Chen and der Klaauw 2006). The rise in disability beneficiaries in the United States in the 1990s led to a decrease in the size of the labor force that lowered the measured unemployment rate (Autor and Duggan 2003). A study of South Africa found that the disability grant program appeared to be responsible for part of the decline in employment of people with disabilities over the 1998–2006 period (Mitra 2008). In contrast to some prior studies, a Canadian study found that increased benefits were not linked to decreased labor force participation of older men (Campolieti 2004).

report negative attitudes or behaviors. In addition, a review of more than a dozen empirical studies of wage differentials concluded that "a substantial part of the wage differential" can be attributed to disability-related discrimination (Baldwin and Johnson 2006). A study in France found that employers were much less likely to respond positively to job applications from people with paraplegia than to otherwise-identical applications from able-bodied people (Ravaud et al. 1992).

- *Corporate culture*: Apart from direct discrimination, many aspects of corporate culture – organizational practices and the attitudes of managers, supervisors, and co-workers – limit employment opportunities for people with disabilities (Schur, Kruse, and Blanck 2005). Personnel managers and supervisors may feel uncomfortable around people with disabilities, and this discomfort may be manifested in a reluctance to hire, retain, or promote them. Employers may believe that a worker with a disability will not be well accepted by co-workers and therefore will be less productive in teamwork situations. These concerns are reflected in a survey of U.S. employers, among whom 29% reported that the attitudes of co-workers are a challenge in hiring people with disabilities and 20% reported that attitudes of supervisors are a challenge (numbers that may be understated by social desirability bias, as noted) (Domzal et al. 2008: 13). Employers may hold strong stereotypes about the types of jobs or industries that are appropriate for people with certain types of disabilities and may have biases about the attitudes, aspirations, and potential for further human capital development of workers with disabilities. For instance, among 13 laboratory experiments, 10 showed that evaluators were overly pessimistic about the future performance and promotion potential of employees with disabilities (Colella et al. 1998). In addition, among employers who made changes to enhance the employment of people with disabilities, in a national survey 32% indicated it was difficult or very difficult to change supervisor and co-worker attitudes (Bruyère 2000).

- *Need for accommodations*: Employers may be reluctant to expend time or money on necessary accommodations for employing people with disabilities, despite legal requirements that employers make reasonable accommodations (e.g., Title I of the Americans with Disabilities Act in the United States). Data on employer concerns, the actual costs and benefits of accommodations, and the effects of legislative mandates for employers to provide accommodations (the Americans with Disabilities Act in the United States and the Disability Discrimination Act in the United Kingdom) are discussed in the next chapter.

Finally, on both the supply and demand side, lack of information is an important problem in the lower level of employment among people with disabilities. Some people with disabilities do not know what jobs they might be able to do and how to obtain the necessary training. They may not be aware of their legal rights and available government programs to facilitate employment. Likewise, employers often do not know where to go to hire people with disabilities or what resources are available to assist them (e.g., employee training from government and nonprofit agencies, and information on how to provide accommodations). Employer ignorance may be aggravated by recruitment specialists ("headhunters") who discriminate by failing to find and represent people with disabilities.

2. What Are the Prospects for Higher Employment Levels?

There is both good news and bad news in current labor market trends that will shape the prospects for economic inclusion of people with disabilities. First the bad news:

- *Lower job growth in occupations where people with disabilities are concentrated*: People with disabilities tend to be underrepresented in growing occupations and overrepresented in declining occupations in the United States (Kruse et al. 2010). The fastest-growing occupations are predominantly white-collar, professional jobs that require college degrees and technical expertise, such as network systems analysts and computer programmers, and the declining occupations are predominantly blue-collar production jobs, such as operating textile machines. People with disabilities are underrepresented in 17 of the 20 fastest-growing occupations projected for the 2008–2018 period in the United States and overrepresented in 19 of the 20 fastest-declining occupations. If the distribution of people with disabilities by occupation stays the same, their job growth from 2008 to 2018 will be only 9.0% (representing 825,000 new jobs total), lower than the projected job growth among all workers of 10.1% (15.3 million new jobs). The job growth of people with disabilities will increase only if many of them are able to move into the growing occupations.[27] While there is no direct information on disability and job growth outside of the United States, it is likely that these general projections apply to other countries. Job growth in Europe is expected to be strong in highly skilled occupations (Cedefop 2010), and it is likely that people with disabilities are underrepresented in these occupations due to their lower levels of education on average (OECD 2010: 27–28).

- *Greater job growth in low-paying occupations for people with disabilities*: A further bit of bad news is that people with disabilities are overrepresented in low-paying occupations, and a large share of their job growth will be in these occupations. Among employed people with disabilities in the United States in 2008, 58% were in occupation with low or very low wages (with a median wage in the lower

---

[27] See Stapleton et al. (2003) for an assessment of the relation of disability to changes in job requirements over the 1975–2000 period, concluding that these changes cannot explain much of the decline in the employment rate of people reporting work disabilities.

half of all occupations), and 74% of their projected job growth from 2008 to 2018 is in such low-paid jobs (Kruse et al. 2010). For example, 110,000 of the projected new jobs for people with disabilities are those of health aide or personal and home care aide, which tend to be low-paid positions.

There are, however, several pieces of good news showing the potential for growth in good jobs for people with disabilities.

- *Substantial job growth in occupations where disabilities are irrelevant*: There will be strong job growth in the United States in occupations where several cognitive abilities – quantitative abilities, memory, perceptual abilities, and spatial abilities – have low importance or where only a low level of the ability is useful (Kruse et al. 2010). For example, there will be 7.9 million new jobs in which only a low level of memory is required and this is not a highly important skill for job performance. In addition, there will be substantial growth in occupations where many of the psychomotor and physical abilities have low or no importance, providing good opportunities for people with mobility impairments. For example, manual dexterity has low or no importance in 3.3 million of the new jobs, and only a low level is somewhat important in 5.0 million of the new jobs, which offers promise to many people with quadriplegia, cerebral palsy, or other conditions that limit their manual dexterity. As another example, gross body coordination has low or no importance in 5.6 million of the new jobs, and only a low level is somewhat important in 5.2 million of the new jobs. These projections offer promise to people using wheelchairs or crutches and to others who generally lack the ability to coordinate all of their limbs easily. It should be noted that these estimates probably reflect lower bounds on the number of jobs that can be performed by people with disabilities, since many accommodations and technologies open up further opportunities for people with specific impairments.

- *Growing importance of computers and new information technologies*:
  These technologies have special benefits for workers with disabilities,
  helping compensate for physical, sensory, or cognitive impairments
  (e.g., using screen readers and voice-recognition systems) and substantially increasing the productivity of many workers with disabilities
  (Blanck 2012). A study of people with spinal cord injuries found that
  people with computer skills at the time of the injury returned to work
  faster than did those without such skills. Furthermore, post-injury
  computer use especially enhanced earnings among people with spinal cord injuries – in fact, they earned the same as other computer
  users, whereas a substantial pay gap was associated with spinal cord
  injury among people who did not use computers at work (Krueger
  and Kruse 1995). Most of the new jobs created between 2008 and
  2018 in the United States will be in occupations where computer
  skills are important, potentially creating good opportunities for people with disabilities given that computer skills can help overcome and
  even erase some of the disadvantages associated with many disabilities (Kruse et al. 2010). As will be discussed in Chapter 5, however,
  there are disturbing gaps between people with and without disabilities in access to computers and the Internet.
- *Increased specialization creating more niches for workers with
  disabilities.* New technologies often create new types of jobs that
  can take greater advantage of the skills of people with disabilities. In some jobs a particular disability may even be an asset. For
  example, people with autism may "flourish in jobs which require
  some very specialized set of skills and which focus their energies
  on a specialized set of tasks" (Cowen, 2011: 17).[28]
- *Increased use of telecommuting, part-time, and flexible work arrangements*: New information technologies have made home-based

---

[28] Cook (2012) describes a growing company that employs a large number of autistic
individuals who are especially good at very specific, detail-oriented tasks that require
a high degree of concentration.

work more productive, and can create special benefits for people with disabilities – particularly those with transportation problems or medical concerns that require them to be close to home. In addition, there has been continued interest in and experimentation with other types of flexible work arrangements that help promote work–family balance and accommodate the needs of people with disabilities, such as job sharing, flexible schedules, and temporary employment. The growth of part-time and home-based jobs by 2018 is projected to be strong, slightly exceeding overall job growth (Kruse et al. 2010). While such jobs often have disadvantages and it is clear that workers with disabilities should have full access to standard full-time jobs, the growth of several types of flexible and contingent jobs may enhance the employment of many people with disabilities who benefit from these arrangements. People with disabilities are more likely to take part-time and home-based jobs, as discussed in the next chapter.

- *Growing attention to workplace diversity*: Most large corporations today have diversity programs, and a growing number are including disability as one of the criteria for a diverse workforce.

These trends may signal a fundamental change in the nature of work over the next several decades.[29] The next chapter delves into several of these issues more intensively – examining the employment barriers and opportunities facing people with disabilities and the policies that may increase economic inclusion.

---

[29] See Barnes (2000, 2004, 2012) and Barnes and Mercer (2005) for further reviews of changes in work and discussions of how work may need to be reconceptualized (going beyond paid employment) in order to provide greater inclusion and status for people with disabilities.

3

A Closer Look at Employment

A. INTRODUCTION

Employment plays a critical role in the economic inclusion of people with disabilities. We saw in the preceding chapter that people with disabilities are less likely to be employed than otherwise similar people without disabilities, and their prospects for higher employment are uncertain, with both positive and negative trends at work. Given the importance of employment, in this chapter we delve more deeply into several interconnected issues and the barriers and opportunities they present to the employment of people with disabilities.

We start by examining alternative work arrangements among people with disabilities, which can provide flexibility needed by many. We then explore workplace disparities in pay, job security, and other job characteristics, which leads to a review of discrimination models and evidence. We discuss the ways in which disparities may be linked to corporate cultures, summarizing recent research on workplace policies, practices, and attitudes affecting people with disabilities, with lessons on barriers to and facilitators of the inclusion of employees with disabilities. Since many employees with disabilities require and benefit from workplace accommodations, we review the research regarding accommodations, including the evidence on legislative mandates for accommodations in the U.S. Americans with Disabilities Act (ADA) and the UK Disability Discrimination Act (DDA). We conclude with an overview of policies that may promote employment among people with disabilities.

B. ALTERNATIVE WORK ARRANGEMENTS

Many individuals with disabilities need flexibility in their schedules. Some disabilities are associated with an increased need for medical or physical therapy appointments, or with greater physical demands or time spent on self-care, that make a standard full-time schedule difficult to manage. In addition, people with mobility impairments can face transportation problems or public transportation schedules that make rigid work schedules difficult and increase the attractiveness of setting their own schedules and working for themselves at home.[1]

Employers have increasingly used alternative work arrangements, often as part of work–life programs, to help employees balance their jobs with their spousal, parental, caregiver, and other roles (Bond et al. 2005). When employees must cope with personal and family issues, standard inflexible work arrangements may lead to increased employee stress and injury, absenteeism, turnover, and lower productivity. Work–life balance is an important issue for workers with disabilities, given the many ways that disability can increase demands and challenges in organizing one's daily life. The advantages of flexible work arrangements for workers with disabilities are recognized in company ratings.[2] We consider five types of alternative work arrangements: part-time work, temporary work, telecommuting and other home-based work, jobs with flexible hours, and self-employment.

---

[1] This section draws on material presented by the National Council on Disability (2007), based on a report written by the Rutgers Program for Disability Research.

[2] For example, flexible work arrangements are common in nine of DiversityInc's 2012 "Top 10 Companies for People with Disabilities," www.flexjobs.com/blog/post/top-companies-for-people-with-disabilities-are-also-flexible-workplaces (accessed August 28, 2012).

1. Part-Time Work

Part-time work places lower demands on time and energy than does full-time work, making it appropriate for many people with disabilities. Two examples are described in Schur (2003):

> A woman who was born with a balance disorder works in a local grocery store for only 10 hours per week due to fatigue ("I couldn't work a bunch more hours. I'm pretty exhausted when I get home from work").

> Another man with schizophrenia said that the pressure in his prior full-time computer job brought on schizophrenic episodes, and that his current job as a gas station cashier allows him to avoid stress and control the effects of his illness.

Part-time work can be part of a transition to full-time employment after an illness or injury:

> A man who broke his back in a work accident ... said that he eventually was able to return to a full-time managerial job because his employer gave him a part-time schedule when he first came back to work: "Part time work was a good way to make the transition. If I worked for another type of employer they wouldn't have taken me back. There's a good chance that I'd [still] be out on disability."

People with disabilities are more likely than those without disabilities to have part-time jobs, as shown by data for 29 developed countries in Figure 3.1. Part-time employment is especially high among people with cognitive impairments and those who have difficulty with activities of daily living inside the home or getting around outside the home.[3]

---

[3] Data from the 2009 U.S. American Community Survey show that part-time employment as a percentage of all employment is 21% among people without disabilities, 26% among those with a hearing impairment, 26% among those with a vision impairment, 34% among those with a mobility impairment, 46% among those with a cognitive impairment, 47% among those with difficulty getting dressed or bathed, and 46% among those with difficulty going outside alone (Kruse et al. 2011).

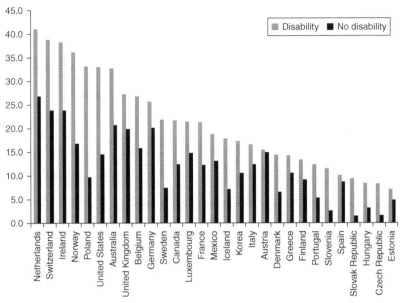

Figure 3.1. Part-time employment as a percentage of all employment by disability status, mid-2000s.
Source: Drawn from OECD, 2010, Figure 2.3.

The high rate of part-time employment among people with disabilities may partly reflect constraints from earnings limitations imposed by disability income programs, such as the U.S. SSDI program. Higher monthly earnings limitations and increased availability of Medicaid health insurance in the 1990s in the United States help explain a rise in part-time employment among those reporting work disabilities (Hotchkiss 2004a). People with disabilities may also be restricted to part-time jobs if they encounter employer discrimination or reluctance to hire them full time. It appears, though, that the high rate of part-time employment among people with disabilities is driven primarily by the preference of many people with disabilities for part-time work. This is indicated by a U.S. study examining changes in employment as labor markets tightened and jobs became more available, giving workers increased power to choose the types of jobs they wanted.

The increased employment among people with disabilities as labor markets tightened in the United States in the late 1990s took the form primarily of part-time employment, while people without disabilities were more likely to take full-time jobs, indicating a generally higher preference for part-time work among people with disabilities (Schur 2003). Likewise, a United Kingdom study of part-time employment among people with disabilities found that it "provides an important way of accommodating a work-limiting disability rather than reflecting marginalization of the disabled by employers" (Jones 2007).

The rise in part-time work therefore presents opportunities for many people with disabilities.[4] While part-time work has the advantage of placing fewer demands on time and energy, it has the disadvantages of generally lower pay when compared with full-time employment (10% less per hour on average), a much lower likelihood of receiving employer benefits (particularly employer health insurance and pension coverage), and a lower likelihood of receiving employer-sponsored training (Schur 2002: 608; Frazis et al. 1998).

2. Telecommuting and Other Home-Based Work

The rapid development in computer and Web-based information technologies over the past 25 years has made home-based work more productive and attractive to employers and employees. A 2005 survey of U.S. employers found that about one-third allow at least some employees to work part of the workweek at home occasionally (34%) or on a regular basis (31%) (Bond et al. 2005). Only 3%, however, offer this option to most or all employees.

---

[4] The increase in part-time work was 15.5% over the 1995–2008 period among a selected set of OECD countries (OECD 2010: 29). Also, on the basis of occupational projections for the United States, the growth rate of part-time jobs is projected to be slightly higher than for all jobs over the 2008–2018 period (Kruse et al. 2010).

Home-based work can help accommodate the needs of a wide range of employees, including those with and without disabilities. It may have special benefits for people with mobility impairments who find it difficult or costly to travel outside the home, for those who may need to take frequent breaks from work, and for those who must remain close to medical equipment at home. The advantages are illustrated by two stories:

> Many disabled workers say they consider telecommuting to be the single most important factor enabling them to work. Robert O'Byrne, a senior applications specialist for New York Life and a quadriplegic, said he would be on public assistance if his employer had not allowed him to work from home. Mr. O'Byrne, 41, who taught himself programming, goes to the office for occasional meetings, driven there by his father in a specially equipped van. But, he said, the hour-and-a-half commute from his home in Wyckoff, N.J., to the company's offices in Manhattan, would be too exhausting. The job at New York Life "gave me a sense of purpose," he said.
>
> Janet Pearce, a producer at NBC News, was diagnosed with muscular sclerosis nearly a decade ago. But she has rarely missed a day of work even as her illness has progressed, making her unable to walk. A vital reason she has remained gainfully employed is telecommuting. About two years ago, NBC gave Ms. Pearce the option of working at home when she needed to, and today she splits her time, spending three days a week at the office and two at home. After 36 years at NBC, Ms. Pearce said she could not imagine leaving her job, even when she found herself overwhelmed by her disease, her medical appointments, the physical therapy and the adjustment to a wheelchair. (Tahmincioglu 2003)

Workers with disabilities are more likely than those without disabilities to usually work at home. As shown by U.S. data presented in Figure 3.2, 5.3% of workers with disabilities in 2010 reported that they usually work at home, compared with 4.1% of workers with disabilities. Not surprisingly, the rate is high among those with mobility impairments (6.3%), especially those who have difficulty going outside the home alone (7.1%). Self-employed workers are more likely

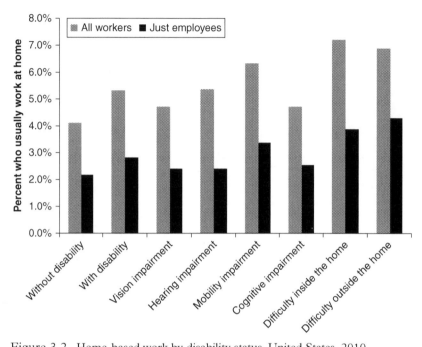

Figure 3.2. Home-based work by disability status, United States, 2010.

than employees to be working at home.[5] Excluding the self-employed, Figure 3.2 shows that employees with disabilities remain more likely than those without disabilities to usually work at home (2.8% compared with 2.2%), with the highest likelihood again among people with difficulty going outside alone (4.3%). These differences remain after demographic factors are controlled for and are strong enough that sampling error can be rejected as an explanation (Kruse et al. 2011).

The numbers in Figure 3.2 present a lower bound on home-based work, however, since they reflect only those who "usually" work at

[5] Based on analysis of the 2010 American Community Survey, U.S. Census Bureau. Among the self-employed, the percentage of those usually working at home is 22% among people without disabilities, 23% among those with a hearing impairment, 21% among those with a vision impairment, 27% among those with a mobility impairment, 23% among those with a cognitive impairment, 28% among those with difficulty getting dressed or bathed, and 30% among those with difficulty going outside alone (Kruse et al. 2011).

home. Using a broader definition of home-based work, about one-eighth (12.7%) of workers reporting work disabilities stated in 2001 that they do at least some paid work at home, compared with one-twelfth (8.4%) of workers without work disabilities (National Council on Disability 2007). Therefore, workers with disabilities appear to be about one and a half times as likely as workers without disabilities to do home-based work. While computers can have special advantages for people with disabilities (as will be covered in Chapter 5), their high rate of home-based work is not fully explained by computer use: only half of home-based workers with disabilities were using computers in their paid home-based work in 2001, compared with four-fifths of home-based workers without disabilities. Data on home-based work outside of the United States are limited. A 2009 survey of UK employers revealed that 20% had made or planned to make an accommodation that allowed working from home (Dewson et al. 2010).

There are several advantages of home-based work from the employer's perspective: the ability to tap into a labor pool that is not available for on-site work; possible savings on office space and equipment; the ability to meet transportation demand management guidelines or regulations; and possibly more motivated and loyal employees. The disadvantages for the employer can include increased difficulty in monitoring quality of work and possible increased costs in providing necessary equipment at home. For the employee, the advantages of flexibility and reduced transportation expense must be balanced against the reduction in social interaction at work, possibly reduced chances for training and promotion, and difficulties in drawing a boundary between work and family life. Working at home can be a reasonable accommodation under the ADA for some employees with disabilities, but workers with disabilities are not automatically entitled to work at home (Blanck et al. 2009).[6]

---

[6] The reasonableness of home-based work as an accommodation depends on whether the disability necessitates work at home and whether the essential job functions can be

3. Temporary Employment

Temporary jobs can provide economic resources and useful work experiences without substantial training or commitments tied to a specific job or employer, and often with flexibility in deciding whether and when to work. One example is work obtained through a temporary employment agency – this industry has developed in the past two decades to help firms meet immediate but possibly short-lived needs for ready supplies of skills. Temporary employment includes on-call and day labor, in which workers may be hired at short notice to work for one or a few days, as well as other jobs that are not expected to last long.

Along with the potentially greater flexibility of temporary employment compared with standard jobs, such jobs can also be a way of testing one's abilities and interests in different work environments and of "auditioning" for permanent jobs when openings arise. Temporary employment may be a way for people with disabilities to ease their transition into work after an injury or illness. The following stories, from a study of Manpower Inc., illustrate the benefits that temporary employment can have for people with disabilities and their employers (Blanck and Steele 1998):

> An accident in the military resulted in the amputation of Greg Alden's right arm.... [Despite an associate degree in micro-computers], Greg spent the next several months applying for jobs in his field but had no luck.... [A temporary agency assessment] indicated that Greg had exceptional computer skills.... At his job [obtained through a temporary agency], Greg is responsible for testing educational software that is designed for children. "My disability is not a factor.... Even when there was a cutback in the number of temporaries on this assignment, I remained on the job," he says. "I like the work, I'm paid well, and I find it interesting and challenging."

performed at home. The factors to consider are discussed by the Equal Employment Opportunity Comission (EEOC) at www.eeoc.gov/facts/telework.html.

Valerie Meyer graduated from college with an associate degree in business management and marketing. But Valerie [who uses a wheelchair] found it difficult to find employment. [After several temporary assignments], Valerie was hired as a permanent customer service representative. Her supervisor said "Valerie was one of 60 people that Manpower provided us for the particular project that we had. We knew that when the project ended we were going to hire one person. After observing Valerie's work, we knew that she was the right person for the job."

As with part-time and home-based work, people with disabilities are more likely than those without disabilities to have temporary jobs. Looking just at temporary help agencies, 0.8% of U.S. workers with disabilities held temporary jobs in 2008–2009, compared with 0.6% of workers without disabilities (Kruse et al. 2011). While the difference in percentage points is small, it indicates that workers with disabilities are about one-third more likely than workers without disabilities to have such jobs. The difference holds up after demographic factors are controlled for and is strong enough for sampling error to be rejected as an explanation.

Looking broadly at temporary employment, evidence from the United States in 2001 shows that workers with disabilities are about twice as likely as those without disabilities to hold some type of temporary or contingent job (as temporary agency employees, on-call and day laborers, workers provided by contract firms, independent contractors working primarily for one company, and workers who expect their jobs to last for a limited time). About one-fifth (20.8%) of workers with disabilities reported such arrangements, compared with slightly more than one-tenth (20.8%) of workers without disabilities (Schur 2003: 597–598). In addition, permanent full-time employees with disabilities were about twice as likely as those without disabilities (7.9% compared with 4.1%) to have started working with their current employer as a temporary or contract worker, supporting the idea that these jobs are an important part of a transition to permanent employment for many people with disabilities.

There are, however, downsides to temporary employment for employees apart from the lack of job security. About one-fourth of temporary employees say they are in a temporary job because it is the only type of work they could find; in addition, about three-fifths say they would prefer a standard job (Schur 2002, 2003). Like part-time employees, temporary employees earn less than permanent employees (10% less per hour on average) and are much less likely to receive health insurance or pension coverage from the employer.

4. Flexible Schedules

Some jobs allow workers a degree of control over work hours, either by giving them some discretion over when to start and stop work each day or by allowing them to choose or design a schedule that meets their needs but remains fixed each week (such as evening or night shifts or compressed workweeks). A 2005 survey of U.S. companies showed that many employers allow at least some employees to change starting and quitting times on a daily basis (34%) or periodically (68%) or to have control over which shifts they work (39%) (Bond et al. 2005). Such arrangements give employees with disabilities the flexibility to accommodate expected appointments (e.g., weekly physical therapy) and unexpected events (e.g., transportation or medical difficulties).[7]

A U.S. study using 1996 data found no general difference between workers with and without disabilities in the likelihood of working day, evening, night, or rotating shifts (Presser and Altman 2002). Similarly, there is little overall difference by disability status in flexibility of hours for employees: in a 2001 U.S. survey, about one-third of employees

---

[7] Part-time and flexible schedules can be a type of reasonable accommodation for an employee with a disability, if those schedules allow the essential job functions to be performed and do not impose an undue hardship on the employer. The EEOC provides guidance at www.eeoc.gov/types/ada.html.

with and without disabilities could vary or make changes in when they began and ended work, and about one-eighth were part of formal flextime programs (National Council on Disability 2007: 109). The occupational pattern, however, masks some underlying differences. Employees with disabilities are more likely to be in occupations that do not provide flexible hours (production, service, and clerical jobs) and are underrepresented in managerial, professional, and technical jobs where flexible hours are more common. Within occupations, however, employees with disabilities are in fact slightly more likely than their co-workers to have flexible hours.[8] In other words, workers with disabilities have less access to the types of jobs that commonly provide flexible hours, but within a given job, they are more likely than their co-workers without disabilities to be able to vary or make changes in the times they begin and end work. This may reflect formal or informal accommodations to help meet the needs of employees with disabilities.

5. Self-Employment

While employees with disabilities overall do not seem to have more flexible hours than employees without disabilities, some people with disabilities gain extra flexibility by becoming self-employed. The advantages of self-employment are illustrated by the following case:

> Allen, who previously worked for a large electronics company, spent approximately forty hours per week at that job. After the onset of

[8] Based on analysis of the 2001 U.S. dataset by the authors, employees with disabilities are on average about 5 percentage points more likely to be able to vary or make changes in their start and end times compared with co-workers without disabilities in the same occupation. The differences are highest in service (39% compared with 25% for employees with and without disabilities) and blue-collar occupations (29% compared with 19%). Accounting for occupational patterns does not, however, make a difference in access to formal flextime programs as measured by the survey.

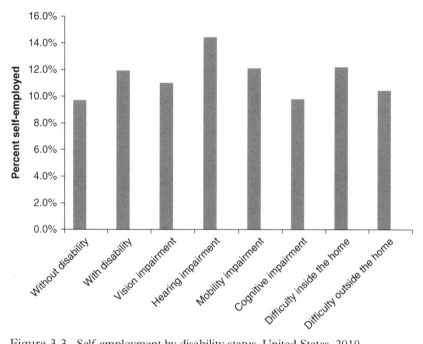

Figure 3.3. Self-employment by disability status, United States, 2010.

his disability, Allen began his own electronic repair business and was required to work sixty hours per week to maintain it. Allen says that although he works longer hours, he enjoys the flexibility of being self-employed and able to design his work and home life schedules. (Blanck et al. 2000: 1632)

Among employed people, those with disabilities are more likely than those without disabilities to be self-employed, as shown in Figure 3.3 based on U.S. data. Almost one-eighth are self-employed, compared with one-tenth of workers without disabilities. The rate of self-employment is highest among those reporting a hearing impairment, followed by those with a mobility impairment and those who have difficulty inside the home.

While there are no hard estimates, it is clear that self-employment is common among people with disabilities in the developing world. One informal estimate is that "for each disabled person employed in the formal sector, at least four are generating income as a result of their own enterprises" (Harris 2003).

Self-employment is a preferred choice among many people with disabilities.[9] The reasons for self-employment often cited by people with disabilities include flexibility, independence ("being one's own boss"), being able to earn more money, and being able to accommodate one's disability through arrangement of working conditions, physical access, communication, personal assistance, and transportation (Montana RRTC 2001; Work Incentives Support Center 2004; Office of Disability Employment Policy 2005; Arnold and Ispen 2005, Hagner and Davies 2002). While people without disabilities also commonly cite the value of flexibility and independence (Schur 2003), these factors may be especially salient for many individuals with disabilities.

Although most self-employed people with disabilities say they are satisfied with self-employment,[10] some feel limited to it. Among self-employed independent contractors, those with disabilities were more likely than those without disabilities to say they would prefer to work for someone else (15% compared with 9%). Also, among workers with disabilities, the self-employed were more than twice as likely as other employees to report encountering job-related discrimination within the past five years (26% compared with 12%), indicating that some individuals may choose self-employment after encountering perceived disability discrimination at work or in searching for jobs

---

[9] When people with disabilities in rehabilitation programs had the ability to choose their potential employment outcome, between 20 and 30 percent of the participants chose self-employment (Rizzo 2002; Arnold and Ispen 2005).

[10] In a U.S. survey, 91% of self-employed people with disabilities said they enjoyed operating their own business, 73% said they were satisfied with their business, and 56% reported that the business met or exceeded their initial expectations and was successful (Montana RRTC 2001).

(Schur 2003).[11] The idea that self-employment is not the preferred form of employment for many workers with and without disabilities is supported by the finding that the likelihood of self-employment decreases as labor markets tighten and more job opportunities are available (Schur 2003).

While self-employment provides greater flexibility and freedom in designing one's work, there are a number of potential barriers to self-employment, including inability to access capital (particularly given the low income and asset levels of people with disabilities), the possible loss of disability income and health care, the possible loss of housing and other subsidies, a lack of information on starting a business, and a lack of assistance and support from self-employment and small business entities (Office of Disability Employment Policy 2005). A number of programs have been designed to address these barriers in the United States (National Council on Disability 2007). In addition, a number of initiatives have sought to address the barriers to self-employment in developing countries. A study in the 1990s found 76 initiatives across 31 developing countries that encouraged self-employment, business start-ups, or worker cooperatives among people with disabilities (Harris 2003). Such programs can provide training, financial support (such as loans or subsidies), and other services to support business success.

C. PAY, JOB CHARACTERISTICS, AND EMPLOYEE ATTITUDES

What happens to people with disabilities in the workplace? Do they receive the same level of earnings as employees without disabilities, and do they have the same opportunities?

---

[11] Other studies also find that people with disabilities turn to self-employment because of a perceived lack of other employment opportunities (Blanck et al. 2000; Wagner and Davies 2002).

A number of studies indicate that employees with disabilities, relative to those without disabilities, tend to have:

- lower pay, both before and after education and other productive characteristics are controlled for;[12] and
- lower job security, measured both as perceptions of security and as actual rates of job loss.[13]

There is only limited research on other job characteristics, with only a few studies showing that employees with disabilities tend to have:

- lower likelihood of employer-provided benefits such as health insurance and pension plans;[14]
- fewer opportunities for training;[15]

---

[12] For the United States, see the review in Baldwin and Johnson (2006), plus subsequent studies in Bennett (2009), Schur et al. (2009, 2011), and Baldwin and Choe (2010). For Australia, see Brazenor (2002). For Canada, see Butler et al. (2006) and Campolieti and Krashinski (2006). For the United Kingdom, see Kidd et al. (2000) and Jones (2006) (the latter concluding that the pay gap appears to be explained by productivity differences). For Spain, see Malo and Pagan (2007) (as reported in Pagan and Malo 2009). In studies that track workers before and after the onset of disability, wage losses tend to be smaller for those who receive accommodations and those who return to their pre-injury employer (Butler et al. 2006; Campolieti and Krashinski 2006). Higher levels of education appear to narrow the pay gap between workers with and without disabilities, but a gap still remains (Hollenbeck and Kimmel 2008). Relative wages of workers with disabilities in the United Kingdom were found to be increased by equal opportunity policies, but decreased by workplace accommodations (Jones and Latreille 2010). Rigg (2005) found lower earnings growth among British workers with disabilities. For comparisons of average wages in the United Kingdom, see Table B7 at odi.dwp.gov.uk/roadmap-to-disability-equality/indicators.php (accessed May 22, 2012).

[13] Based on U.S. data in Baldwin and Schumacher (2002); Kaye (2010); Mitra and Kruse (2010); Schur et al. (2009); Yelin and Trupin (2003).

[14] Based on U.S. data in Schur (2002); Lustig and Strauser (2004).

[15] Based on UK data in Rigg (2005) and U.S. data in Schur et al. (2009). Another U.S. study finds that differences in perceived training opportunities disappear when

- lower likelihood of participating in decisions at the job, department, or company level;[16]
- similar levels of job autonomy, although a lower likelihood of having jobs classified as "economically and psychologically rewarding";[17]
- similar levels of promotion opportunities;[18]
- similar levels of perceived work–life balance, organizational commitment, and turnover intention;[19] but
- more negative views of treatment by management[20] and
- generally lower job satisfaction.[21]

These disparities are related to each other. In a study of U.S. employees, the lower job satisfaction of employees with disabilities was found to be predicted by their more negative views of management, which in turn were strongly related to their lower job security (Schur et al. 2011). The importance of views of management is consistent with another U.S. study finding that perceived company fairness to all employees has an especially favorable impact on the satisfaction, turnover intention, and organizational commitment of employees with disabilities (Schur et al. 2009).

occupation is controlled for (Schur et al. 2011). See Rankhumise (2010) for a discussion of progress in training and advancing people with disabilities in South Africa.

[16] Based on U.S. data in Schur et al. (2009).

[17] Based on U.S. data in Yelin and Trupin (2003: 28).

[18] Based on U.S. data in Schur et al. (2009, 2011), although Rigg (2005) finds lower "upward occupational mobility" for British workers with disabilities.

[19] Based on U.S. data in Schur et al. (2011).

[20] Based on U.S. data in Schur et al. (2011).

[21] For Canada, see Burke (1999); Renaud (2002); and Uppal (2005). For the United States, see McAfee and McNaughton (1997a, 1997b) and Schur et al. (2009, 2011), although Perry et al. (2000) found slightly higher job satisfaction among employees with disabilities than among nondisabled employees after controlling for perceived discrimination in access to employment. For Spain, Pagan and Malo (2009) found higher job satisfaction after controlling for detailed job characteristics, which they attributed to lower job expectations among workers with disabilities.

There are several possible reasons for the these disparities in pay, job security, benefits, training, and participation in decisions. One potential explanation is that the disparities reflect systematically different preferences between employees with and without disabilities, leading many people with disabilities to accept some disparities in exchange for other desired job characteristics – for example, lower pay in exchange for greater flexibility (creating what economists call compensating wage differentials). The limited evidence indicates, however, that this is unlikely. Both employed and nonemployed people with disabilities in the United States express views similar to those of their counterparts without disabilities about the relative importance of a number of job characteristics: high income, job security, promotion chances, working independently, having an interesting job, and being able to help others or society in one's job (Ali et al. 2011, Schur et al. 2011).

Some trade-offs may occur as people with disabilities accept lower-paying part-time or temporary work to accommodate concerns about time, effort, and flexibility. But studies continue to find lower pay and benefits for workers with disabilities when looking just at full-time employees (Baldwin and Johnson 2006; Schur 2002). The idea that the disparities reflect employee preferences is also contradicted by the findings of lower job satisfaction, since the satisfaction of employees with disabilities should not be lower if they are simply choosing to trade off one characteristic for another.

A second possible explanation for these disparities is that people with disabilities have lower levels of productivity due to education, training, functional abilities, or health. If this is the case, employees with disabilities may be more likely to be stuck in jobs with less desirable characteristics where their satisfaction is lower. A number of the studies have controlled for educational levels and years of work experience, but it is possible that remaining unmeasured differences in skill or health help to account for the disparities.

Differences in productivity may reflect job mismatch, in which employees with disabilities have not been able to obtain jobs that effectively utilize their skills or have not been granted necessary accommodations to improve their performance. Job mismatch may occur for any employee but may be especially likely for employees with disabilities, as employers may find it difficult to assess their prospective productivity, which can vary with the particular disability, its severity, the exact requirements of each job, and the cost effectiveness of potential accommodations. This may help explain the higher rates of job loss among employees with disabilities, as employers who find that they have made a bad match will tend to lay those workers off before other workers. A United Kingdom study found that job mismatch appears to be especially high for workers with disabilities, helping account for their lower earnings (Jones and Sloane 2010), although a Spanish study found no relation between disability and job mismatch (Blazquez and Malo 2005).

A third possible explanation for these disparities is stigma and discrimination, which may operate in part through job mismatch.

D. DISCRIMINATION MODELS AND EVIDENCE

Among people with disabilities in the United States, more than two-fifths (43%) reported in 2010 that they had encountered job-related discrimination due to disability, most commonly due to being paid less than similar workers with similar skills (18%) and being refused a job (17%) (Kessler/NOD/Harris 2010: 56). Restricted just to workers, over the 1986–2004 period between 22% and 32% reported having experienced job-related discrimination at some point in their lives (NOD/Harris 1998, 2004).[22] Among those who reported having encountered job-related discrimination in a 2000 survey, more than

---

[22] Also see Snyder et al. (2010) for a study finding that employees with disabilities in a large university were more likely than other employees to report both overt and subtle discrimination.

one-third (37%) reported taking some action against it, ranging from verbal or written complaints to working with lawyers and contacting politicians (Schur 2002).

In the United Kingdom, almost one-fifth (19%) of workers with disabilities reported unfair treatment at work in 2008, compared with one-eighth (13%) of workers without disabilities.[23] While these reports are useful measures of employee perceptions, they represent only one side of the story and will be overstated if they reflect general discontent over low pay or lack of employment opportunities. The numbers may also be understated, however, as some people may not be aware of discriminatory treatment they have received, are reluctant to report discrimination, or have been socialized in ways that hinder them from perceiving poor treatment as discrimination. For more in-depth understanding, we turn to models of discrimination with other types of evidence.

There are three basic models of discrimination, each based on different assumptions about the mechanisms that generate and support discriminatory behavior. The first model is based on simple prejudice, where people with a stigmatized characteristic are denied opportunities because others are uncomfortable being around them. Some support for the prejudice version of discrimination theory comes from studies finding lower wages for people whose disabilities have lower social acceptability rankings after productive characteristics are controlled for (Baldwin and Johnson 2006). Consistent with this, a Canadian study found that people with disabilities reported that perceptions of disability impede securing and maintaining employment (Shier et al. 2009).

A second model is statistical discrimination, where group averages are assigned to individuals based on imperfect information about individual characteristics. Employers may believe, rightly or wrongly, that

---

[23] odi.dwp.gov.uk/roadmap-to-disability-equality/indicators.php, Table D1 (accessed May 22, 2012).

people with disabilities are less productive on average and may make individual employment decisions based on this belief. Greater uncertainty about the future performance of people with disabilities makes statistical discrimination more likely.

The third model of discrimination is based on employer power or monopsony, where employers can pay certain groups less due to limited job mobility. For example, people with disabilities may face higher costs in switching jobs because of transportation problems or difficulties in attaining accommodations with a new employer. This would allow their current employers to underpay them, given a lower risk of turnover. One survey casts some doubt on this model as a general explanation for the disparities noted earlier, since people with disabilities were not more likely than those without disabilities to say they would have difficulty finding a similar job at another organization, but the employer power model may still apply in some situations (Schur et al. 2011).

The prejudice and statistical models of discrimination are given some support by psychological studies showing that supervisor and co-worker attitudes affect the workplace experiences of people with disabilities (Colella 1996, 2001; Colella et al. 1998; Marti and Blanck 2000; Ren, Paetzold, and Colella 2008). These attitudes can reflect stereotypes about the personalities and abilities of employees with disabilities, as well as discomfort if the disability involves particularly stigmatized conditions such as mental or cognitive impairments (Colella 1996).

Among employers in a 2008 U.S. national survey, the potential role of prejudice, discrimination, and unwelcome corporate cultures was indicated by the 34% who cited "attitudes of customers," 32% who cited "discomfort or unfamiliarity," 29% who cited "attitudes of co-workers," and 20% who cited "attitudes of supervisors" as challenges in hiring people with disabilities (Domzal et al. 2008: 13). Another recent survey found that 47% of employers said attitudes of co-workers are a reason employers don't hire people with disabilities

(Kaye et al. 2011). These results are consistent with earlier surveys: one-fifth (20%) of employers reported that the greatest barrier to people with disabilities finding employment is discrimination, prejudice, or employer reluctance to hire them (Dixon et al. 2003), while 22% of employers reported attitudes and stereotypes are a barrier to employment of people with disabilities in their own firms (Bruyère 2000).

It is likely that these figures understate the problem due to "social desirability" bias and the frequent discrepancy found between the attitudes employers express towards people with disabilities on surveys and their actual hiring practices (Wilgosh and Skaret 1987). The importance of stereotypes is also indicated by interviews with corporate executives revealing that "most employers hold stereotypical beliefs not consistent with research evidence" (Lengnick-Hall et al. 2008: 255) and by the finding that prior positive experiences with co-workers with disabilities are linked to more positive expectancies and affective reactions toward people with disabilities (Scherbaum et al. 2005).[24]

In a French study in 1989 that strongly points to employer discrimination, a representative sample of employers were sent job applications that varied by whether the (fictitious) applicant had paraplegia and whether the applicant was highly or modestly qualified for the position. With otherwise identical job applications, the highly qualified able-bodied applicants were 1.78 times more likely than those with paraplegia to receive a positive response, while the modestly qualified able-bodied applicants were 3.2 times more likely to receive a positive response (Ravaud et al. 1992).[25] The positions were all compatible with having paraplegia, indicating that the lower

---

[24] For further discussion of evidence on discrimination against workers with disabilities see Paludi et al. (2011).

[25] This methodology is currently being used by the authors and Meera Adya of Syracuse University for a study of U.S. employer responses to job applications from people with either spinal cord injuries or Asperger's syndrome, in positions where the disability will not limit productivity.

likelihood of a positive response is due to discrimination rather than productivity concerns.

The idea that negative attitudes shape the workplace disparities and experiences of employees with disabilities fits with the recent scholarship suggesting the importance of corporate culture, to which we turn in the next section.

E. CORPORATE CULTURE

"When individuals with disabilities attempt to gain admittance to most organizational settings, it is as if a space ship lands in the corporate boardroom and little green men from Mars ask to be employed."

– John, a 58-year-old employed man with paraplegia
(Boyle 1997, p. 263)

There has been growing recognition over the past two decades of the importance of corporate culture – the explicit and implicit attitudes, norms, policies, and practices in an organization. A company's culture helps determine not only who gets hired, but also employee treatment, performance, attitudes, turnover, and other outcomes. Corporate cultures fundamentally shape policies, attitudes, and opportunities. The evidence cited earlier on attitudes of employers, supervisors, and co-workers strongly suggests that the values and norms underlying many corporate cultures may reflect a basic discomfort with disability, which in turn creates tangible and intangible barriers that often marginalize employees with disabilities (Robert and Harlan 2006; Schur, Kruse, & Blanck 2005).

Some efforts to remake corporate culture focus on increasing diversity. As noted by the U.S. Supreme Court, "Major American businesses have made clear that the skills needed in today's increasingly global marketplace can only be developed through exposure to widely diverse people, cultures, ideas, and viewpoints" (*Grutter v. Bollinger*

2003: 330). Some of the efforts are partly motivated by a desire to reduce the potential for lawsuits with catastrophic consequences (Ramirez 2000) or to enhance corporate image (as indicated in a UK study by Dibben et al. 2002). The efforts include diversity training for all employees; scholarships, mentoring, and efforts to recruit members of underrepresented groups; and developing products and services that appeal to and benefit diverse communities (National Council on Disability 2007).

While some of the diversity research includes disability as a category of interest, the focus remains on gender, race, and sexual orientation, and disability is often overlooked (Klein et al. 2005; Ball et al. 2005; Knowling 2003; ITAA 2003). A study of the Fortune 100 companies in the United States found that 92 have workplace diversity policies, but only 39 of these policies expressly mention people with disabilities (Ball et al. 2005). While there is no solid research on the effects of these policies, one survey found that "companies with workplace diversity programs had twice as many people with disabilities in management positions (2%) as companies without diversity programs (1%)" (NOD 2003).

Apart from diversity programs, employee experiences are profoundly shaped by the extent to which a company has a bureaucratic structure with many fixed rules and procedures, and pits the fairness of treatment for all employees against the personalized consideration of employees with disabilities (Stone and Colella 1996). In companies with a more bureaucratic culture, accommodations for people with disabilities are more likely to be viewed as unfair by co-workers, especially if they are seen as making the accommodated person's work easier, making the co-worker's job harder or less desirable, or causing co-workers to lose competitive rewards.

A bureaucratic culture often includes detailed job descriptions that identify ideal job characteristics rather than essential job characteristics, which makes it more difficult for employees with disabilities to show they can perform the jobs (Stone and Colella 1996; Boyle 1997).

Employees with disabilities may respond to unfriendly or indifferent corporate cultures with a range of strategies that include concealing the disability, making extra efforts to communicate about the disability to reduce discomfort and clarify norms, emphasizing similarity to others, becoming a "superworker" to dispel stereotypes and modify others' expectations, and taking an activist approach to changing organization policies on their own or in concert with others (Stone and Colella 1996; Sandler and Blanck 2005).

People with disabilities are likely to do better in flexible organizations that value diversity, cooperation, and the personalized consideration of employee needs (Stone and Colella 1996). In company cultures that are based on personal needs, with a stress on individual autonomy and letting employees decide how to perform their own work, accommodations to the needs of all employees become the norm, and disability accommodations do not stand out as exceptions. Employers may, for example, combine a number of work–life policies and programs to create a "culture of flexibility" (Bond et al. 2005; Schur, Kruse, & Blanck 2005).[26]

The importance of corporate culture for people with disabilities receives support from laboratory studies (Colella 2001; Colella et al. 1998) and from a study of almost 30,000 employees in more than 250 worksites which found that employees with disabilities had more negative attitudes and a higher likelihood of quitting only at worksites where employees in general gave low ratings for company fairness and responsiveness to employees (Schur et al. 2009). As noted in the latter study, the results indicate that "workers with disabilities fare better in companies viewed as fair and responsive to the needs of all employees, in part

---

[26] In a 2002 survey of U.S. employees, almost one-third (31%) of employees in large companies perceived high workplace culture support for a culture of flexibility, compared with one-fifth (18%) of employees in small companies. At the other extreme, one-sixth (16%) of employees in large companies perceived low support for a culture of flexibility, compared with one-fourth (26%) of employees in small companies (Bond et al. 2005: 8–9).

because workplace accommodations are less likely to be viewed as special treatment, while employees with disabilities are likely to fare worse in unresponsive and more rigid organizations" (Schur et al. 2009).

F. WORKPLACE ACCOMMODATIONS

People with disabilities may need accommodations for some jobs, either to do the jobs at all or to do them as productively as possible. This depends on the job and type of disability. For example, workers who use wheelchairs need ramps or elevators in place of steps, and people with visual impairments often need Braille signage and peripheral software for computers. While many people with disabilities are able to perform their jobs without any changes to the job or workplace, there is a wide and growing range of accommodations available that can enable people with disabilities to be productive (Schartz et al. 2005, 2006).

The usefulness of accommodations is not limited to people with disabilities. Accommodations are often made as part of broader work–family programs designed to better meet all employees' needs. A 2005 survey of U.S. employers found that employers provide an average of 14.5–16.7 weeks of job-guaranteed family leave; 66% have employee assistance programs to help employees deal with personal and family issues; 47% provide health/wellness programs; and close to one-third provide assistance in locating child care (32%) or elder care (29%), while 7% provide on-site child care (Bond et al. 2005). In addition, workers' needs may be met by flexible work arrangements, as previously discussed. Several studies point toward positive effects of work–life programs on productivity, absenteeism, and other outcomes (e.g., Appelbaum et al. 2005; Corporate Leadership Council 2000, 2003; Klaus 1997; Konrad and Mangel 2000).

Employees without disabilities often request accommodations, although employees with disabilities are more likely to do so. Between one-eighth and two-thirds of U.S. employees with disabilities have received accommodations according to several studies.[27] Only one study has examined accommodations for employees without disabilities, finding that more than one-fourth of U.S. employees without disabilities had requested an accommodation (defined as a change in the job or workplace "to better meet your personal needs"), which was about half the rate for employees with disabilities.[28]

The financial costs of most disability accommodations are low, although a small percentage are expensive. Surveys of U.S. employers, including users of the federally sponsored Job Accommodations Network that provides free advice to employers, have shown that a majority of accommodations cost less than $500, while no more than 5% of accommodations cost more than $5,000.[29]

---

[27] Among workers with disabilities aged 50 or older in the 1992, 1998, and 2004 cohorts of the Health and Retirement Survey, 26% reported receiving a workplace accommodation if disability onset was before the implementation of the ADA, compared with 30% for those whose disability onset was after ADA implementation (Burkhauser et al. 2012). Hernandez et al. (2009) found that 65% of employees with disabilities in retail establishments had received accommodations compared with 27% of employees without disabilities. Data from the 1994–1995 National Health Interview Survey show that just 12% of workers with disabilities reported receiving any type of workplace accommodation (Zwerling et al. 2003), while more recent data from the 2007–2008 California Survey of People with Disabilities show that 31.3% of employed people with disabilities had discussed accommodations with their employers and 22.6% had received accommodations (H. Stephen Kaye, personal communication).

[28] Among more than 5,000 employees in six case study companies, 28% of those without disabilities had requested an accommodation from their current employer, compared with 62% of those with disabilities (Schur et al. 2013).

[29] A 2003 national survey of employers found that the average cost of accommodations was less than $500 for a majority of employers (29% reported $100 or less; 32% reported $100–$500; 11% reported $500–$1,000; 11% reported $1,000–$5,000, and 4% reported $5,000+) (Dixon et al. 2003). Only 14% reported that the cost was higher than they originally anticipated. A 2004–2005 survey of employers who used the Job Accommodations Network (JAN) found that the initial and first-year disability-related costs of accommodations were zero for 59% of employers, between

The benefits of accommodations have received less attention, in part because many of the benefits are hard to quantify. In two studies using U.S. data, a majority of managers, co-workers, and employees requesting accommodations report that disability accommodations help to improve employee productivity or retain qualified employees, while many also report that accommodations have eliminated the cost of training a new employee, increased employee attendance, decreased employee stress at work, improved interactions with co-workers, or increased overall company morale.[30]

Additional studies based on U.S. data have found that accommodations increase expected job tenure and reduce the speed of application for Social Security Disability Income (SSDI) benefits following the onset of a work-limiting disability (Burkhauser et al. 1995; Burkhauser 1999). A detailed examination of employee attitudes found that accommodations appear to have a spillover effect, improving not only the attitudes of

$1 and $500 for another 19%, and greater than $5,000 for only 5% of employees (Schartz et al. 2006). A 2008 national survey of employers who had not used JAN found that 24% reported no one-time or annual cost for disability accommodations, 55% reported a one-time cost, and 18% reported an annual cost (Solovieva et al. 2011). Across all respondents the median one-time cost was $50 with a mean of $1,480, and the median annual cost was $0 with a mean of $2,674. This survey also attempted to measure indirect costs related to the accommodation, "such as lost time because of training, supervisor's time, and loss of production." Slightly more than half of employers (54%) reported no indirect costs, while 35% reported indirect costs (11% did not know), with an overall median indirect cost of $510 and mean of $7,053.

[30] In a survey of U.S. employers, the percentage of those citing benefits of accommodations were 91% for retaining a qualified employee, 71% for increasing the employee's productivity, 56% for eliminating the cost of training a new employee, 46% for increasing the employee's attendance, 40% for improved interactions with co-workers, and 35% for increased overall company morale (Solovieva et al. 2011). In surveys of managers, co-workers, and employees requesting accommodations, strong majorities said that accommodations improved employee productivity, retention, and morale or job satisfaction, while more than one-third said accommodations improved employee attendance, interactions with co-workers, and workplace safety (Schur et al. 2013).

accommodated workers, but also the attitudes of other employees in the worker's unit (Schur et al. 2013). This supports the idea that accommodation policies may be an important aspect of corporate culture, consistent with arguments of Stone and Colella (1996). When employers were asked to quantify the value of the benefits, the median benefit reported was $1,000, compared with a median cost of $25 (Schartz et al. 2006). Another U.S. study found that a majority of U.S. employers estimated the direct benefits as more than $1,000, and one-third estimated indirect benefits of more than $1,000 (Solovieva et al. 2011).

Do the costs of accommodations deter employers from hiring people with disabilities? In reporting challenges to hiring people with disabilities, 64% of U.S. employers said that not knowing how much an accommodation will cost is a challenge, and 62% said that the actual accommodation cost is a challenge (Domzal et al. 2008: 13). The ADA's requirement to provide reasonable accommodations has been controversial since the ADA was passed, with critics claiming that the requirement increases the cost and decreases the likelihood of hiring people with disabilities.

Two early studies found that employment of people with disabilities declined at the time the ADA went into effect, which was interpreted as evidence that the accommodations mandate discouraged hiring (Acemoglu and Angrist 2001; Deleire 2000). Subsequent studies using these and other datasets, however, showed that there was no decline at this time when other measures and techniques were used (Kruse and Schur 2003; Beegle and Stock 2003; Houtenville and Burkhauser 2004; Hotchkiss 2003, 2004; also see similar results following passage of the UK DDA in Jones and Jones 2008; Jones 2009; and Donahue et al. 2011) and that any ADA-related decline in employment was temporary, while the SSDI system played a larger role in the overall trends (Jolls and Prescott 2004; Bound and Waidmann 2002).[31]

---

[31] A study of obesity suggested positive effects of the ADA, with increased employment of obese people after a court ruling that obesity is covered by the ADA (Carpenter 2006).

Similarly, employer concerns about accommodation costs may have contributed to a short-term decline in employment of people with disabilities in the United Kingdom after the DDA was implemented in 1996, but relative employment rates improved after 2000, possibly because of tighter labor markets and/or a growing realization that accommodation costs tend to be low (Bell and Heitmueller 2009).

In sum, workplace accommodations are a key topic and concern in employing people with disabilities. The fears over accommodation costs may be overstated by many employers, since the large majority of accommodations are not expensive, and recent studies show that accommodations have a number of benefits not only for the accommodated worker, but also for the workplace in general.[32]

G. POLICIES TO INCREASE EMPLOYMENT OPPORTUNITIES

What can be done to improve employment opportunities for people with disabilities? The possible policies may be put into several categories (drawing from WHO/World Bank 2011: 240–252).[33]

1. Laws
   - *Antidiscrimination statutes*: One goal of civil rights laws is to reduce discrimination that limits the hiring, promotion, and retention of people with disabilities, and thereby increase their employment opportunities. There are legislative or constitutional

---

[32] See Moon and Baker (2012) for a discussion of barriers to workplace accommodations and policies to address the barriers.

[33] For a description and analysis of policies in European countries designed to increase employment among people with disabilities, see Priestley and Roulstone (2009). For an additional review and analysis of policy options see Rimmerman (2013: 83–96).

prohibitions against disability discrimination in Australia, Brazil, Canada, Germany, Ghana, New Zealand, South Africa, the United Kingdom, and the United States. There has been mixed evidence over the success of the United States and United Kingdom laws (as reviewed earlier). While these provide important protections that enable people with disabilities to obtain or retain their jobs, they do not by themselves appear to have had a dramatic effect on the overall rate of employment of people with disabilities.

- *Affirmative action*: Some laws go beyond civil rights protections, requiring affirmative action for people with disabilities in which employers take steps to increase employment of people with disabilities. Such affirmative action requirements exist in Brazil, Israel, and Portugal, but there are no studies of their effects (WHO/World Bank 2011: 241).

- *Quotas*: Some countries attempt to ensure employment of people with disabilities by establishing employer quotas for the percentage of employees within a firm who have disabilities. "Over one-third of OECD countries have some type of quota, ranging from 2 percent in Spain and Korea to 6 percent in France and Poland, and even 7 percent in Italy," although the quotas are often unfulfilled (the average fulfillment is 50–70%) (Mont 2004: 20–21). The requirement for quotas often excludes small firms. Those who don't meet the quota are often required to pay a fine, which can be used for programs to increase the employment of people with disabilities. The quotas are often controversial, both among employers who may resist filling a quota and among disability advocates who are concerned that requiring employers to hire people with disabilities creates a stigma and decreases the perception that people with disabilities are valuable resources. There is no solid evidence on the effects of quotas on the employment of people with disabilities (WHO/World Bank 2011: 242).

2. Targeted programs

- *Vocational rehabilitation programs*: Such programs provide training, counseling, and job placement services for people with disabilities. They are generally found to have positive effects on the
  return to work and earnings of participants (see, e.g., evidence
  based on Australian data in Mavromaras and Polidano 2011;
  evidence based on Swedish data in Heshmati and Engstrom
  2001; evidence based on U.S. data in Hollenbeck and Huang
  2006 and Dean et al. 2011; a review of randomized trials on
  people with schizophrenia in Twamley et al. 2003; and a more
  general review in Pruett et al. 2008). There have been a variety
  of approaches to enhance the effectiveness of training, including
  having training done by community members and peers (e.g.,
  by rural village entrepreneurs in Cambodia), early interventions
  after disability onset (e.g., computer training for people with spinal cord injuries in Australia), and mentoring (e.g., internships
  for young people with disabilities in the United States) (WHO/
  World Bank 2011: 246).
- *Employer incentives*: These incentives can lower the cost of
  employing people with disabilities through wage subsidies,
  sub-minimum wages, or partial or full payment of disability accommodation costs. The evidence on wage subsidies is
  mixed – while they can lower the cost of employing targeted
  groups, the effect on hiring may be small, and the subsidies may
  create or reinforce stigma for the targeted group (see the review
  in Rimmerman 2013: 85–88). Paying people with disabilities
  below the minimum wage is permitted in the United States only
  in sheltered industries for people with severe disabilities, but it is
  permitted in Israel in competitive employment and in Australia
  in both sheltered and competitive employment (Soffer et al.
  2011). This approach is controversial, since some people see it
  as discriminatory and stigmatizing (Rimmerman 2013: 94–96).
  Regarding accommodation costs, small businesses in the United

States are eligible for up to $5,000 in tax credits for expenditures to increase workplace access.[34] In addition, U.S. employers are entitled to free advice on how to accommodate people with disabilities.

- *Supported employment programs:* These programs provide people with disabilities, particularly those with intellectual impairments and developmental disabilities, various types of assistance to maintain jobs in the competitive labor market. The assistance can include training, working with job coaches, assistive technology, and transportation to and from work. Studies of supported U.S. workers with intellectual disabilities have found that the benefits of supported employment exceed the costs for both the workers and taxpayers (Cimera 2010a, 2010b).

- *Sheltered employment:* This provides jobs in organizations or worksites where all employees have disabilities, typically with government support (Blanck et al. 2002). These are focused on persons with the most severe disabilities and are often controversial because they "segregate people with disabilities and are associated with the charity ethos" (WHO/World Bank 2011: 243). There has been a shift from sheltered employment to supported employment (WHO/World Bank 2011: 243). United States studies have found that workers with intellectual disabilities in sheltered employment earn less and cost more than supported employees in competitive employment (Cimera 2011a, 2011b).

- *Increased access to employment agencies:* Employment agencies have increasingly been required to serve all job seekers with disabilities, as opposed to having the job seekers go to special placement services. For example, in the United States the "one-stop

---

[34] askjan.org/media/tax.html (accessed January 27, 2012). See also www.worksupport. com/Topics/downloads/taxcredits.pdf for other employer incentives in the United States.

centers" created under the Workforce Investment Act were developed to bring together employment and training services within one place and are required to serve people with and without disabilities.

- *Disability management programs*: Such programs provide specialized services to people with disabilities, including "effective case management, education of supervisors, workplace accommodation, and an early return to work with appropriate supports" (WHO/World Bank 2011: 244). The services may be tailored to people with different types of impairments. Policies that encourage training and labor market activity soon after disability onset can interrupt a self-reinforcing cycle that keeps people out of the labor force, as indicated by results from a Canadian study (Oguzoglu 2012). A successful example is provided by the Return to Work program in Malaysia, where financial support combined with physical and vocational rehabilitation helped 60% of those injured at work to return to employment (WHO/World Bank 2011: 245).

3. Self-employment and microfinance

A number of programs throughout the world assist people with disabilities in becoming self-employed. These programs often provide microfinance (small amounts of money as loans or grants) and training in business skills to enable individuals to start a business. While such programs are often successful for low-income people in general, there is no solid evidence on how effective they are for people with disabilities (WHO/World Bank 2011: 247).

4. Disability income and other social protection

Disability income programs provide a minimal level of support for people with disabilities but have mixed effects on the likelihood of employment. The programs provide economic security that enables people after disability onset to get new training or otherwise prepare for employment, but also the programs often create disincentives for employment by providing a nonemployment source of income that may be decreased or eliminated as people become employed. As the costs of disability income programs have risen, many countries have experimented with their programs to encourage greater return to work. The changes include stronger financial incentives to work, such as making the benefits time-limited (e.g., in Germany, the Netherlands, and Norway), allowing beneficiaries to maintain their government-provided health insurance after becoming employed (e.g., in the United States), and providing tax credits for employed people with disabilities (e.g., in the United Kingdom). The changes also include employment supports to help overcome other barriers to employment (e.g., providing assistance with transportation or attendant care).

Such assistance may be most productive as "early intervention" at the time of disability onset, before a person has gone through a lengthy process of establishing that he or she has a condition limiting the ability to work (Burkhauser and Daly 2011: 105–106).[35] The World Health Organization and World Bank note, "Evidence from Hungary, Italy, the Netherlands, and Poland suggests that tighter obligations for employers to provide occupational health services and to support reintegration, together with stronger work incentives for workers and better employment supports, can help disability beneficiaries into work" (WHO/World Bank 2011: 248). Another policy idea is to institute "experience-rating" of U.S. employers so that the amount paid into the SSDI system is higher among employers when more of their injured employees move into the SSDI system (Burkhauser and Daly 2011: 109–113). This would provide an incentive for employers to accommodate injured workers so that they can continue their employment, as well as to create safer conditions that minimize the number of work-limiting disabilities.

5. Corporate culture and accommodations

Companies can adopt policies and practices to increase accommodations and create more welcoming corporate cultures. These

---

[35] A study from Sweden, however, casts doubt on the value of early intervention based on the signaling of health problems from applying for disability benefits (Engstrom et al. 2012).

include centralized offices in large companies that serve as information clearinghouses and technical assistance centers on disability issues; centralized accommodations funds so that costs do not fall on department or unit budgets; disability training for managers and co-workers; and encouragement and support of disability networks and affinity groups. A number of prominent U.S. companies have adopted these practices (National Council on Disability 2007).[36] Employer associations have been formed in several countries to share and promote practices for creating more inclusive cultures, such as the Employers' Forum on Disability in the United Kingdom, the Business Leadership Networks in the United States, and similar groups in Australia, Germany, South Africa, and Sri Lanka (WHO/World Bank 2011: 249).

In sum, while people with disabilities face a variety of barriers in the labor market, there are also promising trends that may help improve their employment opportunities and outcomes. As will be discussed in the next chapter, employment and economic empowerment are closely linked to political inclusion – the responsiveness of the political system and the ability and willingness of people with disabilities to vote and engage in other activities to further their political interests.

---

[36] For example, IBM and Microsoft have centralized accommodations funds; IBM, Microsoft, American Airlines, General Motors, JPMorgan Chase, and Nike provide support for networks and affinity groups for employees with disabilities; Giant Eagle and Microsoft train all employees in disability awareness and sensitivity; American Airlines, IBM, and JPMorgan Chase have structured processes and managerial training for accommodations; and Hewlett Packard, IBM, and Merrill Lynch develop recruiting methods and advertise job positions that target people with disabilities (National Council on Disability 2007: 11). For further examples see DiversityInc's 2012 "Top 10 Companies for People with Disabilities" (www.diversityinc.com/diversity-management/the-diversityinc-top-10-companies-for-people-with-disabilities-2/) (accessed August 28, 2012).

4

Political Inclusion

The actions of the disabled, their militancy, and their reliance on social protest demonstrate that they are independent rational beings, capable of self-determination and political action. These actions symbolically assault the prevailing common-sense (and sociological) imagery of passivity and victimization.... Unlike other responses to stigma and disability, political activism creates an ideology which repudiates societal values and normative standards, and in so doing creates a viable self-conception for participants. (Anspach 1979: 773).

[T]hose of us who engage in political debates ... have the obligation to enhance the abilities of ... our fellow citizens with disabilities to participate in the life of the United States as political and moral equals with their nondisabled peers – both for their own good, and for the good of democracy, which is to say, for the good of all of us. (Berube 2009)

A. INTRODUCTION

The representation of disadvantaged groups is a fundamental issue in a democracy. "Democracy's dilemma" is the recurrent theme of unequal participation and unequal engagement of minority groups with misunderstood political needs or, worse, silenced political voices (Lijphart 1997). As discussed, disability is, by definition, a perceived deviation from societal norms and as such often results in stigma and discrimination (Goffman 1963; Bonwich 1985; Fine and Asch 1988).

A historic barrier for people with disabilities has been the assumption that they cannot or should not participate in civic life. Public policies, often in the guise of paternalistic concern, have frequently isolated people with disabilities and excluded them from citizenship (U.S. Commission on Civil Rights 1983: 17–22). For example, many jurisdictions around the world have laws disqualifying people with mental and other disabilities from voting and serving on juries (Prince 2007: 16), as have many states in the United States (Schriner et al. 1997; Carey 2009). These laws have their origin in a judgment that people with intellectual disabilities do not deserve the basic rights of citizenship. This view was articulated in a 1927 Supreme Court case concerning the right of the state to prohibit procreation: "In his impassioned court decision, Justice Oliver Wendell Holmes Jr. gave unwavering support for the state's authority to deny basic civil rights, including the rights to privacy, parenthood, and bodily integrity, to people with intellectual disabilities" (Carey 2009: 4–5). While substantial progress has been made in the past century, people with intellectual disabilities still receive mixed messages in laws and policies about the extent of their rights of citizenship (Carey 2009: 9–11).

Even when laws or policies have not explicitly excluded people with disabilities, the arrangement of public space has often reflected an unexamined assumption that they will not participate (Hastings and Thomas 2005; Hahn 1988). One of the clearest examples of this is the inaccessibility of many polling places in the United States, despite the legal requirements for accessibility (GAO 2009). As another example, political information is often presented only in written formats, which make it difficult for many people with visual and cognitive impairments to learn about political candidates and issues.

There are two fundamental forms of political inclusion: (1) recognition of the civil rights of people with disabilities as members of the political community who should be treated with equality and dignity and (2) active participation in the political process. We first review the emergence of civil rights protections for people with disabilities and then address factors behind disability activism and other forms of political participation.

B. CIVIL RIGHTS PROTECTIONS

Grassroots activism and protest by people with disabilities formed the basis of the disability rights movement, which has led to important legislation and policy initiatives in many countries around the world. In the United States the first major civil rights protections for people with disabilities were contained in the 1973 Rehabilitation Act. Section 504 of this law prohibits discrimination against people with disabilities by the federal government, federal contractors, or any organization receiving federal funds and requires these entities to make accommodations (Blanck et al. 2009). The U.S. government, however, refused to issue the necessary regulations accompanying the Act, fearing they would be too costly. This delay led disability activists to engage in high-profile protests, culminating in 1977 with the occupation of government offices, which resulted in the signing of the regulations (Scotch 2001).

Thirteen years later, with bipartisan support and relatively little opposition, Congress passed, and President Bush signed, the Americans with Disabilities Act (ADA) of 1990.[1] Modeled on the Rehabilitation Act, the ADA prohibits private employers (with at least 15 employees), state and local government entities, and "public accommodations" (private commercial entities of any size) from discriminating against people with disabilities in the areas of employment, services, and access to public venues and commerce.

---

[1] See Young (2012) for a discussion of the support across the ideological spectrum for disability rights legislation.

By 2008, however, Congress recognized that the ADA was not as effective as intended in combatting disability discrimination, particularly with regard to employment, largely because the U.S. Supreme Court had narrowed the definition of disability and courts had become focused on whether an employee had a legally recognized disability and not on whether the employer had engaged in discrimination. Consequently, Congress passed the ADA Amendments Act (ADAAA) in 2008 with the "primary purpose" of "mak[ing] it easier for people with disabilities to obtain protection under the ADA."[2] With the passage of the ADAAA, Congress redirected courts to focus less on the question of whether plaintiffs have legally recognized disabilities and pay more attention to whether employers "have complied with their obligations" or engaged in unlawful discrimination.[3] Since the ADAAA does not apply retroactively (to any discrimination occurring before the act's 2009 effective date), it is too soon to evaluate its full impact. Early rulings, however, suggest that the ADAAA is indeed making it easier for plaintiffs to prevail in disability employment discrimination lawsuits (Hays and Kirby 2012).[4]

On the international level, the United Nations has become increasingly involved with disability issues since it was founded.[5] In 1993,

---

[2] For example, the ADAAA requires judges to interpret the definition of disability in favor of "broad coverage of individuals under the Act" and requires evaluation of a plaintiff's disability without regard to "the ameliorative effects of mitigating measures," such as hearing aids or medications. ADAAA Title 42 Chapter 126 Sec. 12102(4)(E)(i).

[3] ADAAA Title 42 Chapter 126 Sec. 12101(b)(5).

[4] See for example, Katz v. Adecco USA, Inc. 2012 WL 78156 (S.D. N.Y. 2012), Molina v. DSI Renal, Inc. 2012 WL 29348 (W.D. Tex. 2012), Eldredge v. City of St. Paul, 2011 WL 3609399 (D. Minn. 2011), Medvic v. Compass Sign Co, L.L.C. 2011 WL 3513499 (E.D. Pa. 2011).

[5] For a history of the UN's involvement in disability issues, see www.un.org/disabilities/default.asp?id=121 (accessed May 4, 2012). Apart from the 2006 UN Convention, there are 15 international human rights conventions and covenants that protect the rights of people with disabilities and are binding upon those who have ratified the instruments (www.un.org/esa/socdev/enable/disovlf.htm; accessed May 9, 2012). In

the UN adopted the nonbinding "Standard Rules on the Equalization of Opportunities for Persons with Disabilities," which along with the ADA served as a model for developing antidiscrimination legislation in a number of countries (Degener and Quinn 2002; South-North Dialogue 2006). Some examples of disability rights laws enacted in the 1990s are Australia's Disability Discrimination Act in 1992, India's Persons with Disabilities Act in 1995, and the United Kingdom's Disability Discrimination Act in 1995.[6] In addition, some countries, such as Austria, Brazil, and Germany, amended their constitutions to include prohibitions against disability discrimination (Degener and Quinn 2002).

A major accomplishment for the disability rights movement was the adoption of the UN Convention on the Rights of Persons with Disabilities in 2006. The UN Convention "is intended as a human rights instrument with an explicit, social development dimension. It adopts a broad categorization of persons with disabilities and reaffirms that all persons with all types of disabilities must enjoy all human rights and fundamental freedoms."[7]

The UN Convention was initially signed by 82 countries and has 155 signatories as of January 2013.[8] It takes a broad approach, stating in the preamble that all human rights are "universal, indivisible,

addition, a number of international instruments that pertain to disability are technically nonbinding but "express generally-accepted principles and represent a moral and political commitment by States" (ibid.).

[6] For a listing of legislative initiatives see www.dredf.org/international/ and "Compilation of Legislative Measures Undertaken in the Implementation of the Convention on the Rights of Persons with Disabilities: 2011 Update" at www.un.org/disabilities/documents/COP/crpd_csp_2011_crp.5.doc (accessed May 9, 2012). The United Kingdom's 1995 Disability Discrimination Act was updated in 2005 and replaced by the Equality Act of 2010.

[7] www.un.org/disabilities/default.asp?navid=14&pid=150 (accessed January 18, 2013).

[8] www.un.org/disabilities/countries.asp?navid=12&pid=166 (accessed January 18, 2013).

interdependent, and interconnected."[9] It emphasizes respect for the inherent dignity of individuals with disabilities and espouses the principles of "full and effective participation and inclusion in society on an equal basis with others" (Article 1). Among other provisions, the Convention includes the right to equal access to the physical environment, including buildings, roads, transportation, and technology (Article 9), and the right to choose one's place of residence, and where and with whom one will live (Article 19). It declares that all people have a right to education and that students with disabilities shall "not be excluded from the general education system on the basis of disability.... The goal is full inclusion" (Article 24).

The UN Convention also prohibits employment discrimination and requires employers to provide reasonable accommodations (Article 27). People with disabilities have the right to participate fully in cultural, public, and political life (Articles 19, 29, and 30). Among other provisions, this means that voting procedures, facilities, and material must be accessible and easy to understand and use, and that people with disabilities have the right to vote by secret ballot (Article 29). The Convention is more fully explained and analyzed in Kayess and French (2008) and Schulze (2010). Following its adoption, the UN Convention has helped stimulate disability legislation in many of its member countries.[10]

There is great variation in disability rights laws and their enforcement, and some do not provide adequate protections or penalties for violators.[11] Nonetheless, these initiatives for people with disabilities

---

[9] The UN Convention can be found at www.un.org/disabilities/default.asp?id=259 (accessed May 9, 2012).

[10] See "Compilation of Legislative Measures Undertaken in the Implementation of the Convention on the Rights of Persons with Disabilities: 2011 Update" at www.un.org/disabilities/documents/COP/crpd_csp_2011_crp.5.doc (accessed May 9, 2012). Also see Flynn (2011) for a discussion of how the Convention has helped stimulate and shape national disability strategies in a number of countries.

[11] Reports indicate a low level of compliance with accessibility laws (WHO/World Bank 2011: 173).

represent a greater recognition of their rights as citizens and are an important move toward political inclusion. Apart from these policy gains, it is important to consider another aspect of political inclusion: the degree to which people with disabilities participate through voting and other means. Any underrepresentation raises concerns that people with disabilities are being "sidelined" from the political process, and their needs and interests are being neglected and ignored by government officials and policy makers.

C. RESPONSES TO DISABILITY AND THEIR POLITICAL IMPLICATIONS

How are political views and experiences shaped by living with a disability? When examining political participation among people with disabilities, it is useful to start with three questions that apply to political participation in general (Verba et al. 1995):

1. "Are you able to participate?" The answer to this question depends on resources such as money, education, time, and energy. As discussed, people with disabilities tend to have lower incomes and education levels than people without disabilities, and their financial resources are often further constrained by higher expenses for medical care and special equipment. In addition, physical and mental abilities are themselves resources, and for many people with disabilities it takes extra time and effort to participate in community and political activities.

2. "Did anyone ask you to participate?" Political recruitment among people with disabilities is limited by their relative isolation and social exclusion. As will be seen in Chapter 5, they are more likely than people without disabilities to live alone and face transportation problems, and are less likely to be involved in community and social activities. The relative lack of participation in voluntary group

activities, which help build "social capital" (Putnam 2001), discourages political involvement. Isolation can be exacerbated by discriminatory practices such as disenfranchisement and physical barriers, frequent neglect by candidates and parties, and negative messages about disability conveyed through the media and public policy.

3. "Do you want to participate?" The desire to participate in politics is strongly influenced by feelings of political efficacy – both the belief that one is competent to participate (which political scientists call "internal political efficacy") and the belief that the political system is responsive to people like oneself ("external political efficacy"). People with disabilities in the United States tend to report lower levels of both types of political efficacy than do people without disabilities (Schur et al. 2003). Their lower level of internal efficacy is explained largely by lower levels of education and employment, but their lower level of external efficacy remains after these factors are controlled for. Lower levels of external efficacy are reflected in the greater likelihood of people with disabilities reporting that they do not receive equal treatment from public officials or have equal influence in politics, indicating that people with disabilities tend to feel the political system is not responsive to their interests.[12] Such perceptions may result from internalized "social constructions" of disability, which are popular images shaped by public policies that send negative messages (e.g., by stereotyping people with disabilities as dependent, needy, and unable to work) (Schneider and Ingram 1993). Lower levels of political efficacy may be part of a vicious cycle: people with disabilities may respond to the lack of concern exhibited by politicians by withdrawing further from the

---

[12] The situation may be different in the United Kingdom, where people with disabilities are about as likely as those without disabilities (71% vs. 73%, respectively) to believe they have been treated with respect and consideration by their local public services. odi.dwp.gov.uk/roadmap-to-disability-equality/indicators.php, Table D3 (accessed May 22, 2012).

political process, and this withdrawal, in turn, may lead politicians to pay even less attention to the needs and interests of people with disabilities.

At the extreme, the lack of personal efficacy can lead to fatalism, the belief that we are helpless products of external forces, with no capacity for initiative or control over what happens to us. For example, in a qualitative study of political participation among people with spinal cord injuries, one young man who experienced chronic pain and extreme isolation said, "[I] don't think anyone has control over their life.... I think things are more of a ... destiny. Whatever is going to happen is going to happen to you and I don't think you have control" (Schur 1998: 12). He added that he follows politics "not too much at all" and that, while he appreciates the work of disability rights activists, his life is not affected by decisions made by politicians: "To be honest with you, I really don't feel any effect [from] anything" (Schur 1998: 12).

Many people with disabilities are reluctant to identify with a stigmatized group or engage in political activity stemming from that identity (Hahn 1988; Scotch 1988; Young 2012). Borrowing from the sociologist Erving Goffman, Richard Scotch (1988) claims that many individuals practice "role distance," seeking to separate themselves as much as possible from others with disabilities, principally because of the image of helplessness and incompetence traditionally associated with "the disabled." This is expressed by one woman with a spinal cord injury who said:

> "I don't go to all of those special meetings with a bunch of other people sitting in wheelchairs 'cause to me that's too depressing.... I'm lucky enough that I have my friends and my family so it helps me keep my mind off of this stupid wheelchair.... So by staying away from other people in wheelchairs it kind of ... makes me feel like I'm having a normal day." (Schur 1998: 13)

A less extreme response to disability is "normalization." Normalizers emphasize that they are "superficially different but basically the same as everyone else" while ignoring, minimizing, or rationalizing the stigma placed on disability (Anspach 1979: 769). This is illustrated by a man who emphasized that he is "still the same person" he was before his disability and that it has not "changed my life drastically other than, yeah, I can't walk." He went on to say:

> "It's not something I dwell on. I get up in the mornings and I go about my life.... [T]he only time you can say you look at yourself as a disabled person is when, hey, I'm entitled to that parking spot, not you. But as far as looking at myself as disabled, no." (Schur, 1998: 13)

Normalizers may report high levels of efficacy and are likely to engage in standard forms of political participation such as voting, but they are unlikely to engage in disability activism.

While responses such as the ones quoted here discourage activism, many people respond to disability-related problems and experiences by becoming politically active on disability issues. Anspach describes disability activists as individuals who identify strongly with others who have disabilities and maintain a positive self-concept while reject-ing society's devaluation of people with disabilities. Identification is a necessary but insufficient condition for political activism on behalf of a subordinate group (Miller et al. 1981). Group identification with-out politicization is illustrated by a woman who began to "enjoy life" when she became a peer counselor, teaching other people with spi-nal cord injuries how to become "as independent as possible" and "to be advocates, to get out there and get the things that are needed for them" (Schur 1998: 13–14). While she strongly identifies with other people who have spinal cord injuries, her focus is almost exclusively on self-help. She claimed she is completely uninterested in political issues: "I am not politically oriented in any way, shape, or form."

Disability activism requires not just identification with others who have disabilities, but also awareness of the group's position in society, dislike for its low status, and belief that social injustices rather than individual failings are to blame for the group's low social position. According to Scotch (1988: 166), blaming the environment rather than the individual for disability-related problems is a basic part of the social model of disability, which he claims is a "prerequisite to activism."

Some writers argue that traditional rehabilitation programs discourage disability activism because they promote normalization and "depoliticize" disability by focusing on modifying the individual rather than altering the environment (Anspach 1979; Hahn 1985: 88–9). It is clear, however, that rehabilitation experiences can also raise political issues that spur activism. For example, one woman's negative rehabilitation experiences led her to embark on a personal campaign to force rehabilitation hospitals to design more individualized programs and to refrain from discharging patients prematurely.[13]

During rehabilitation, people meet others who are in similar circumstances, which can lead to strong bonds and political awareness. For example, one veteran described how he went through a "metamorphosis" during rehabilitation at a hospital where there was a "special energy" and camaraderie among the patients that gave him "a lot more of a political consciousness." Despite his growing political awareness, he did not view his disability in political terms at first:

> "I think initially becoming involved with [the disability rights organization] was not a political decision by any means. It was, hey, this seems like a good group that can help me and is helping other people and it seemed like a good group to be involved in … but the

---

[13] She said the hospital tried to discharge her too soon, just as she was starting to recover some function, and claimed the rehabilitation system "treats everyone the same – they don't individualize anything.... You're like a herd of cattle.... They really don't care." As part of her fight to regain control over her life, she waged a one-woman campaign to raise public awareness and try to change laws regarding rehabilitation. Her response can be described as "lone wolf activism," since initially she refused to speak with any politicians or work with disability groups to promote her views, although eventually she worked with legislators to further her goals (Schur 1998).

realization that, you know, a lot of what [the organization] does is political is a thing that's kind of grown over the years. It's not really something that was kind of instantaneous." (Schur 1998: 16)

His work with the disability organization exposed him to new information and role models that gradually led him to understand the political dimensions of disability and become a committed disability rights activist. He has worked for the organization for more than twenty years and now holds a full-time leadership position. As part of his political evolution, he developed a new understanding of discrimination; he said he does not think that anyone is "born with" a knowledge of discrimination but that "you have to learn when somebody's not treating you right." His personal response to disability has been to try to find a "balance," paying attention to physical needs and disability-related problems (unlike normalizers), but not letting his disability rule his life as the fatalists do.

While discrimination may lead to feelings of alienation and passivity, another disability activist described how discrimination was a political catalyst for her. As a wheelchair user, she found she was unable to get into any of the changing rooms at a major department store and was told she could buy the clothes, take them home, and return what she didn't want. She said, "I picked up the clothes, I threw them on the floor, I said, 'I don't have to do that. Nobody else has to do that'" (Schur 1998: 15). She went on to create one of the first disability organizations in the state and worked on changing the state code (prior to the ADA) so that there is a paragraph requiring accessible dressing rooms. She found that her own experiences with discrimination drew her away from her original career plans and toward disability issues: "I did not realize that I had lost my rights once I became disabled. They don't tell you that. So when I did experience discrimination, I was appalled."

Four basic perceptions appear to be linked to disability rights activism. First, there must be recognition of the importance of disability-related problems. This is undermined by normalization, when people minimize or rationalize such problems. Second, in contrast to people with a fatalistic response, activists have a sense of efficacy. They believe that many disability-related problems are not an inherent part of living with a disability but are socially constructed and can be eradicated. Third, they perceive that their problems are widely shared and have a strong sense of identification with others who have disabilities. Finally, activists perceive that many disability-related problems require political rather than purely individual solutions. They emphasize changing policies, practices, and laws rather than relying on self-help strategies such as developing a "positive attitude" or learning how to put nondisabled people at ease.

Disability activism, in turn, may change self-conceptions and societal conceptions of the participants: Phillips (1985: 54) argues that political activism can give people with disabilities a "new belief in their ability to control their own destinies without capitulating totally to normalization." In other words, activism may increase feelings of personal control and efficacy, as well as counteract fatalism stemming from disability-related problems. It also directly challenges stereotypes of people with disabilities and is an "assault upon taken-for-granted popular conceptions of deviants as helpless and powerless" (Anspach 1979: 765–766). The idea that political involvement can have a transformative effect on participants has a long history, starting with Aristotle .(1962: 2), who argued that political participation "completes and fulfils the nature of man," and continuing on to modern advocates of participatory democracy who claim that "human growth and development ... [are] stimulated through involvement in politics and in governmental decision making" (Conway 1991: 60). It may have particular value for members of disadvantaged groups who have experienced a history of marginalization, disempowerment, and political invisibility.

Just as there are different ways people with disabilities become politically active, there also are a variety of disability organizations, with different goals, strategies, and approaches. On the basis of work developed by Oliver (1990), Barnes and Mercer (2010) constructed a typology of disability organizations, divided into organizations primarily *for* and those primarily *of* disabled people. The former include partnership/patronage organizations focused on charity and the provision of disability services, and economic/parliamentarian organizations that focus on a single issue and conduct lobbying, research, and/or legal work. The latter include self-help groups, populist organizations focused on empowerment, collective action, and consciousness raising, and umbrella organizations made up of various disability groups (Barnes and Mercer 2010: 162).

D. DISABILITY MODELS AND POLITICAL ACTIVISM

Both individual and societal responses to disability have been profoundly shaped by the disability rights movement and its reframing of disability-related issues. As noted in Chapter 1, the social model views disability as created by society and people with disabilities as a distinct group with a shared experience of oppression, and it has provided a sense of unity and solidarity that has motivated generations of activists around the world.

The universalist model of disability has different implications for political activism. This model views impairments as existing on a continuum and emphasizes that almost all people will experience impairments at some point in their lives. The universalist model sees the reality of oppression as complicated, since different groups, and individuals within groups, may experience disability in different ways and face different issues. As noted, many people with impairments may not identify themselves as having disabilities. This may be particularly true for older people who gradually develop limitations and become politically involved in issues related to their conditions or impairments. In addition, this model is inclusive of people who do not currently experience disability but may be politically involved in disability issues out of a recognition that disability touches everyone's life at some point.

Both models are valuable, given the diversity of people with disabilities and the problems they face. The social model, which focuses on society as the source of disabling barriers, may be the most effective for uniting people across disabilities to raise awareness and fight for disability rights. The universalist model may be more relevant after basic disability rights are in place, helping people with disabilities form coalitions with other groups around common interests, such as work–family balance or affordable health care, that address concerns of large numbers of people both with and without disabilities.

E. EVIDENCE ON DISABILITY ACTIVISM

How many people with disabilities engage in disability activism? As shown by the preceding discussion of qualitative evidence, disability-related problems can both discourage and encourage activism. While people in many countries have become disability activists, the only available quantitative evidence on how many people with disabilities have engaged in disability advocacy is from the United States, showing that about one-sixth have engaged in disability activism (Table 4.1) (Kessler/NOD/Harris 2010; Schur 2003a).

Both qualitative and quantitative studies have explored the characteristics of disability activists (Schur 1998, 2003a). People who become politically active on disability issues are more likely to meet regularly with disability groups. As noted, such groups provide education on disability issues, political recruitment networks, and a supportive environment for the development of a sense of efficacy and identification with others who have disabilities. Disability activists are more likely than other people with disabilities to say they have directly experienced disability discrimination, which partly reflects a broader definition of discrimination. For example, activists tend to define discrimination not just in terms of intentional behavior, but also in terms of policies or practices that have discriminatory effects, such as

Table 4.1. *Evidence on Disability Activism among People with Disabilities*

Ever participated in group or organized activity that advocates for rights of people with disabilities (2010 U.S. survey)	17%
In past year, engaged in political activity on a disability issue (1998–2000 U.S. surveys)	10%
In past year, took action against private organization on disability issue (e.g., talking to business owners, filing lawsuits) (1998–2000 U.S. surveys)	9%
Either of above two in past year (1998–2000 U.S. surveys)	15%

architectural standards that make buildings inaccessible. They are also less likely to believe that people with disabilities get equal respect from public officials. Nevertheless, disability activists also express greater life satisfaction and a greater sense of control over their lives, and experience higher levels of internal and external political efficacy than other people with disabilities.

The most committed activists have lived with their disabilities for a longer period of time on average, consistent with findings on the psychological impact of disability onset. While some people describe becoming activists after being galvanized by a particular experience (e.g., an act of discrimination or denial of needed services), others describe going through a slow process in which they gradually learned to come to terms with living with a disability, fully accept themselves, and identify with others who have disabilities. Early in this process they may go through stages of fatalism, role distance, and/or normalization but then learn to develop broader views of disability and discrimination, as well as an appreciation for the value of political action.

Some people originally join disability groups for nonpolitical reasons but become politically active after being exposed to new issues and meeting politically active people who serve as role models. The gradual politicization of many activists suggests that there are no apparent prerequisites for who can become active in disability rights politics and that circumstances – the types of groups, information, and opportunities that are available – often play a large role in politicization.

One noteworthy finding on disability activism in the United States is that it is highest among young people with disabilities (Schur, Shields, and Schriner 2005). This may reflect generational differences in the experience of disability: older generations were socialized during a time of greater segregation and stigma for people with disabilities, while the younger generation has been socialized during a time of increased emphasis on disability rights, more laws prohibiting discrimination, and greater access to equal education. These different experiences suggest that disability activism may increase as older cohorts of people with disabilities are replaced by younger cohorts.

Disability protests appear to be more common in the United States than in other countries: over the 1970–2005 period Barnartt (2010b) identifies 1,247 disability protests in the United States compared with 689 outside of the country.[14] She attributes this difference largely to the U.S. organization ADAPT, which commonly uses public protests in its advocacy efforts. The non-U.S. protests increased substantially after 1989, with most occurring in Canada and the United Kingdom. About half of the protests included people with a range of disabilities, while the other half involved people with specific types of disabilities (most commonly lack of or limited mobility, deafness, and blindness).

It appears that early political efforts are often motivated by the goal of increasing government benefits and needed services rather than redressing past discrimination or promoting civil rights. For example, Rimmerman and Herr (2004) write that the main goal of the 1999 disability strike in Israel was to improve disability benefits for people with the most severe disabilities, while in Japan the first disability groups in the early 1960s were motivated by the goal of

---

[14] Barnartt (2010b) notes that there are methodological problems in international comparisons; for example, the search for disability protests was based primarily on English-language news reports, although some were obtained from non-English sources.

increasing the welfare pension for people with disabilities (Hayashi and Okuhira 2001).

Similarly, efforts by advocates in former Communist countries in Eastern Europe remain primarily focused on improving services for people with disabilities (Holland 2008). Gayle and Palmer contend that the demand for services may be based on the premise that people with disabilities feel they have a right to the services which will in turn enhance their development and participation in society (Gayle and Palmer 2005: 127). In other words, it may not be uncommon for disability organizations to begin with relatively narrow and service-based agendas and gradually develop a broader focus as their members gain political efficacy and a broader conception of discrimination through their political efforts. Some disability scholars maintain there is a risk, however, that once disability organizations gain more widespread social and political acceptance, their priorities may tend to shift and their radicalism diminish in terms of both political aspirations and activities (Barnes and Mercer 2010).

It would be a mistake to overgeneralize regarding trends in disability activism. First, even in developing countries where people with disabilities receive few services, disability activists sometimes focus on specifically "political" goals. For example, in Lebanon disability rights organizations conducted a nonpartisan nationwide campaign to safeguard and promote voting rights of citizens with disabilities on the eve of the 2005 governmental elections (Wehbi and El-Lahib 2008).

Furthermore, when looking at disability rights activism, it is a mistake to separate "nonpolitical" issues (such as the receipt of government benefits and services) from overtly "political" issues (such as access to voting). As noted, a fundamental aspect of the disability rights movement is the recognition that many disability-related problems that are traditionally viewed as private, personal issues are in fact caused by "disabling" social and political barriers and ought to be addressed through public action.

F. POLITICAL PARTICIPATION IN GENERAL

How much do people with disabilities participate in political activities in general, apart from disability activism? We begin by looking at voting, since "[p]articipating in elections is the essential starting point of any democratic system" (Prince 2007: 5). As discussed, participation may be limited by lower levels of resources and greater social isolation. In the United States, fewer people with disabilities vote than do people without disabilities, and they are less likely to engage in other political activities such as working with others on community problems, contacting public officials, attending political meetings, contributing money to political causes, writing letters to newspapers, and participating in political protests or demonstrations. Table 4.2 presents evidence on U.S. voter turnout, and Table 4.3 presents evidence on other forms of political participation, from surveys over the past 20 years.[15]

The U.S. disability gap in voter turnout may not extend generally to other political systems that have higher turnout in general: across European Union countries in 2007, people with disabilities were just two percentage points less likely than those without disabilities to participate in national elections (Grammenos 2010: 45).

There were, however, substantial differences across countries, with especially low participation by people with disabilities in Finland

---

[15] In Table 4.2, study 1 is based on a survey of New Jersey residents with spinal cord injuries (SCIs) (Schur and Kruse 2000); numbers 2, 6, 8, 10, and 12 are based on surveys by Louis Harris and Associates (Kessler/NOD/Harris 2010: 133); numbers 3, 4, and 5 are based on nonemployed respondents to national surveys who answered an employment question by saying they have a disability (Shields et al. 1998; LoBianca 1998); numbers 7 and 9 are based on broader samples of people with disabilities (Schur et al. 2002; Schur, Shields, and Schriner 2005); and numbers 11 and 13 are based on large broad samples in the U.S. Census Bureau's Current Population Survey (Schur and Adya 2012). The data in Table 4.3 on other forms of political participation are based on an analysis of national surveys conducted at Rutgers University following the elections in 1998 and 2000, and the 2008 CPS Civic Engagement Supplement conducted by the U.S. Census Bureau.

Table 4.2. *Disability and Voter Turnout*

Election Year	Disability Sample	Disability Turnout	Nondisability Turnout	Gap
1. 1992	People with SCIs	56%	71%	15%
2. 1992	Broad disability sample	45%	56%	11%
3. 1994	Nonemployed	33%	54%	21%
4. 1992–1996	Nonemployed	57%	71%	14%
5. 1996	Nonemployed	44%	65%	21%
6. 1996	Broad disability sample	33%	50%	17%
7. 1998	Broad disability sample	54%	60%	6%
8. 2000	Broad disability sample	70%	82%	12%
9. 2000	Broad disability sample	41%	52%	11%
10. 2004	Broad disability sample	52%	56%	4%
11. 2008	Broad disability sample	57%	64%	7%
12. 2010	Broad disability sample	59%	59%	0%
13. 2010	Broad disability sample	43%	46%	3%

Note: "SCI" denotes spinal cord injury.

and Italy, and especially high participation in Estonia and Slovenia. A United Kingdom study found that people with disabilities were significantly less likely to vote than citizens without disabilities in the 2005 national elections (Clarke et al. 2006). UK data also indicate that people with disabilities are slightly less likely to have engaged in some form of civic involvement over the 2005–2010 period.[16] Another

---

[16] In 2009–2010, 55% of people with disabilities and 60% of people without disabilities had engaged in one or more activities related to volunteering, civic participation (contacting officials, taking part in public meetings or protests, or signing petitions), civic consultation (completing a questionnaire or attending a public meeting or discussing local services), and civic activism (holding some type of local government position or being part of a group making decisions about local services). Breakdowns by category, however, show little difference in the latter three categories by disability status, while people with disabilities are less likely than those without disabilities to engage in volunteer activities. odi.dwp.gov.uk/roadmap-to-disability-equality/indicators.php, Table E2 (accessed May 22, 2012).

Table 4.3. *Disability and Other Forms of Political Participation*

	1998–2000		2008	
	Disability	No Disability	Disability	No Disability
Contacted a public official	31%	41%	11%	11%
Worked with others on community problem	22%	29%		
Contributed money to organization trying to influence government policy or laws	17%	24%		
Attended political meeting or rally	13%	17%	9%	11%
Contributed money to political party or candidate	13%	17%		
Wrote letter to newspaper	8%	8%		
Otherwise worked with groups or on one's own to change government laws or policies	15%	19%		
Participated in protest or march	4%	5%		
Worked on or contributed to political campaign			14%	16%
Took part in march, rally, protest, or demonstration			2%	3%

study focused on the east of England found that only 34% of those with learning difficulties were registered to vote in the 2005 elections, compared with 51% of other potential voters (Keeley et al. 2008). Yet another British study found that one in five people with a "learning impairment" thought staff at polling stations were unhelpful (Scott and Crooks 2005). A Swedish study found that only 31% of citizens with intellectual disabilities voted in the 1994 elections, compared with 86% of the total Swedish population (Kjellberg 2002).

The estimated disability gaps in voter turnout and other political participation in the United States are maintained and, in fact, often grow larger when demographic characteristics and other predictors of participation are controlled for. For example, the disability turnout gaps of 7% and 3% in the 2008 and 2010 U.S. elections both widen to 12% when a comparison is made between otherwise similar people with and without disabilities.[17]

Why are people with disabilities less likely to vote and to engage in other political activities? Several studies indicate that lower levels of resources (especially income and education), recruitment, and internal and external efficacy help account for their lower participation (Shields et al. 2000; Schur 2002; Schur et al. 2002; Schur, Shields, and Schriner 2005).[18] Consistent with these results, people with disabilities are less likely to say they frequently discuss politics with family members or friends, reflecting their greater likelihood of living alone and greater isolation in general (to be reviewed in Chapter 5).[19] Social isolation also makes it less likely they will be asked to participate by political parties and by friends, family members, and acquaintances. Furthermore, voting among people with disabilities can be discouraged when family members or caregivers make informal "gatekeeping" decisions to vote for particular candidates or not providing needed assistance with registering or casting a ballot (Tokaji and Colker 2007; Wehbi and El-Lahib 2008).

These factors do not, however, fully explain the gap in voter turnout. Voting among people with disabilities can be discouraged by barriers getting to or using polling places. The U.S. GAO (2009) found

---

[17] The narrower overall gaps of 7% and 3% partly reflect the fact that people with disabilities have higher average ages, and age in general is linked to higher voter turnout. Comparing people of the same age, however, creates a higher estimated gap of 12% (Schur and Adya 2012).

[18] See Young (2012) for additional discussion of the political participation of people with disabilities.

[19] Among people without disabilities, 45% reported discussing politics with family or friends at least a few times a week, compared with 36% of people without disabilities. Based on analysis of the 2008 CPS Civic Engagement supplement, conducted by the U.S. Census Bureau.

that only 27% of polling places in 2008 had no potential impediments to access by people with disabilities, a slight improvement from 16% in 2000.[20] In the 2000 election survey, 6% of people with disabilities who had voted in the past 10 years reported encountering problems in voting at a polling place, while one-third (33%) of all others with disabilities said they would expect problems, compared with only 2% of people without disabilities. Reported problems included difficulty in getting to or inside the polling place, difficulty once inside the polling place, and general mobility limitations. Inaccessible polling places, apart from the practical difficulties they present, convey the message that people with disabilities are not fully welcome in the political sphere and can create feelings of alienation and resentment. For example, one woman who uses a wheelchair described the ramp at her polling place as a "ski slope" and now votes by absentee ballot, "which she calls a 'second-class ballot' that forces her to cast votes before she's made up her mind" (Korte 2012).

The continuing problems in polling places were recognized in a 2012 U.S. District Court ruling that ordered New York's Board of Elections to improve accessibility. The ruling described problems such as steep wheelchair ramps, accessible entrances that were locked, automatic door openers that did not work, physical obstructions to voting equipment, and voting booths too close to the wall for people in wheelchairs to use.[21] Election officials who are ignorant about disability issues or reluctant to help citizens with disabilities are also part of the accessibility problems that can inhibit citizens with disabilities from voting (Ward et al. 2009).

---

[20] The views of election officials are more positive: a survey found that 88% of polling places were reported to be physically accessible to people with disabilities in the 2006 elections, and 85% were reported to allow a visually impaired voter to cast a ballot in private. www.eac.gov/assets/1/AssetManager/2006%20EAVS%20Access%20to%20 Voting%20for%20the%20Disabled.pdf, accessed January 18, 2013.

[21] United Spinal Association v. Board of Elections in City of New York, F.Supp.2d-, 2012 WL 3222663 S.D.N.Y., 2012. August 08, 2012.

Voting by mail can be an attractive alternative for people with mobility impairments or other difficulties in getting to and using polling places. Several studies have found that voting by mail is higher among people with disabilities, particularly those with mobility impairments.[22] Election policies regarding voting by mail appear to make a difference: the turnout of people with disabilities was especially high in the 2010 U.S. elections in jurisdictions where everyone voted by mail or no-excuse mail ballots were available (allowing citizens to avoid any stigma of having to cite a disability in order to obtain a ballot); also, there were fewer reports of not voting due to illness or disability in these jurisdictions (Schur and Kruse 2012). Tokaji and Colker (2007) discuss the advantages of voting by mail for many people with disabilities, but also the limitations of the current process. For example, people with visual or cognitive impairments may have trouble following complicated written instructions, and those with limited fine motor skills may find it hard to record their vote (Tokaji and Colker 2007: 1036).

Even with the option of voting by mail, the percentage of people who vote is especially low among people with mobility problems. Turnout is particularly low among those who report difficulty going outside their homes alone and among people who are not able to drive. Voting does not depend on being able to go outside alone (since one can vote by mail or be taken to the polling place by others), suggesting that greater ease of mobility may have important social and psychological effects through increased interaction, feelings of efficacy, and identification with mainstream society.

Recent onset of disability also appears to discourage political participation, consistent with studies of the effects of other major life transitions on participation (Stoker and Jennings 1995). Learning to live

---

[22] From the studies cited in Table 4.2, voters with SCIs in 1992 were five times as likely as voters in the general population to vote by mail (35% vs. 7%), while other samples show that voters with disabilities were about twice as likely as those without disabilities to vote by mail (13% vs. 7% in 1994, 14% vs. 8% in 1998, and 20% vs. 11% in 2000).

with a disability can be difficult, and many people with new disabilities may feel overwhelmed and have less time, energy, and interest available for political activities. Also, Jennings (1999) argues that pain and loss have a depoliticizing effect, which may wear off as people learn to manage their new situations. This is consistent with findings that disability activists tend to have lived with their disabilities for longer periods of time than people with disabilities who are not politically active (Schur 1998).

Employment appears to play a special role in increasing political participation for people with disabilities. Several studies have found that lower turnout is concentrated among nonemployed people with disabilities but that it is almost identical between employed working-age people with and without disabilities. Employment may raise political participation among people with disabilities by increasing resources and recruitment opportunities (through increased income, skills, and social contacts at work) and through psychological effects (such as increasing efficacy, self-esteem, and interest in public issues). Employment may also increase turnout through other, as yet unidentified factors (Schur and Kruse 2000; Schur 2003c).

Legislation in the United States has attempted to reduce barriers to voting among people with disabilities. One effort was the National Voter Registration Act (NVRA) in 1993, which required states to offer voter registration in conjunction with any business at public service or assistance agencies, as well as at offices providing state-funded programs for people with disabilities. In addition, states must provide for mail-in registration procedures. The NVRA went into effect in 1995, but full implementation was delayed and a 2000 survey showed that many agencies were not aware of their NVRA responsibilities.

The Help America Vote Act (HAVA), passed in 2002, encouraged the adoption of computer technologies, requiring each polling place to have at least one fully accessible voting system by January 1, 2006. In addition, HAVA promotes election access by requiring that each state allow electronic voter registration at disability agencies, that all voting-related materials be available in alternative formats, and that poll workers be given disability etiquette training.

On the international level, as mentioned earlier, the UN Convention's Article 29 commits nations to "ensure that persons with disabilities can effectively and fully participate in political and public life on an equal basis with others" and requires "[e]nsuring that voting procedures, facilities and materials are appropriate, accessible and easy to understand and use" and "[p]rotecting the right of persons with disabilities to vote by secret ballot in elections and public referendums without intimidation."[23] While the Article spells out the general requirements, it remains up to the individual countries to implement the provisions. This Article has been used by both international and local organizations to monitor and improve election procedures, such as in Mexico, Bosnia-Herzegovina, and the Philippines.[24] Efforts to implement it often involve diverse groups of stakeholders – "non-governmental organizations, democracy activists, election management professionals, political party representatives, disabled advocates, media specialists, and others" – who work to interpret and implement Article 29 in "locally relevant ways" (Tucker 2009: 1).

Along with potentially making it easier for people with disabilities to vote, new computer technologies may help to increase their overall political participation through increased access to information, networking, and recruitment. For example, government entities, from the federal to the local level, are increasingly using the Internet to facilitate access to and delivery of governmental information and services (Jaeger 2006). Section 508 of the U.S. Rehabilitation Act, which took effect in 2001, requires members of the public with disabilities "seeking information and services from a Federal department or agency to have access to and use of information and data that is comparable to" that of other members of

---

[23] www.un.org/disabilities/default.asp?id=289 (accessed August 28, 2012).
[24] See www.article29.org (accessed August 28, 2012).

the public. However, implementation of Section 508 has been slow (Jaeger 2006).

The positive effect of the Internet on political participation among people with disabilities is also muted by their more limited access to computers (Kaye 2000; Dobransky and Hargittai 2006), which probably explains why people with disabilities are less likely than people without disabilities to say that the Internet has affected their own political activity (Schur and Adya 2012). The European Union has also identified a disability gap in computer access in its member nations (Vincente and López 2010). The fact that relatively few people with disabilities have access to computers is due both to economic factors, such as lower income levels, and to technological barriers (Jaeger 2006).

The Internet has, however, been a tremendous tool for political mobilization among disability activists. It has been used extensively by UK disability groups to influence disability policy development (Power and Power 2010). As another example, Women with Disabilities Australia uses the Internet to connect members across a large geographical area (Meekosha 2002), and the Disabled Women's Network in Ontario describes its mission as "fostering virtual activism and individual empowerment," using the Internet to educate and organize members and allies.[25]

In analyzing the reasons for lower political participation in general among people with disabilities, it is important to note that there is an interesting interaction between disability and age. As shown in Figure 4.1, young people with disabilities (aged 18–34) were at least as likely as their counterparts without disabilities to have engaged in some political activity apart from voting in 2008, while older people with disabilities were less likely than their counterparts without disabilities to have done so (consistent with the pattern for 1998–2000 data found in Schur, Shields, and Schriner 2005).[26]

[25] dawn.thot.net/what.html, access January 18, 2013.
[26] The nonvoting political activities include those in the 2008 column in Table 4.3. The disability gaps among those aged 18–34 and 35–49 are not statistically significant at

As suggested in the earlier discussion of the higher level of disability activism among young people with disabilities, this pattern may indicate generational differences, with greater perceptions of stigma among older generations and greater commitment to disability rights among the younger generation, leading to greater political activism among young people with disabilities. This indicates that the disability gaps in political participation found in Table 4.2 may decrease over time as tomorrow's seniors with disabilities become more active than today's seniors with disabilities (Schur, Shields, and Schriner 2005).

G. POLITICAL INTEREST AND VIEWS

People with disabilities generally express the same level of political interest as those without disabilities (Schur and Adya 2012). When asked how disability has affected their political views, about half of people with disabilities say it has had no effect (Gastil 2000). Among those who say it has affected their views, about half say it has increased their interest in disability issues, while smaller percentages say it has made political participation more difficult, has made them more cynical and antigovernment, or has made their political views more liberal (Gastil 2000). People with disabilities do not report that they have less exposure to news through the newspaper, television, or Internet, but they are less likely to say the Internet has affected their own level of political activity.

As members of a historically disadvantaged group, it might be expected that people with disabilities in the United States would tend to favor Democrats, since the Democratic Party has traditionally been associated with the expansion of civil rights and social programs. Some early evidence supported this (Gastil 2000), but more recent national

conventional levels (p =.15 and .38), while the gaps among those aged 50–64 and 65+ are highly significant (p <.0001). Based on analysis of the CPS Civic Engagement Supplement, conducted by the U.S. Census Bureau.

evidence suggests that people with disabilities are no more or less likely to identify with the Democratic Party, and their average score on a scale of liberal to conservative is similar to that of other Americans (Schur and Adya 2012).

Despite being no more likely than non-disabled people to identify themselves as Democrats, people with disabilities appear to prefer a greater role for government in general, compared with people without disabilities. In line with their low employment rates and generally greater need for health care, they are more likely to say it is the responsibility of government to provide a job for everyone who wants one and to provide health care for the sick (Schur and Adya 2012). They are also more likely to say the government has the responsibility to keep prices under control, help industry grow, give aid to university students from low-income families, and provide decent housing for those who can't afford it.

When asked about government policies and spending, there are only two policies on which people with disabilities differ from nondisabled respondents: they are less likely to favor decreased government regulation of business (perhaps reflecting the perceived importance of the ADA and antidiscrimination legislation) and are more likely to favor increased spending on health care. In addition, people with disabilities express a stronger belief in civil liberties: they are more likely to say revolutionaries should be allowed to hold public meetings and publish books, and less likely to say government should be allowed to detain people without trial, to tap telephone conversations, or to stop and search people at random to protect against a terrorist act. The higher priority given to civil liberties among people with disabilities may reflect their perspective as part of a marginalized group whose privacy has often been violated.

The Americans with Disabilities Act was passed with broad public support, and disability appears to still be a salient issue for many people in the general population. A national survey before the 2012 United States elections found that 41% of people said they would be

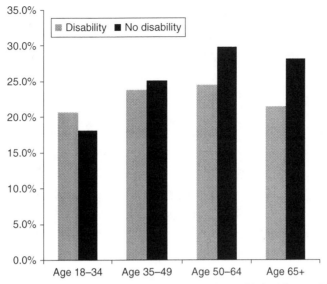

Figure 4.1. Political participation by disability and age, United States, 2008.

more likely to vote for a Congressional candidate who "is committed to making policies and programs to help those with disabilities a national priority," while only 2% said they would be less likely to vote for such a candidate.[27] The support was higher among Democrats (51% compared with 22% among Republicans and 30% among Independents), and among people who know someone with a disability (48% compared with 33% among those who do not know someone with a disability).

H. CONCLUSION

In sum, overall political participation is lower among people with disabilities than among the general population in the United States and

[27] "Public Opinion on Disabilities," Greenberg Quinlan Rosner Research and Laszlo Strategies, September 19, 2012, laszlostrategies.com/docs/National LikelyVoterPollDisabilityGQR_Laszlo_2012.pdf, accessed January 20, 2013.

some other countries. This is due in part to lower resource levels, fewer recruitment opportunities, and a weaker sense of political efficacy. Political participation among people with disabilities can be encouraged by policies that decrease social isolation and increase resource levels – in particular by creating better educational and employment opportunities.

Other barriers, such as inaccessible public buildings and transportation, as well as legal disenfranchisement, stigma, and other forms of discrimination also limit participation. The barriers that discourage many people with disabilities from fully participating in political life, however, also motivate others to become politically active. While some people view disability-related problems as purely personal concerns, many others perceive political dimensions in the problems they face. Disability groups play a particularly important role by reframing disability-related problems as political issues, providing role models, building group identification and social capital, and increasing exposure to political information and opportunities for participation.

In short, the evidence in this chapter provides a mixed message on the political inclusion of people with disabilities. While countries have increasingly provided disability rights protections, people with disabilities are still less likely to participate in the political process and remain political outsiders in many respects. Their lower political participation both reflects and contributes to social isolation and lack of needed resources and supports, the subject of the next chapter. Many political activities by disability activists directly focus on social issues, such as accessible technologies and transportation, home-based care services, and inclusive education. Social inclusion, in turn, has a direct relation to political inclusion. When people are fully part of their communities, they are less likely to feel isolated and they are more likely to form networks with others, share information, and engage in civic and political activities.

5

Social Inclusion

"Social inclusion" is a fluid term with a variety of meanings (Bates 2002; Rimmerman 2013). There have been several efforts to conceptualize social inclusion and exclusion, all of which recognize that they have many dimensions (reviewed in Rimmerman 2013:33–44). Social inclusion means in part that people with disabilities have "full and fair access to activities, social roles, and relationships directly alongside non-disabled citizens" (Bates and Davis 2004: 194). This includes the right to receive an education, live independently in the community, receive adequate and appropriate support services, and obtain accessible technology and transportation. Social inclusion also encompasses more intangible factors, such as being treated with dignity and respect, being able to form and maintain friendships and intimate relationships, and generally being able to live as equals in the broader community (Bates and Davis 2004: 196).

There is an important distinction between community access and true inclusion. Many people with disabilities participate in their communities while still maintaining the status of outsiders. They are "spatially proximal yet socially distant," living "in but not of their local communities" (Milner and Kelly 2009: 48). On the basis of a qualitative study of people with disabilities in New Zealand, Milner and Kelly (2009) identified important prerequisites of a sense of community inclusion. These include "control over the timing or form of participation (as opposed to the when, where and how of participation being determined by service providers), establishing a sustained presence at ordinary times and places, reciprocity, and a sense of psychological safety" (Milner and Kelly 2009: 58).Social inclusion, therefore, encompasses a psychological sense of connection to others along with physical access and social interaction. A review of 15 studies identified six themes in social inclusion as expressed by people with disabilities: (1) being accepted as an individual; (2) having personal relationships with family, friends, and others; (3) being involved in recreation, leisure, church, and other activities; (4) having appropriate living accommodations; (5) having good jobs; and (6) having needed formal and informal supports (Hall 2009). We covered employment as part of economic inclusion in Chapters 2 and 3, and in this chapter we examine a range of topics that address the other themes just listed. We first review the concept of social stigma that underlies social exclusion and then focus on important aspects of social inclusion for people with disabilities: independent living, social contact, transportation, computers, assistive technology, universal design, and education.[1] As will be seen, several of these topics not only are aspects of social inclusion, but are key factors that also contribute to economic and political inclusion.

A. SOCIAL STIGMA

Stigma is "any persistent quality of an individual or group that evokes negative or punitive responses from others" (Westerholm et al. 2006a: 1503). As a deviation from societal norms, disability has long been recognized as a source of stigma, and hundreds of studies have documented and analyzed the stigma associated with different types of disability (see overviews in Yuker 1988; Nowicki and Sandieson 2002; Muzzatti 2008; Scior 2011; Thompson 2011; Westerholm et al. 2006a, 2006b). The stigma of disability has been measured in a variety of

---

[1] See Rimmerman (2013) for a complementary review of many of these topics.

ways, including experiences of discrimination, perceptions of stigma by others, internalized stigma, and stigmatizing practices (Antonak and Livneh 1988; Van Brakel 2006).

One common way to measure stigma is by "social distance," reflecting how comfortable a nondisabled person feels in interacting with someone who has a particular disability. A high social distance score indicates a desire for avoidance, that is, a lot of discomfort in being around a person. The common finding is that social distance scores are highest for people with mental illness (e.g., schizophrenia) but also are high for people with intellectual disabilities compared with those with mobility or sensory impairments (Yuker 1988, 1994; Kersh 2011; Scior 2011).

Stigma can be manifested in many ways, from simple avoidance of people with disabilities to overt discrimination and violence (Fitzsimons 2009). One illustration of stigma is provided by a 2010 U.S. survey which found that 27% of people with disabilities said that people generally treated them differently after learning of their disability, with 14% saying that people would generally avoid further contact (Kessler/NOD/Harris, 2010). Hate crimes are the clearest and most severe negative expression of stigma; Quarmby (2011) documents and analyzes a number of cases in the United Kingdom in which people were brutalized or killed as a result of having a disability.

Stigma against people with disabilities has been found in studies across many cultures and countries, but the degree of stigma varies (Westerholm et al. 2006b; Scior 2011). Cultures differ in their popular understandings or beliefs of the origin of disability, how people with disabilities fill social roles, and the rights and responsibilities of people with disabilities. For example, people with disabilities may face greater stigma in societies based on individualistic values that emphasize independence and self-reliance, as well as in cultures where disability is viewed as a character defect or punishment for a transgression committed by oneself or one's parents or ancestors (Westerholm et al. 2006b). People with disabilities may also experience greater stigma in cultures characterized by traditional and inflexible gender roles (Peters and Opacich 2006), as will be discussed in Chapter 6.

Stigma appears to be more common when people lack awareness about a disability, so that stereotypes or prejudices play a greater role in shaping attitudes toward a person with a disability (Scior 2011). Media portrayals of people with disabilities often reflect and perpetuate common stereotypes, such as the "Tiny Tim" stereotype of a helpless person who deserves pity and assistance, the "sinister and evil" stereotype of a person warped by disability, and the "supercrip" stereotype of an individual who courageously triumphs over the disadvantages of a disability (Barnes 1992; Shapiro 1993; Rimmerman 2013: 55–712). To combat such stereotypes and prejudices in the media, one strategy is to promulgate media guidelines to prevent biased and negative images, and another is to use techniques that "reduce the sense of 'difference' between people with and without disabilities," such as matching (showing how people with and without disabilities are similar), likeability (creating an emotional bond), celebrity (using a famous person to portray a person with a disability), incidental inclusion (including a character for whom the disability is not the focus of the story), and brief educational or informational pieces (Rimmerman 2013: 149–175). Studies of "Kids on the Block," a puppet show that educates children about different types of disabilities, have found that it has positive effects on attitudes toward students with disabilities (Rimmerman 2013: 160–162).

More broadly, two methods of improving awareness and information are greater contact with people with disabilities and educational efforts. A number of studies, including structured interventions to increase contact or provide accurate information, have found that these can be effective in decreasing negative responses (e.g., anxiety and awkwardness) and improving attitudes toward people with disabilities (Westerholm et al. 2006a; Scior 2011; Kersh 2011).

Many of the studies, however, have methodological limitations (e.g., use of self-selected samples), and it is not clear that these methods have led to changes in actual behavior (Scior 2011; Kersh 2011). The effects of greater contact and education may also depend on the ways they occur, as well as on individual and situational factors. Greater contact is more likely to improve attitudes toward people with disabilities when the people interacting have equal status (e.g., co-workers, not supervisor and subordinate) and are involved in cooperative or interdependent tasks where they are treated equally by teachers or supervisors (Kersh 2011; Novak and Rogan 2010). In addition, context matters; for example, as discussed in Chapter 3, when company cultures are based on attention to the individual needs of all employees, co-workers are less likely to resent the granting of accommodations to employees with disabilities as "special treatment" (Novak and Rogan 2010; Kersh 2011; Schur et al. 2013).

B. INSTITUTIONAL VERSUS COMMUNITY-BASED INDEPENDENT LIVING

One of the most blatant forms of social exclusion is to segregate people with disabilities by putting them into asylums, nursing homes, separate schools, and other institutions. Religious enclaves established hospices for blind people as early as the fourth century in Turkey, Syria, and France; asylums for people with mental disabilities were established in the eighth century in Baghdad, Cairo, and what is now Morocco; and mental hospitals were established in many European countries in the Middle Ages (Braddock and Parish 2001: 17–20).

In the United States and Europe many residential facilities for people with disabilities were opened in the 1800s as part of a search for institutional solutions to social problems. These included residential schools for students with disabilities, such as the first school for the deaf in the United States, founded by Gallaudet and Leclerc in 1817 (Braddock and Parish 2001: 31). Many U.S. states opened psychiatric institutions, many of which had become overcrowded by the end of the nineteenth century.

The institutionalization of people with disabilities was fueled in part by the rise of the eugenics movement, which sought to segregate people with disabilities and prevent them from procreating. Institutionalization continued in the United States in the twentieth century, with many accounts of abuse of institutionalized people with disabilities, such as at Willowbrook in New York, where residents were unknowingly exposed to hepatitis as part of an experiment (Braddock and Parish 2001: 42).

Some U.S. court decisions and public policies in the 1960s and 1970s established greater rights and better treatment for institutionalized people with disabilities and encouraged downsizing of institutions in favor of community-based living with expanded community services. These developments were propelled in large part by the growth of the independent living movement, which began in Berkeley, California, in the 1960s. This early history is well described by Shapiro (1993), Scotch (2001), Barnartt and Scotch (2001), and Nielsen (2012).

Ed Roberts was a quadriplegic who was initially forced to live in the university hospital while attending college. He organized other students with disabilities at the University of California into a group called the Rolling Quads, which established the first Center for Independent Living (CIL) in the local community to help people with disabilities move out of institutional settings and live independently (Wilson 2009). As noted by Hasler (2006: 931), "The CIL came into being at an institution with a reputation for social radicalism and an era of political radicalism." As a self-help group run by people with disabilities, the Berkeley CIL became a model that inspired the creation of similar initiatives in the United States and throughout the world.

Today, there are hundreds of CILs in the United States and more worldwide. The main goals of CILs are to provide individual and systems advocacy, information and referral, peer support, and independent living skills training.[2] Congress recognized the importance of

[2] See www.ncil.org/about/CentersforIndependentLiving.html (accessed March 5, 2012).

CILs when it amended the Rehabilitation Act in 1978 to create a program that would provide comprehensive services for independent living. A condition of the funding was that people with disabilities would participate in the management of the CILs (Barnes and Mercer 2010: 142). At least 51% of the board of directors of each CIL must be composed of people with significant disabilities.

In addition to providing services, CILs "became sites for consciousness raising and political organization" (Barnes and Mercer 2010: 143). From its beginning, the disability rights movement has stressed the connections between political activism and social inclusion. This is evident from efforts by groups such as ADAPT to pass the federal Community Choice Act, which would allow individuals eligible for nursing homes the opportunity to choose instead "Community-Based Attendant Services and Supports."[3]

The independent living movement began to spread internationally in the late 1970s and varies in different regions throughout the world. As discussed by Hasler (2006: 931), "In most of the developing world independent living has been associated with economic independence, so the movement has focused on employment opportunities, often linked to providing services to other disabled people. In Zimbabwe, for example, a wheelchair manufacturing business provides both work and services for disabled people as well as generating income for the CIL."

A majority of European countries have policies expressing support for independent living, but there is great variation in concrete commitments and progress (Townsley 2009). In Western Europe, CILs have tended to focus on ensuring that people with disabilities have viable alternatives to living in institutions. Most European CILs, as well as the European Network on Independent Living (ENIL), focus on personal assistance as a key component of independent living. In the United Kingdom, CILs have advocated for direct payments for

---

[3] www.adapt.org/.

people with disabilities who need personal assistance services so that disabled people have control over the money used to pay assistants, and the hiring (and if necessary firing) of the people who assist them (Hasler 2006: 931–932).

According to Hasler, one of the challenges facing the independent living movement is how to sustain the energy and commitment that motivated the early CIL pioneers and how to motivate younger people with disabilities to become active in the independent living movement. One method exists in Scandinavia, "where national disabled people's organizations support independent living projects in several developing countries" (Hasler 2006: 934).

While the importance of independent living has been recognized in the United States and many other countries, it is far from universally accepted. For example, in China, despite disability rights legislation, it is not considered the responsibility of the government to help people with disabilities live on their own. Consequently, most people with disabilities who need housing and personal assistance live with their families or in institutions, or are disproportionately homeless (Fisher and Jing 2008).

Even in situations where people with disabilities are not able to live independently, living in community settings is generally considered preferable to institutionalization (if adequate support is provided). The U.S. Supreme Court recognized the value of community living in its landmark 1999 decision *Olmstead v. L.C.* when it held that people with disabilities have the right to live in the least restrictive environment, and states are required under Title II of the ADA to place persons with mental disabilities in community settings rather than in institutions when the state's treatment professionals have determined that community placement is appropriate, the transfer from institutional care to a less restrictive setting is not opposed by the affected individual, and the placement can be reasonably accommodated.[4]

[4] Olmstead v. L. C. (98–536) 527 U.S. 581 (1999) 138 F.3d 893.

Since the *Olmstead* decision, which affirmed the ADA's integration mandate, several federal laws have sought to expand access to home and community-based services, and the percentage of long-term care spending going to such services under the Medicaid program has increased (Carlson and Coffey 2010: 7, 11–15).[5] A 2010 report noted that "the Olmstead decision and its reasoning have become accepted in the community, particularly throughout the network of persons providing aging services ... [who] understand the core of its ruling – that people with disabilities have a right not to be relegated to nursing homes, psychiatric hospitals, and like institutions" (Carlson and Coffey 2010: 2). Despite this, there appear to be a variety of ongoing barriers that make it difficult for people to obtain home and community-based services in place of institutional care (Carlson and Coffey 2010: 20–27).

The number of people with disabilities living in institutions in the United States has decreased over the past several decades. The number in psychiatric hospitals was 559,000 in 1955 and dropped by 200,000 by 1975 (Braddock and Parish 2001: 45), while the number in county- or state-run mental hospitals dropped from an average of 110,125 in the mid-1980s to 49,437 in the early 2000s (Salzer et al. 2006). While there are no solid data on trends in the percentage of people with disabilities living in institutions, the percentage of U.S. adults with disabilities who are now living in institutions under supervised care or custody in 2010 is illustrated in Figure 5.1.[6]

Overall, 6% of adults with disabilities live in institutional settings, with a higher rate among those with cognitive impairments (10%) and

---

[5] Programs to increase access were added or encouraged by the Deficit Reduction Act of 2005, the 2006 reauthorization of the Older Americans Act, and the Patient Protection and Affordable Care Act of 2010 (Carlson and Coffey 2010: 2).

[6] The numbers in Figure 5.1 cover all those in institutionalized group quarters, including medical facilities, prisons and juvenile group homes and treatment centers. Based on analysis of the 2010 American Community Survey, conducted by the U.S. Census Bureau.

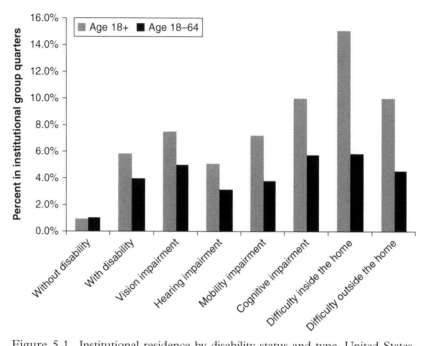

Figure 5.1. Institutional residence by disability status and type, United States, 2010.

an especially high rate for those who have difficulties inside the home with activities of daily living (15%). Those who live in institutions are disproportionately likely to be elderly. Looking just at those aged 18–64, only 4% of people with disabilities live in institutional settings.

While the number of people living in psychiatric hospitals has declined in the United States, deinstitutionalization has often not been accompanied by adequate resources and supports. Consequently, many people with mental disabilities have become homeless and have wound up in prison. A 2003 estimate is that as many as one in five, or about 300,000, of Americans in jail and prison were seriously mentally ill, far outnumbering the number of mentally ill people living in psychiatric hospitals (Human Rights Watch 2003, 2009). The study by Human Rights Watch concluded that jails and prisons are now the country's "default mental health system" as more state hospitals have closed and as the country's prison system has quadrupled over the past 30 years.

While only a small percentage of people with disabilities currently live in institutions, independent living remains a central issue for disability advocates, given that having choices about where to live and the supports to live independently can increase people's sense of empowerment (DeJong 1983; Hahn 1986) and are fundamental to social participation and inclusion.

C. LIVING ARRANGEMENTS AND MARRIAGE

Where people live and who they live with are key factors in their social inclusion. People with disabilities are more likely than people without disabilities to experience social isolation in part because they are more likely to live by themselves. Among those who live in the community (not in institutions or other group quarters), U.S. adults with disabilities in 2010 were twice as likely as those without disabilities to be living alone (24% compared with 12%).[7]

The likelihood of living alone does not vary much by type of disability but does vary by age, as shown in Figure 5.2. Young people are less likely to live alone, and the rate does not vary between young people with and without disabilities, while the disability gap grows among the older age groups. People with disabilities have also been found to be more likely than those without disabilities to live alone in all of the European Union countries; an average of one-sixth (17%) of working-age adults with disabilities lived alone in 2008, compared with one-tenth (10%) of their counterparts without disabilities (Grammenos 2010: 7).

---

[7] These and the following numbers are based on analysis of the 2010 American Community Survey, conducted by the U.S. Census Bureau. The figures exclude those in institutional group quarters.

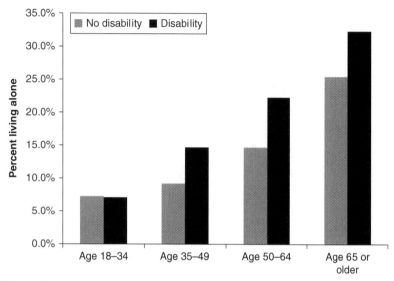

Figure 5.2. Living alone by disability status and age, United States, 2010.

The greater likelihood of living alone among older people with disabilities partly reflects their lower chance of being married with a spouse present. Overall, just two-fifths (41%) of U.S. adults with disabilities are married with a spouse present, compared with slightly more than half (52%) of adults without disabilities. The disability gap in marriage rates exists among all age groups, as shown in Figure 5.3.

People with disabilities have also been found to have lower rates of marriage than people without disabilities in the United Kingdom (Heady 2002: 109), India (Bhambhani 2006), Afghanistan, and Zambia (Trani and Loeb 2012). The pattern does not, however, extend to several other European countries where people with disabilities appear to have a higher rate of marriage (Austria, Germany, Greece, Norway, and Portugal), at least in part due to their higher average age (Heady 2002: 109).

The low marriage rate among people with disabilities in the United States reflects a combination of a lower likelihood of a first marriage and

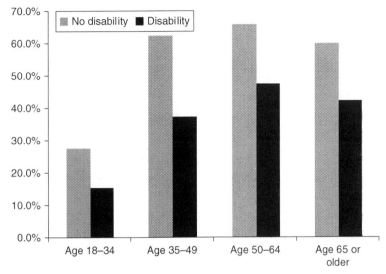

Figure 5.3. Married and living with spouse, by disability status and age, United States, 2010.

a higher likelihood of being separated, divorced, or widowed. Among those aged 65 or older, the disability gap in marriage in Figure 5.3 is explained by a higher likelihood of being widowed; among those under 65, however, the disability gaps represent both lower rates of ever being married and higher rates of being divorced or separated.[8]

Studies in the United States have found a lower likelihood of a first marriage among those who grew up with disabilities and those who had a recent onset of a disability (Dijkers et al. 1995; MacInnes 2011). This may reflect social isolation and stigma, which decrease marriage prospects for people with disabilities. Being unmarried may add to the

[8] The percent never married among those with disabilities (without disabilities) is 74% (65%) if aged 18–34, 31% (17%) if aged 35–49, 15% (9%) if aged 50–64, and 5% (4%) if aged 65 or older. The percent divorced or separated among those with disabilities (without disabilities) is 8% (5%) if aged 18–34, 27% (17%) if aged 35–49, 28% (19%) if aged 50–64, and 13% (12%) if aged 65 or older. The percent widowed among those with disabilities (without disabilities) is 0.3% (0.1%) if aged 18–34, 2% (1%) if aged 35–49, 7% (4%) if aged 50–64, and 38% (22%) if aged 65 or older.

stigma since, as will be discussed in the chapter on gender and disability, unmarried women may be stigmatized in societies with traditional values where women's status is largely dependent on their roles as wives and mothers (Bhambhani 2006).

Apart from the lower likelihood of becoming married, there may be a higher rate of divorce following the onset of a disability (Dijkers et al. 1995; although Charles and Stephens 2004 found no relationship), which may represent a variety of economic, social, and psychological stresses faced by couples in coping with disability-related problems. Finally, the low rate of marriage among people with disabilities may partly reflect the effect of marriage on disability: marriage can decrease the risk of disability by improving access to health care, as well as mental and physical health (Wood et al. 2007).

D. SOCIAL CONTACT

The higher likelihood of living alone and the lower likelihood of being married do not in themselves imply less social contact for people with disabilities. Those who live alone may have active social lives based on networks built through family, friends, neighbors, employment, political work, Centers for Independent Living, and other groups. Overall, however, people with disabilities appear to have less social contact than do people without disabilities.

In the United States, adults with disabilities are less likely than those without disabilities to report socializing with friends, neighbors, or relatives at least twice a month (79% compared with 90%), going to a restaurant at least twice a month (48% compared with 75%) or visiting a department store, mall, or shopping center (23% compared with 41%) (NOD/Harris 2000; Kessler/NOD/Harris 2010). They are less likely to have attended a group or organization meeting in the past 12 months (18% compared with 24%) or to be officers or committee members in groups or organizations (8% compared with 12%).[9] They are also less likely to go to the movies, theater, live music performances, sports events, or events related to hobbies such as dancing, art shows, or events for collectors (NOD/Harris, 2000).

Similarly, a study in Ireland found that respondents with disabilities were less likely to report having had "an evening out" in the previous two weeks (Gannon and Nolan 2007: 1434), while UK data show that people with disabilities are less likely to participate in cultural, leisure, and sports activities, and about one-third report difficulties in gaining access to such activities or other publicly available goods and services.[10] The gaps in socializing and going to a restaurant in the United States do not appear to have changed in the past two decades. An important form of social contact for many people is attendance at religious services. While people with disabilities in the United States are equally likely as those without disabilities to say that religious faith is very important to them (NOD/Harris 2004), they are less likely to attend religious services at least once a month (50% compared with 57% in 2010) (Kessler/NOD/Harris 2010).

One encouraging sign is that there tend to be smaller disability gaps in social contact among young people, and in fact young adults with disabilities appear to be just as likely as their nondisabled peers to socialize with friends, neighbors, or relatives (Kessler/NOD/Harris 2010: 126) and to have attended a group or organization meeting in the past 12 months.[11] As discussed in Chapter 4 with respect to

---

[9] The possible groups or organizations include (1) a school group, neighborhood, or community association; (2) a service or civic organization; (3) a sports or recreation organization; (4) a church, synagogue, mosque, or other religious institution or organization (not counting attendance at religious services); or (5) any other type of organization. Based on analysis of the 2008 CPS Civic Engagement Supplement, conducted by the U.S. Census Bureau.

[10] odi.dwp.gov.uk/roadmap-to-disability-equality/indicators.php, Tables E3 and F4 (accessed May 22, 2012).

[11] Close to one-sixth of young people (aged 18–34) have attended a group or organization meeting in the past 12 months, and there is no statistically significant gap between people with and without disabilities (16% and 17%, respectively). Among

political participation, this may reflect generational differences in the experience of disability: older people with disabilities were socialized in an environment with greater disability stigma, which may depress political and social inclusion, and younger people with disabilities were socialized in an environment more focused on disability rights and participation in mainstream society.

The relationship between disability and social contact may, of course, depend on the context. An Australian study found that people with disabilities who lived outside of cities had lower employment levels and incomes than those who lived in cities, and were less likely to socialize frequently with family members and friends who did not live with them, but they were more likely to do volunteer work and attend community events and had stronger feelings of being part of the community (McPhedran 2011). The social inclusion may have helped compensate for the economic exclusion, given that life satisfaction was broadly consistent between the two groups.

The generally lower levels of social contact among people with disabilities may occur for several reasons. Many people with disabilities may be reluctant to leave their homes and meet people due to the real or perceived social stigma they face, particularly among older people, as previously suggested. They may also feel that social activities require a great deal of physical or emotional effort. Their lower levels of employment may play a role, as both quantitative and qualitative research suggests that employment is linked to greater social inclusion for people with disabilities (Morris and Abello 2005; Schur 2002). Not only are many workplaces important sources of social contact (Morrison 2009), but nonemployed people may reduce their social activities due to embarrassment over their status as well as their limited financial resources. Transportation problems also play a role in

older people, however, there is a significant nine-point gap between people with and without disabilities (18% and 27%, respectively). Based on analysis of the 2008 CPS Civic Engagement Supplement, conducted by the U.S. Census Bureau.

decreasing social contact by making travel more difficult or costly, as discussed in the next section.

E. TRANSPORTATION

Transportation is a key factor in social inclusion because meeting people for socializing, group meetings, and other activities often requires going at least a moderate distance from one's home. Accessible transportation also contributes to economic and political inclusion, as described in Chapters 3 and 4. Many forms of transportation are inaccessible to people with disabilities, particularly those who have cognitive, vision, or mobility impairments. Data from the United States show that one-third (34%) of people with disabilities say inadequate transportation is a problem for them, compared with one-sixth (16%) of people without disabilities (Kessler/NOD/Harris 2010: 117).

The likelihood of transportation problems is higher among those with low incomes (44%) and those with severe disabilities (49%), and it has not lessened over the 1998–2010 period. The trend appears to be slightly better in the United Kingdom, where the percentage of people with disabilities reporting difficulties in transportation decreased from 27% to 23% over the 2005–2010 period.[12] In the European Union overall, people with disabilities in 2007 were slightly less satisfied with the quality of public transport than were people without disabilities (66% compared with 69%) (Grammenos 2010: 7, 51).

Transportation problems that are inconvenient or irritating for people without disabilities may create serious barriers for those with disabilities. For example, an Australian study found that among all people reporting difficulties with transportation, those in the

---

[12] odi.dwp.gov.uk/roadmap-to-disability-equality/indicators.php, Table F2 (accessed May 22, 2012).

"vulnerable/impaired" group (who had worse self-reported health and were more likely to receive disability benefits) traveled less and were more socially excluded as a result of transportation difficulties (Delbosc and Currie 2011).

People with disabilities face difficulties in accessing both private and public transportation. Regarding private transportation, they are less likely than people without disabilities to have or be able to drive a private vehicle (car, van, or truck), so they are dependent on others in areas where private vehicles are needed for mobility (Schur 2004). Vehicles can often be modified to allow people with disabilities to drive (e.g., with hand controls for those with no use of their legs) or use them as passengers (e.g., with ramps and tiedowns for wheelchairs), but vehicle modifications are often expensive. Among people with spinal cord injuries in the United States, for example, more than three-fourths reported having a vehicle modified for their use with an average modification cost of almost $6,500 in 1998 (Berkowitz et al. 1998). These modification costs are sometimes paid or subsidized through insurance or other programs, but often people with disabilities and their families must bear the cost.

Inaccessible public transportation systems have been a target of substantial activism by disability groups. In the United States the fight for accessible transportation began with the rise of the independent living movement. In 1978, after a judge ruled that the public bus system in Denver, Colorado, was not required to become accessible, a group of wheelchair users closed down Denver's bus system for two days until they won agreement that all of the city's new buses would be equipped with lifts. Among other tactics, members of the group chained their wheelchairs to inaccessible buses to protest discrimination. By 1982 the entire Denver fleet was accessible, and the group had grown and become one of the most confrontational and militant disability rights groups, ADAPT (Lamp 2006: 1321).

Air travel has also been a subject of disability activism. In 1986 the Supreme Court ruled that the Rehabilitation Act does not apply to air travel.[13] Disability advocates quickly organized in protest, and just ninety days later Congress passed the Air Carrier Access Act (ACAA). This law requires airlines to provide access for people with disabilities but stopped short of requiring companies to develop accessible aircraft (Lamp 2006).

Four years later, the 1990 Americans with Disabilities Act (ADA) established minimum transportation accessibility requirements in the United States, which improved access to ground transportation for people with disabilities in many parts of the country. Some transportation entities, however, failed to comply with the ADA and were taken to court, while others complied with the letter of the law while leaving many potential users without viable access (Lamp 2006). Four years after the ADA's passage, about 80% of people with disabilities reported that their public transportation system was difficult to use (Hendershot 2005: 11).

A major and ongoing problem in the United States, as well as in other countries, is that while people with disabilities continue to demand accessibility, federal and state governments have often severely cut funding for public transportation. This means that many people with disabilities must increasingly rely on private vehicles such as cars, which as already noted can be expensive to modify and maintain, or private taxi services, which are also expensive and mostly remain inaccessible (Lamp 2006). The growing reliance on private vehicles has led Aldred and Woodcock (2008: 494) to argue that the environmental and disability movement share a common interest in challenging "the car economy" and creating accessible and sustainable public transportation alternatives for people with disabilities and the general public. Continuing problems with public transportation are illustrated by the example of the New York City subway system, which is the largest in North America. Originally built in 1904, the subway system remains largely inaccessible to people with mobility

---

[13] DOT v. Paralyzed Veterans of America, 477 U.S. 597 (1986) No. 85–289.

impairments, as documented by John Hockenberry (2004), a journalist and wheelchair user.

Outside of the United States, many countries fail to provide accessible transportation for people with disabilities, even when there are laws requiring it (WHO/World Bank 2011). Lack of accessible transportation is particularly common in developing countries. The report by the World Health Organization and the World Bank points out, however, that accessibility standards adopted by wealthier developed countries may not be appropriate or affordable in other contexts, and it highlights examples of creative and effective transportation initiatives, not just in developed countries, but also in middle- and low-income nations.

In India, for example, design teams found inexpensive ways to make small vans accessible and developed a type of pedicab that is easier for people with restricted mobility to use. Cities such as New Delhi and Beijing have introduced major policies to upgrade their public rail systems and make them more accessible. Wheelchair-accessible, low-floor buses have been installed in various cities in India, Colombia, Ecuador, the United Republic of Tanzania, and Brazil. Other examples include Helsinki, Finland, which made its tram system accessible by buying new vehicles and renovating stops and stations, and the United Kingdom, which adopted a special initiative to make all taxis in the country wheelchair accessible (WHO/World Bank 2011: 180–181).

The example provided by Curitiba, Brazil, is particularly impressive. In 1970 the city started running an integrated public transportation system designed to provide complete accessibility for people with disabilities through the use of universal design. All buses, terminals, and bus stops in Curitiba are designed to be wheelchair accessible, and the system includes "parataxis" – accessible vans that are available to all passengers (WHO/World Bank 2011: 182).

As noted by Lamp (2006: 1322), early transportation activists in the United States often fought for full access by framing their arguments in terms of a "common" disability population, failing to prioritize the needs of those who "could not be accommodated by mainline transportation systems, such as those with respiratory impairments who cannot wait for buses in temperature extremes." Consistent with the Curitiba example, an instance of flexible solutions in the United States is provided by the New Jersey Middlesex County Department of Transportation, which created a modified fixed-route shuttle program using wheelchair-accessible minibuses that provide curb-to-curb service while operating on a fixed schedule that does not require advance reservations. The shuttle system is intended to provide greater transportation flexibility for senior citizens and individuals with disabilities, and it is also available to the general public.[14]

F. COMPUTERS, INTERNET, AND ASSISTIVE TECHNOLOGY

Technology is a major factor in the social inclusion of people with disabilities (Blanck 2012). Rapid technological change over the past three decades has greatly increased the potential capabilities of people with disabilities in a wide variety of ways. The development of mainstream technologies for the general population, such as faster computers with greater capabilities, may have special benefits for people with disabilities.

Mainstream technologies may, for example, enable people with hearing, speech, and cognitive impairments to communicate more easily through computers or hand-held devices, increase the opportunities for productive high-paying jobs among people in wheelchairs who are restricted in many manual and service jobs, and increase the potential for telecommuting (as discussed in Chapter 3). In addition, many new assistive technologies are designed specifically for people with disabilities to help compensate for their functional limitations; such technologies include screen readers and voice-recognition software that enable

[14] www.co.middlesex.nj.us/transportation/index.asp.

people with limited vision or manual dexterity to read and write more quickly and easily, computer peripherals that allow hands-free use of computers, and remote devices for people with mobility impairments to do tasks around the house or workplace (e.g., opening doors and curtains) (see, e.g., Miesenberger et al. 2012). It is well recognized that these technologies can improve opportunities for employment, group participation, and political activities that enhance the inclusion of many people with disabilities.

Rapid technological change, however, may also paradoxically reduce the social inclusion of people with disabilities. When new technologies are broadly adopted in the general population, they often shape forms of social inclusion. For example, where Internet access is widespread, it can become a prerequisite for effective participation in many groups, organizations, and social networks. As new technologies change our social and economic environment, they also may limit the social inclusion of people with disabilities if they are too expensive or inaccessible, and people with disabilities are left behind.

This is a real concern, since people with disabilities are less likely than those without disabilities to use computers or have Internet access. In the United States, almost half (46%) of households headed by someone with a disability did not have a computer at home in 2010, compared with only 20% of households headed by someone without a disability (U.S. Department of Commerce 2011: 16). In addition, more than half (54%) of households headed by someone with a disability had no Internet access from home, compared with only 25% of households headed by someone without a disability (U.S. Department of Commerce 2011: 16).

Similarly, another U.S. survey found that people with disabilities are less likely to access the Internet from home, work, or other locations (Kessler/NOD/Harris 2010: 156). This is consistent with earlier U.S. data showing lower computer use and training among people with disabilities, despite the benefits that computer use appears to have for return to work, earnings, and quality of life of people with disabilities

(Krueger and Kruse 1995; Kruse and Schur 2002; Kaye 2000; Chung 2006). The situation is similar in the United Kingdom, where almost three-fifths (58%) of people with disabilities lived in households with Internet access in 2010, compared with more than four-fifths (84%) of people without disabilities.[15] In a study of 10 European countries, only one-third (35%) of people with disabilities had Internet access, compared with three-fifths (61%) of people without disabilities (Vicente and López 2010).

Internet access may be limited in part by the accessibility and usability of Web sites (Blanck 2012); in the United States, federal law establishes that governmental Web sites have to be accessible to those using assistive technologies, but this does not generally apply to private Web sites (Chung 2006). According to the World Health Organization and the World Bank, "Few public and even fewer commercial web sites are accessible," with one study finding that only 3 of 100 home pages in an audit of 20 countries met the most basic level of accessibility (WHO/World Bank 2011: 185). More generally, many countries do not have recognized standards for information and communication technologies; only 8 of 36 countries and areas in Asia and the Pacific were found to have accessibility standards or guidelines for information and communication technology, compared with 26 that have standards for the built environment or public transportation (WHO/World Bank 2011: 185; for a discussion of the effect of telecommunications policy on people with disabilities, see Jaeger 2006). Voluntary and consensus Web standards do exist, such as the Web Content Accessibility Guidelines (Version 2.0) supported by the Web Accessibility Initiative (Blanck 2012). But these and other such standards often are not followed by public and private Web service providers.

Apart from standard computers and Internet access, it is important to consider the wide variety of assistive technologies. An assistive

---

[15] odi.dwp.gov.uk/roadmap-to-disability-equality/indicators.php, Table F3 (accessed May 22 2012).

technology device is "any item, piece of equipment, or product system, whether acquired commercially, modified, or customized, that is used to increase, maintain, or improve the functional capabilities of individuals with disabilities" (Gray and Cook 2006: 129). The use of these technologies has expanded greatly since 1980 – more than would be predicted by population growth and changes in age composition (Institute of Medicine 2007: 184). There are nearly 40,000 assistive technologies available to enhance participation in the full spectrum of home, work, school, recreation, and other activities.[16] The most common are mobility devices such as wheelchairs, walkers, scooters, and crutches; other widely used devices include hearing aids, prostheses, adapted furniture, screen readers or other software or devices for those with vision impairments, and voice-recognition technology, adapted keyboards, or other devices for those with limited use of hands or arms (Institute of Medicine 2007: 194–196; NOD/Harris 2004: 110). Some of these technologies, including television remote controls, cordless telephones or speakerphones, closed captioning on television, and automatic door openers, have become mainstream and are used equally by people with and without disabilities (NOD/Harris 2004: 109).

Assistive technology is highly important to people with disabilities, as found in a 2004 U.S. survey; without such devices, one-third of respondents said they would not be able to take care of themselves at home, one-fourth said they would not be able to get around outside of home, one-sixth said they would not be able to attend social gatherings as often, and one-sixth said they would not be as involved in hobbies or other interests (NOD/Harris 2004: 111). Studies have found clear benefits of assistive technology for people with mobility impairments in Uganda, for people with brain injuries in the United Kingdom, and for people with hearing impairments in Nigeria (WHO/World Bank 2011: 101).

---

[16] See www.abledata.com, which is maintained for the National Institute of Disability and Rehabilitation Research, U.S. Department of Education.

For some people with disabilities the technologies appear to reduce the need for personal assistance, particularly informal care (Institute of Medicine 2007: 199–200). The greater use of assistive technology by more highly educated senior citizens in the United States helps explain why they are better able to cope with disability (Cutler et al. 2009). Despite their obvious benefits for many individuals, studies clearly documenting how assistive technology increases independence and community participation are "relatively sparse" (Institute of Medicine 2007: 197).

Cost is a major factor in the adoption of computers and assistive technologies. People with disabilities tend to have lower incomes and a higher likelihood of living in poverty than do people without disabilities, as discussed in Chapter 2, which limits their resources for purchasing these technologies. The costs may be partly or fully paid by insurance, rehabilitation services, government agencies, employers, or private charitable organizations, but more than one-third (35%) of people with disabilities in the United States reported that they fully paid for their most recent assistive technology by themselves (NOD/ Harris, 2004).

In addition, high cost was cited by more than half of people with disabilities who said there is assistive technology that they need but do not have. One United Kingdom study found that cost was the most common reason for people with disabilities who were not using the Internet (WHO/World Bank 2011: 186). The overall costs of assistive technology may be lowered by economies of scale in mass production and purchasing, use of local materials, tax exemptions or subsidies, and reducing duty or import taxes (WHO/World Bank 2011: 118). Vietnam and Nepal are two examples of countries that provide subsidies and reduced taxes to encourage assistive technology use (WHO/ World Bank 2011: 118).

There may be substantial barriers to developing and producing assistive technologies. There may be a small market for some technologies, and consumers may have below-average incomes without health plan coverage to pay for them. Producers may face high costs of research, development, and production, particularly if the product must pass government safety tests (Institute of Medicine 2007: 205). The broader benefits of these technologies have provided justification for government support for research, development, consumer awareness, and financial subsidies for assistive technologies (Institute of Medicine 2007: 205–216).

Apart from access to specific devices, people with disabilities may not have access to assistive technology that is part of the information infrastructure. A survey by the World Federation of the Deaf found that only 21 of 93 countries provided captioning of current affairs programs; in addition, in Europe only one-tenth of commercial broadcasts included subtitles, and closed captioning or sign-language interpretation of news broadcasts in Asia is limited and generally available only in large cities (WHO/World Bank 2011: 184–185).

In the United States, there is pending litigation over the extent to which Web services such as CNN.com must provide captioning on their Web sites or entertainment providers such as Netflix must caption their titles (Blanck 2012). The 2010 Communications and Video Accessibility Act will further require Web services to be accessible and usable by persons with different disabilities (Blanck 2012). Increasingly, accessible and usable Web services will be required for persons with sensory disabilities (blindness and deafness), but also for those with cognitive impairments who require enhanced comprehensibility and ease of use in these crucial services for education, work, recreation (gaming), and civic participation.

G. ACCESSIBILITY AND UNIVERSAL DESIGN

Several of the topics in this chapter, such as housing, transportation, and Web services, highlight the importance of accessible physical and cyber environments. Some environments "disable" people with impairments by limiting or preventing their activities, while the same individuals are not restricted in other environments that have been designed to be barrier free.

At the international level, accessibility has been a key component of disability policy since the World Programme of Action Concerning Disabled Persons was passed by the UN General Assembly in 1983 (Brown 2006). The UN's nonbinding "Standard Rules on the Equalization of Opportunities for Persons with Disabilities," adopted in 1993, led many countries to adopt policies on accessibility, but by 2005 less than half had allocated any financial resources to increasing accessibility (South-North Dialogue 2006; WHO/World Bank 2011: 172). The countries with laws requiring accessibility appear to have a low level of compliance (WHO/World Bank 2011: 173). In the United States, the 1973 Rehabilitation Act created the Access Board to develop standards for physical access to federal facilities, but over time its responsibilities expanded (particularly with the passage of the Americans with Disabilities Act) to cover standards for all public accommodations and information technology (Brown 2006).

While progress has been slow, efforts are being made to improve standards and spread technical knowledge about effective ways to increase accessibility (WHO/World Bank 2011: 172–178). The slow progress is due partly to the difficulty and expense that can be involved in renovating existing buildings or systems, relative to new construction, where "full compliance with all the requirements of accessibility standards is generally feasible at 1% of the total cost" (WHO/World Bank 2011: 173).

The benefits of accessibility underlie the philosophy of universal design (UD). This approach represents an intersection between designers who are creating more accessible environments and rehabilitation technologists who are developing assistive technologies, as described earlier (Story et al. 1998). Universal design seeks to create and promote products and environments that are usable to the greatest extent possible by people of all ages and abilities, based on the value of maximum inclusion (see the Global Universal Design Commission's Web site, www.globaluniversaldesign.org). The seven basic principles of UD are as listed at www.ncsu.edu/project/design-projects/udi/center-for-universal-design/the-principles-of-universal-design:

1) *Equitable Use*: The design is useful and marketable to people with diverse abilities.
2) *Flexibility in Use.* The design accommodates a wide range of individual preferences and abilities.
3) *Simple and Intuitive Use.* Use of design is easy to understand, regardless of user's experience, knowledge, language skills or current concentration level.
4) *Perceptible Information.* The design communicates the necessary information effectively to the user, regardless of ambient conditions or the user's sensory abilities.
5) *Tolerance for Error.* The design minimizes hazards and negative consequences of accidental or unintended actions.
6) *Low Physical Effort.* The design can be used efficiently and comfortably and with a minimum of fatigue.
7) *Size and Space for Approach and Use.* Appropriate size and space is provided for approach, reach, manipulation and use regardless of user's body size, posture or mobility.

Examples of products based on UD principles are kitchen or household implements that can be used by people with limited hand strength or dexterity, such as scissors that distribute pressure evenly across the hand and can be manipulated by people with arthritis (Story et al. 1998). The principles of UD are also applied to building design; for example, the principles call for all houses to have at least one bedroom on the ground level, at least one stepless entry, and weather protection such as a porch roof for people who need extra time to unlock a door (CUD 2006; www.globaluniversaldesign.org). The proponents of UD emphasize that no product or environment will be usable by absolutely everyone, so it "may be more appropriate to consider universal design a process, rather than an achievement" (Story et al. 1998: 2). Mainstream devices are sometimes designed to be compatible with assistive technologies; "often, however, the most economical and effective approach is to have the mainstream device designed so that no additional adaptive equipment is needed, as happens when buildings are designed without steps or when elevators 'announce' their arrival and their stop status" (Institute of Medicine 2007: 203).

While there is no simple way to measure progress, UD appears to be growing in popularity (Institute of Medicine 2007). An example is the wide-ranging effort in four districts of India to make physical spaces more accessible: a local development organization worked with public and private institutions to increase awareness of the value of accessibility, hold workshops to increase knowledge and skills at the local level, do audits of public spaces, and build strategic alliances to advocate for accessibility (WHO/World Bank 2011: 177).

Another example is in the work of the Global Universal Design Commission (www.globaluniversaldesign.org), a not-for-profit corporation established to develop UD standards for buildings, products, and services. The GUDC has developed UD voluntary consensus standards for commercial buildings, which will help expand access to buildings for all people, regardless of physical stature and varying abilities. The UD standards will help corporations and government entities create barrier-free facilities so that diverse users have equal access to commerce, public services, entertainment, and employment.

The principles underlying UD may have value not just for the design of the physical environment, but also for the basis of social policy and law. Bickenbach and Cieza (2012) describe two possibilities: (1) universal health care that provides needed health services to all people on an equitable and flexible basis (they highlight the example of Canada) and (2) universalistic social welfare or social protection that extends services to all people without means-testing, which avoids problems of stigmatization and may result in lower costs due to the avoidance of complex eligibility requirements (they highlight the example of Sweden). They point out:

> Ironically, a universal system of this sort might not have an identifiable "disability policy" at all. But that is as should be expected since "disability policy" is implicitly targeted or selective by its very nature. A universal social support system would likely set standards of participation in major life areas.... Public provision would be universalized by satisfying the principles of equity and flexibility in the provision of basic needs, across the full spectrum of human variability. (Bichenbach and Cieza 2012: 35)

H. EDUCATION

Education is indisputably important in enabling people to obtain better jobs and higher incomes and to engage in political participation. As such, it is a key factor for people with disabilities in achieving economic and political inclusion, as explored in Chapters 3 and 4. Along with this, education may be seen as a form of social inclusion because it is an important institution in which almost all members of society participate, and plays a key role in socializing people into society's norms and standards of behavior. As noted by the World Health Organization and the World Bank, "In some cultures, attending school is part of becoming a complete person" (WHO/World Bank 2011: 205).

While education is valuable for the population in general (Goldin and Katz 2008; Council of Economic Advisors 2011: 69–77), it may be especially beneficial for people with disabilities. One U.S. study found that the wage returns to education were larger for males who experience disability onset after reaching adulthood than for nondisabled men (Hollenbeck and Kimmel 2008). Low levels of education are also a key factor in the high poverty rates among people with disabilities, with a "worrisome vicious cycle of low schooling attainment and subsequent poverty among people with disabilities in developing countries" (Filmer 2008: 141).

Despite the value that education may have for people with disabilities, they have lower levels of education in general. They are less likely to have completed primary, secondary, or post-secondary schooling. Regarding primary schooling, an analysis of 51 countries by WHO found that only half (50%) of men with disabilities and two-fifths (42%) of women with disabilities had completed primary school, compared with 61% and 53% of men and women without disabilities, respectively (WHO/World Bank 2011: 206). People with disabilities also had fewer years of education on average (6.0 and 5.0 for men and women with disabilities, compared with 7.0 and 6.3 for men and women without disabilities), and the gaps were found across all age groups and in both high- and low-income countries (WHO/World Bank 2011: 206–207).

Consistent with the evidence on primary school completion, children with disabilities are less likely to be attending school than their nondisabled peers and are more likely to drop out or fail to be promoted than nondisabled students (WHO/World Bank 2011: 206). For example, studies have found that between one-fourth and two-fifths (24–39%) of children with disabilities aged 5 or older in Malawi, Namibia, Zambia, and Zimbabwe had never attended school, compared with 9–18% of children without disabilities (WHO/World Bank 2011: 207).

The disparity in education exists even in countries with high rates of primary school attendance, such as Bulgaria (96% for children without disabilities compared with 81% for children with disabilities), the Republic of Moldova (97% compared with 59%), and Romania (93% compared with 59%) (WHO/World Bank 2011: 208). Enrollment appears to vary by type of impairment: children with physical disabilities are more likely to attend school than those with intellectual or sensory impairments. For example, in 2006 only 10% of deaf children in Burkina Faso attended school, compared with 40% of children with physical disabilities (WHO/World Bank 2011: 207).

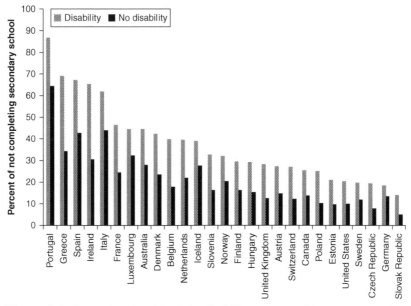

Figure 5.4. Low educational levels by disability status, working-age population, mid-2000s.
Source: Drawn from OECD, 2010, Figure 1.4.

The educational gap continues in secondary school. As shown in Figure 5.4, the percentage of people with disabilities who have not completed secondary school is higher than that of people without disabilities in 27 industrialized countries (OECD 2010: 27). A cause for concern is that the education gaps between people with and without disabilities appear to be getting larger in most countries (one exception being the United States, which passed the Individuals with Disabilities Education Act – IDEA), since the gaps are generally larger among people in their 20s and 30s than among people aged 40 or older (OECD 2010: 28).[17]

Similarly, people with disabilities are less likely to attend college or receive post-secondary degrees than are people without disabilities.

---

[17] For evidence on the lower educational attainment of young people with disabilities in the United Kingdom, see the indicators at odi.dwp.gov.uk/roadmap-to-disability-equality/indicators.php (accessed May 22, 2012).

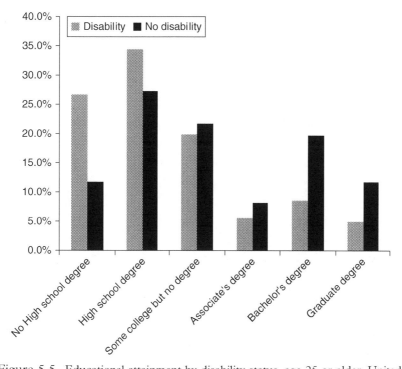

Figure 5.5. Educational attainment by disability status, age 25 or older, United States, 2010.

Figure 5.5 shows that in the United States adults with disabilities are less likely to have completed their education with an associate degree (5% compared with 8% for adults without disabilities), a bachelor's degree (8% compared with 20%), or a graduate degree (5% compared with 12%). Overall, only one-fifth of adults with disabilities have some type of post-secondary degree (19%), which is about half the rate for those without disabilities (40%).[18] In the European Union, only one-fifth (19%) of people with disabilities aged 30–34 have completed post-secondary education, compared with almost one-third (32%) of their counterparts without disabilities (Grammenos 2010: 7).

---

[18] Based on analysis of the 2010 American Community Survey, conducted by the U.S. Census Bureau. The figures exclude those in institutional group quarters.

Consistent with this evidence on educational attainment, current college enrollment among 18- to 24-year-olds in the United States is lower among people with disabilities (40%) than among people without disabilities (62%), with a similar pattern among those aged 18–29 in the European Union (17% compared with 24%) (Grammenos 2010: 7). This outcome in the United States also existed in the 1990s, although two studies found that educational enrollment appeared to increase among young people with disabilities following the enactment of the ADA (Jolls 2004; Honeycutt 2010), and the high school graduation rate among students with disabilities improved over the 1996–2006 period (WHO/World Bank 2011: 213).[19]

Why do people with disabilities have lower levels of education? The causality may run in both directions. Education has been found to influence health and the likelihood of developing a disability (Honeycutt 2010). Those with more education may (1) have generally safer work environments that are less likely to lead to disabling injuries or diseases; (2) have better access to health services and be better able to understand and act on medical information; (3) be more likely to seek preventive care, exercise, and avoid risky behaviors such as tobacco or alcohol abuse; (4) be better able to cope with stress and adversity; and (5) be more likely to use assistive technology and Web and computer services that help people cope with disabling conditions and may reduce the chance of someone reporting that he or she has a disability (Cutler et al. 2009).

While education can affect health and disability, disability also has strong effects on the likelihood and quality of education. Children in low-income families are less likely than other children to be diagnosed with a medical condition should they have one and less likely to receive treatment, and those who develop disabling conditions tend to have a poorer attendance record at school and a greater likelihood of failing or

---

[19] See further U.S. evidence on lower education levels among people with disabilities in Bennett (2009).

dropping out (Case et al. 2002, 2008; Currie and Stabile 2006; Currie et al. 2010).

There is also a long history of direct exclusion of children with disabilities from getting an education or confinement to institutions where the quality of education is low or nonexistent. In the United States the first special schools for children with sensory impairments were established in the early nineteenth century. A similar pattern occurred in other countries. By the middle of the nineteenth century, "children were taken out of almshouses and family settings and sent to 'specialized' schools developed specifically for children with auditory or vision impairments or mental retardation" (Hamlin and Simeonsson 2006: 567). While the stated mission of these schools was to help disabled children become productive members of society, most of these institutions were more accurately characterized as "warehouses" that provided minimal services and where people with disabilities were often neglected and sometimes languished for years (Hamlin and Simeonsson 2006).

This pattern of segregated schooling continued through the first half of the twentieth century. In the 1950s there was a growth of parent groups in the United States advocating for better services for their disabled children, which contributed to a shift in policy against institutionalizing children with disabilities in the late 1960s and early 1970s. This movement against institutionalization was also fueled by media exposure of widespread neglect and abusive conditions at residential institutions such as the Willowbrook State School in 1972.

In 1975 the U.S. Congress passed the Education for All Handicapped Children Act, which established a right to a free and appropriate public school education for all children with disabilities. Subsequent studies, however, found that special education programs did not provide children with equal opportunity and that many children with disabilities were still completely excluded from public schools (Hamlin and Simeonsson 2006). In response Congress revised the 1975 law and renamed it the Individuals with Disabilities Education Act (IDEA, mentioned earlier) in 1990, which guaranteed children with disabilities an education in the "least restrictive environment." This meant for the first time that children with disabilities should attend school in the most integrated setting possible and that specialized placement should be used only when necessary (WHO/World Bank 2011: 210).

The UN Convention in 2006 further recognized the right of all children with disabilities to be included in the general education system and to receive the individual supports they need.[20] In most Western countries the inclusion of students with disabilities in regular schools has been achieved, at least to some extent, especially in the primary grades (Hollenweger 2006b). For example, Finland, which has a reputation for having an excellent public school system, has embraced the principle of including students with disabilities in regular public school classrooms (Hollenweger 2006a).

In poorer countries, education tends to be less common in general and children with disabilities (especially girls) often face the possibility of not attending school at all. As Hollenweger (2006a) notes, UNESCO's 1994 initiative to ensure "Education for All" requires countries to increase the percentage of disadvantaged and disabled young people who receive schooling. This is to be achieved by passing legislation that increases resources for early childhood intervention and special education.

India provides an example of a country that has recognized the right to education for people with disabilities. Sharma and Deppeler (2005) note that "with the passage of the Persons with Disabilities Act, India is committed to the provision of individualized education for disabled children through initiatives to provide teacher training, collaboration among government ministries, changing examination requirements, and involvement of nongovernmental organizations in implementation efforts."

---

[20] See Haines and Ruebain (2010) for a detailed treatment of disability and education policy.

Different countries have taken different approaches to educating children with disabilities.[21] These include special schools and institutions, integrated schools, and inclusive schools. In Europe, 2.3% of pupils are educated in a segregated setting. Some countries place most children with special needs in separate schools (e.g., Belgium and Germany), while others appear to generally place children with special needs in regular classrooms with their peers (e.g., Cyprus, Lithuania, Malta, Norway, and Portugal) (Cooney et al. 2006). There appears to be a "general movement in developed countries towards inclusive education ... [while] in developing countries the move towards inclusive schools is just starting" (Cooney et al. 2006).

Mainstream schooling is generally recognized as a key policy in the promotion of social inclusion, helping create the least restrictive environment for most children with disabilities that will facilitate their full integration into society (Hamlin and Simeonsson 2006). Research on the value of inclusive versus segregated education, however, is inconclusive; studies have not been widely carried out and those that have been conducted often suffer from methodological or other problems, so there is a need for well-conducted research in this area (WHO/World Bank 2006: 211).

Some studies point to benefits for students with disabilities in acquiring better communication, social, and behavioral skills in inclusive settings (WHO/World Bank 2011: 211–212). Also, there is some evidence that students with intellectual disabilities can benefit from being placed in supportive mainstream classes, and inclusive education is more cost effective than creating separate programs and schools (WHO/World Bank 2006: 212, 220). Inclusive education can succeed, however, only if the school provides a safe and supportive environment.

---

[21] For a discussion of education of children with disabilities in European countries, see Ebersold (2011).

An example of the problems that can occur in inclusive education comes from Scotland. A comparison of perceived stigma among teenagers with intellectual disabilities in mainstream and segregated schools in Scotland showed that while both groups reported bullying in their neighborhoods, the mainstreamed group reported experiencing significant additional stigma at school (Cooney et al. 2006).

Barriers to education for children with disabilities include systemwide problems and schoolwide problems. Systemic problems include divided ministerial authority (where special education is included in a different department than education in general), lack of legislation, policy, planning, and targets, and inadequate resources. Schoolwide problems include inflexible approaches to curriculum and teaching, inadequate teacher training and support, physical barriers, negative attitudes, labeling, and violence, bullying, and abuse (WHO/World Bank 2011: 212–216).

Systemwide efforts to overcome barriers include legislative and policy initiatives, and providing adequate funding for implementation. For example, since the 1970s, Italy has had legislation supporting inclusive education for students with disabilities, which has led to high inclusion rates and positive educational outcomes. In Vietnam, the Center for Special Education has worked with a nongovernmental organization to set up pilot projects to demonstrate the feasibility of inclusive education for children with disabilities (WHO/World Bank 2011: 217).

Examples of effective initiatives at the school level include a training program on special education needs set up in 1992 in Ethiopia with support from the Finnish government and a training program in Mongolia run for teachers and parents with support of specialist teachers. The Mongolian program resulted in highly positive attitudes toward inclusion among the teachers and a doubling of the number of children with disabilities enrolled in mainstream primary and preschools (WHO/World Bank 2011: 223).

Communities, families, disability organizations, and young people with disabilities all play important roles in creating sustainable inclusive education. For example, community-based rehabilitation programs in Uganda and Kenya include educational programs for children and work toward the goal of inclusion. A Norwegian parents' organization has encouraged parents of disabled children in Zanzibar to collaborate with the education ministry in introducing inclusive education. In Panama, a parents group pressured the government to change the law requiring children with disabilities to attend school in segregated settings. In 2003, as a result of this campaign, the government introduced a policy to make all schools inclusive (WHO/World Bank 2011: 223–225).

In summary, education is a crucial area for all forms of inclusion for people with disabilities, and much of their economic, political, and social exclusion can be tied to their lower levels of educational attainment. While people with disabilities have often been forced into segregated schools, there are a variety of initiatives around the globe to increase the opportunities of people with disabilities to obtain high-quality schooling in inclusive settings, enabling them to learn, grow, and become more fully integrated into society.

This chapter reveals many of the disparities people with disabilities face in social inclusion. Issues of inclusion may be further complicated by gender, race, and other characteristics. The next chapter explores how such characteristics can influence the experiences of disability and how they often create greater barriers to inclusion.

6

Gender, Race, Ethnicity, and Disability

A. INTRODUCTION

The experience of disability varies widely, both among individuals and among groups. This chapter explores the interactions of disability with gender, race, and ethnicity, drawing on the theory of "intersectionality," which explores how biological, social, and cultural categories interact with and contribute to social inequality (Crenshaw 1991; Collins 1998).

Early disability theorists tended to assume there was a basic dichotomy between people with and without disabilities, simplifying the complexities that characterize people's lived experiences and glossing over aspects of identity such as gender, race, and ethnicity (Barnes and Mercer 2010: 85). In the words of Asch and Fine (1988: 3), according to this view:

> Having a disability presumably eclipses these dimensions of social experience.... [It is] not merely a "master" status but apparently the exclusive status of disabled people.

Over the past several decades there has been widespread and growing recognition that it is simplistic to view people with disabilities as a monolithic group. Degener (2011: 31), for example, writes of the need for greater awareness of "multidimensional discrimination":

> Discrimination at the intersection of race, gender and disability will rarely be composed of discrete jigsaw pieces corresponding

exactly to the three separate grounds. More commonly, it will be based on a mélange of overlapping and undefined prejudices and stigmas.

Similarly, Aybars (2011: 80) writes of situations that occur "when two or more discrimination grounds or identities combine to create a unique situation that is more complex and represents more than just the sum of its parts."[1]

Women with disabilities, for example, may have different experiences than men with disabilities based on the different ways women and men are socialized and the different roles they are expected to fulfill. In particular, women may face challenges "not only because of their weak position within labour markets, but also because within the highly skewed distribution of domestic labour most of the responsibility for parenting and care giving falls on them" (Pokempner and Roberts 2001, cited in Emmett and Alant 2006: 451).

B. GENDER

Feminist disability scholars called attention in the 1980s to the "double handicap" faced by women with disabilities – the fact that they fared significantly worse economically, socially, and psychologically than either men with disabilities or women without disabilities (Deegan and Brooks 1985; Fine and Asch 1988). Recent literature tends to use the term "multiple" or "intersectional" discrimination rather than "double discrimination" or "double handicap" (Degener 2011: 34). The realities facing women with disabilities were found to include lower employment, education, and income levels, fewer opportunities for vocational training, and receipt of lower disability income benefits. In addition, women with disabilities were found to be more likely to live alone, to be

---

[1] For a further exploration of multidimensional discrimination in the European Union, see Schiek and Lawson (2011).

viewed more negatively, and to have more negative self-concepts than men with disabilities.

Disparities associated with gender and disability exist around the globe: "The status of women with disabilities varies from one society to another; however, everywhere disability poses additional challenges for women" (Nagata 2003: 10). As noted, these disparities may not simply combine in an additive way, but can interact in ways that create unique forms of disadvantage (Hanna and Rogovsky 1993).

The UN Convention on the Rights of Persons with Disabilities recognized that people with disabilities may be "subject to multiple or aggravated forms of discrimination on the basis of sex, race, national, ethnic, indigenous or social origin," as well as other characteristics, and that "women and girls with disabilities are often at greater risk, both within and outside the home, of violence, injury or abuse, neglect or negligent treatment or exploitation."[2] The difficulties faced by women with disabilities may be especially pronounced in conservative countries where the status of women is relatively low to begin with and women in general tend to have few options relative to men (Nagata 2003).

1. Prevalence of Disability

Women are more likely than men to have disabilities. Across 50 countries covered in the World Health Survey, almost one-fifth (19.2%) of women are estimated to have disabilities, compared with about one-eighth (12.0%) of men (WHO/World Bank 2011: 28).[3] The rate

---

[2] www.un.org/disabilities/default.asp?id=260, Parts (p) and (q) (accessed May 9, 2012).

[3] The definition of disability is based on survey questions about degree of difficulty in eight domains of functioning and presence of chronic diseases such as arthritis, angina, asthma, diabetes, and depression. Respondents were classified on a scale of 0 to 100, with 0 indicating no functioning difficulty and 100 indicating complete

of disability is especially high for women in lower-income countries (22.1% compared with 13.8% for men), but also women are more likely than men to have disabilities in higher-income countries (14.4% compared with 9.1% for men).[4]

The higher overall rate of disability among women appears to be explained largely by age: women tend to outlive men, so a greater proportion of older people are women with impairments. Along with being older on average, women with disabilities are more likely to have degenerative impairments (such as osteoarthritis), while men are more likely to have disabilities caused by injuries (such as from traffic accidents) (Meekosha 2006b). The higher rate of disability among women may also be partly due to lower levels of care and support in many cultures; in some communities girls with impairments receive less food, medical care, and rehabilitation services than boys with impairments (Emmett and Alant 2006: 455). After age is accounted for, women are slightly

difficulty. People were classified as having a disability if they had a score of 40 or above, since 40 was the average score for those reporting one of the chronic diseases or extreme difficulty in one of the eight domains. For further details see World Bank (2011: 290–291).

[4] Also see Mitra et al. (2011), who found a higher prevalence of disability among women than among men in each of 15 developing countries. Some earlier surveys found a lower prevalence of disability among women than among men in developing countries, and it was suggested that this may reflect underreporting of disability in some cultures where females are identified primarily with domestic labor and where impairments affecting housework, cooking, and child care are not publicly visible and therefore not considered to be disabilities (Emmett and Alant 2006). The more recent surveys capture a broader range of activity limitations. "The suggestion that lower rates of disability among women in developing countries may be related to higher mortality rates for women and girls in these countries receives some support from the demographic phenomenon of the 'missing women' that emerges from Amartya Sen's work on poverty and inequality.... Sen (1990) showed unusually higher age specific mortality rates for women in some developing countries, particularly in South and West Asia, North Africa and China.... [He] attributes these gender specific mortality rates to 'the comparative neglect of female health and nutrition, especially – but not exclusively – during childhood' " (Sen 1999, quoted in Emmett and Alant 2006: 455).

more likely than men to have disabilities.[5] The pattern is similar in the United States, where 2010 data show that women have a higher overall rate of disability than men (15.7% compared with 14.5%), but this reflects their greater average age and they are less likely than men to have disabilities if they are under the age of 75.[6]

2. Economic Inclusion

Women's generally lower employment and income levels can combine with disability to create extra disadvantage. The decrease in employment and income levels associated with disability may, however, present particular challenges to men, who have the traditional breadwinner role in most societies.

Disability is linked to low employment rates for both men and women. Men without disabilities have the highest employment rates, and women with disabilities have the lowest rates, as shown in Figure 6.1 based on the World Health Survey (WHO/World Bank 2011: 238). Disability appears to lower the employment rate slightly more for men (from 65% to 53%) than for women (from 30% to 20%). This larger drop for men is more pronounced in high-income

[5] This is reflected in statistics across the world as well as specifically within high-income countries and low- and middle-income countries. Estimates from the Global Burden of Disease study show that women are more likely to report severe disabilities among those aged 60 or older (10.5% compared with 9.8% for men) and those aged 15–59 (2.8% compared with 2.6%). Counting moderate disabilities as well, women remain slightly more likely than men to report moderate or severe disabilities among those aged 60 or older (46.3% compared with 45.9%) and those aged 15–59 (15.7% compared with 14.2%) (World Bank 2011: 30).

[6] The disability rate for those aged 5–17 is 3.9% for girls and 6.6% for boys; for those aged 18–64 it is 9.9% for women and 10.5% for men; for those aged 65–74 it is 25.8% for women and 26.8% for men; and for those aged 75 or older it is 55.1% for women and 50.2% for men. Based on analysis of the 2010 American Community Survey, U.S. Census Bureau.

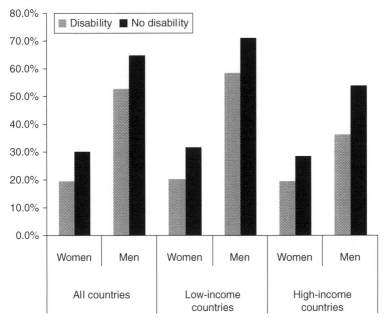

Figure 6.1. Employment by disability and gender, 2004. World Health Survey.

countries (from 54% to 36% among men and from 28% to 20% among women).[7]

This general pattern is evident in U.S. data from 2010, where disability appears to lower the employment of men more than that of women, but women with disabilities still have the lowest employment rate. Figure 6.2 shows that slightly less than one-third (31%) of working-age women with disabilities were employed in 2010, compared with more than one-third (36%) of men with disabilities, while

---

[7] These figures are consistent with a study of European data that showed disability linked to an employment drop of 19 points for men and 12 points for women (OECD 2010: 31). The World Health Survey data include all individuals aged 18 or older. In addition to women with disabilities having the lowest employment rates, their employment is less stable, being more sensitive to the business cycle than that of men with disabilities or women or men without disabilities, which may reflect the greater likelihood that women with disabilities have contingent jobs (OECD 2010: 31).

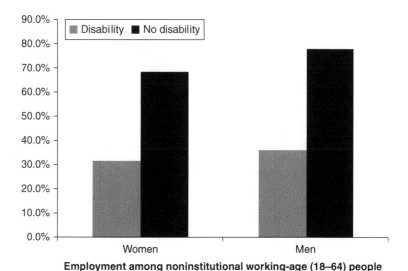

Figure 6.2. Employment by gender and disability, United States, 2010.

more than two-thirds of women without disabilities (69%) and more than three-fourths of men without disabilities (78%) were employed.[8]

In every country where data are available, women with disabilities are more likely to be outside the paid workforce (Meekosha 2006b). Among those who are employed, women with disabilities face disproportionately lower pay in U.S., UK, and Welsh studies (Baldwin and Johnson 1995; Jones et al. 2006a, 2006b).[9]

Low employment rates help explain high levels of poverty among women with disabilities. Figure 6.3 shows that almost one-fourth (23%) of women with disabilities lived in poverty in the United States in 2010, compared with about one-fifth (19%) of men with disabilities.

---

[8] Based on calculations from 2010 American Community Survey, U.S. Census Bureau, for people not living in institutional group quarters.

[9] In addition, Stoddard et al. (1998) found that women with disabilities who were employed were concentrated in non-union, low-wage jobs. Another study found that while employees with disabilities were much less likely than those without disabilities to receive benefits, there were no gender differences in the receipt of benefits among employees with disabilities (Lustig and Strauser 2004).

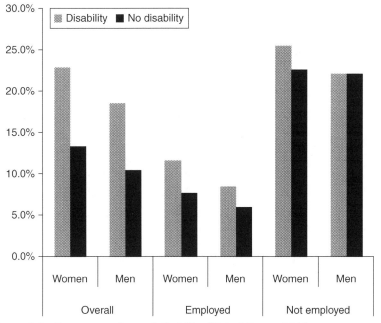

Figure 6.3. Poverty, gender, and disability, United States, 2010.

The poverty rates among women and men without disabilities were substantially lower (13% and 11%, respectively). This figure also shows that employment reduces poverty rates but that disability is linked to higher poverty rates even among employed people. This reflects lower average levels of pay and higher likelihood of part-time work among workers with disabilities, particularly among women.

The higher poverty rate among women with disabilities may be explained in part by their lower likelihood of receiving the main form of public disability income, Social Security Disability Insurance (SSDI), which is tied to pre-disability work earnings (Mudrick 1988; Baldwin 1997). Across the globe women are less likely than men to receive disability benefits in most, though not all, countries (OECD 2010: 73).

The high rate of poverty is only one indicator of hardship among women with disabilities. A U.S. study found that, in every income category, they are more likely than women without disabilities to experience food insecurity (e.g., skipping meals for lack of money), housing insecurity (e.g., being unable to pay rent), and inadequate health care (e.g., postponing medical or dental care) (Parish et al. 2009).

The pattern of greater economic disadvantage and hardship for women with disabilities exists around the world (Emmett and Alant 2006). In poorer nations, poverty tends to affect women with disabilities more severely than men with disabilities because of patriarchal property ownership laws and customs (Emmett and Alant 2006). Women with disabilities are less likely than men with disabilities to receive rehabilitation services (Meekosha 2006b: 768) and were found to be less likely to have access to assistive devices in Malawi and Zambia (WHO/World Bank 2011: 103).

There is, of course, substantial variation among countries in the relative employment and income of women and men with disabilities, as the following examples illustrate. In the oil-rich country of Kuwait, a 1994 study found that while only 2% of women with disabilities reported working outside the home, a majority of the employed women worked in professional and technical fields. In contrast, among the 20% of Kuwaiti men with disabilities who were employed, most worked in lower-paying jobs as service or clerical workers or laborers (Nagata 2003: 12). This gender difference may reflect the relative privilege of employed Kuwaiti women with disabilities, a high percentage of whom earned good salaries and held socially prestigious jobs. Kuwaiti men, in contrast, with or without disabilities, may be under more pressure to work, no matter what jobs are available to them (Nagata 2003: 12–13).

In contrast to the situation of women with disabilities in Kuwait, those in Lebanon (a resource-poor, non-oil-producing country) find it difficult to find well-paying jobs, and those who are employed frequently report discrimination and harassment at work and while taking public transportation (Nagata 2003: 13).

In Turkey, it is estimated that only 7% of women with disabilities are employed (compared with 32% of men with disabilities), and women with disabilities tend to be more socially isolated than men with disabilities (Aybars 2011: 89, 94). In France, which has stronger employment protections and programs to increase employment among people with disabilities, among all people reporting "limitations in their work capacity," 38% of women are employed compared with 50% of men, and the employed women are more likely to have part-time jobs (Aybars 2011: 89).

In India, piecework is the most common form of employment for women with disabilities. Under the piecework system, materials are delivered to the women's homes and the finished products are collected by agents. "Examples of piecework by disabled women and girls include labor intensive and poorly paid activities such as weaving, basket making, sewing and assembling toys" (Rao 2004: 3). The women are paid according to the number of products they make and receive no legal or social protections from fraud, abuse, and exploitation (Rao 2004: 3).

3. Political Inclusion

Both women and men with disabilities are slightly less likely than their nondisabled counterparts to be politically active in the United States. Figure 6.4 shows that women without disabilities were the most likely to vote in both the 2008 and the 2010 U.S. national elections, exceeding the turnout of women with disabilities (by nine and five points, respectively), while the turnout gaps of men with and without disabilities were smaller (five points and one point, respectively).[10]

As noted in Chapter 4, these voting gaps are strongly affected by demographic factors such as age and education – in particular, the higher average age of people with disabilities tends to increase their

---

[10] This figure is based on analysis of the CPS Voter Turnout supplement for November 2010, conducted by the U.S. Census Bureau.

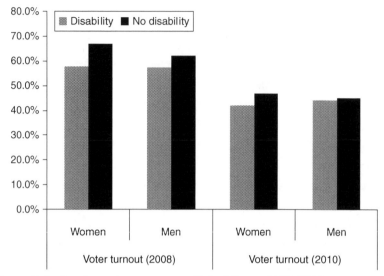

Figure 6.4. Gender and voter turnout, United States, 2008–2010.

voter turnout, while their lower average level of education tends to decrease their turnout relative to that of people without disabilities. However, disability has an independent effect on turnout. When age, education, and other demographic factors are held constant, disability is linked with lower turnout among both women and men.

The relationship between disability and forms of political participation other than voting appears to be similar for women and men. As shown in Chapter 4, young people with disabilities are at least as likely as their peers without disabilities to engage in nonvoting forms of political activity, which is true for both young women and men with disabilities.[11] Among older people, both women and men with

---

[11] Among young women (aged 18–34), the percentage engaging in at least one political activity in the past year is 21% for those with disabilities and 19% for those without disabilities, while the comparable numbers for young men are 21% and 17%, respectively. The disability gaps are largest among those aged 65 or older (20% compared with 26% for women with and without disabilities, and 24% compared with 30% for men with and without disabilities).

disabilities are less likely than people without disabilities to engage in other political activities. As discussed, this difference in the age pattern may reflect generational differences in the experience of disability, which appears to operate similarly for women and men.[12]

Gender differences emerge, however, in perceptions of disability discrimination and responses to it. A U.S. survey in 2000 found that women with disabilities were less likely than men with disabilities to report having experienced discrimination in the past five years (15% compared with 21%), but the women who did experience discrimination were significantly more likely than the men to take action against it (50% compared with 26%), especially among younger women (59% compared with 25% among young men) (Schur 2003a). The greater reports of discrimination and disability activism among younger women suggests that they are less likely than their mothers and grandmothers to have been socialized with negative views of disability and are less likely to "normalize," which is encouraging for future efforts to improve the status of women with disabilities.

There is little information outside of the United States on how disability and gender relate to voter turnout and other direct measures of political participation. We have examples, however, of political strategies and efforts to empower women with disabilities. These include the emergence of organizations run by and for women with disabilities in many countries. Examples include groups in Pakistan, India, Nepal, Hong Kong, Canada, and Australia,[13] as well as regional organizations such as Disabled Women in Africa (DIWA), the Network of

---

[12] One study found that lower participation among older women with disabilities was tied to a lower average sense of internal efficacy, suggesting that many women with disabilities may have internalized negative messages about their capabilities and that efforts to empower women with disabilities through group training and peer counseling can help increase their political engagement (Schur 2003a).

[13] These organizations are Canadian Disabled Women's Network; Women with Disabilities Australia; Society for Disabled Women Pakistan; Association for Women with Disabilities India; Nepal Disabled Women's Association and Association for Disabled Women in Hong Kong.

South Asian Women with Disabilities (NSAWWD), and the European Disability Forum (EDF).

These organizations provide sources of information, support, and validation for women with disabilities, who sometimes feel alienated from disability groups that are dominated by men, and also from feminist groups, which sometimes fail to address disability issues (Meekosha 2002). As an activist from Women with Disabilities Australia (WWDA) explained:

> "Many women with disabilities experience ... an enormous degree of lack of agency, lack of autonomy ... so having an organization which is run by women with disabilities focusing specifically on the issues is enormous.... [T]he issues for women with disabilities in particular are trivialized and women with disabilities themselves are trivialized and so to be taken seriously in a national organization, to make your own analysis of what's happening and to have a vehicle to take that forward is a very empowering thing." (Sue, quoted in Meekosha 2002: 68).

Groups run by and for women with disabilities can be effective vehicles for political mobilization. For example, in 1999, WWDA began a campaign to redefine involuntary sterilization of women with disabilities as a human rights issue, which gained support from the Australian government the following year (Meekosha 2002: 83). WWDA has also successfully advocated for increased access of women with disabilities to services related to violence, particularly women's shelters (Meekosha 2002). In 2002, WWDA won the Australian national Human Rights Award. The organization has depended on the Australian government for grants and has struggled financially while also struggling to maintain its political independence and focus on advocacy. Despite difficulties, it has provided a valuable forum for women with disabilities to express their concerns and engage in political action.

Another example is provided by Disabled Women in Africa (DIWA), the independent women's wing of the Pan-African Federation of the Disabled, the umbrella of Disabled People's Organizations in Africa.

DIWA was founded in Dar-es-Salaam in 2002. DIWA's activities include lobbying for the rights, visibility, and empowerment of women with disabilities in Africa, developing networks of women with disabilities, and working to ensure that gender issues are addressed by disability organizations and included in development policy and government disability programs (DIWA 2010).

One recent project undertaken by DIWA is providing support for women with disabilities to lobby for a gender-balanced implementation of the UN Convention in eastern and southern African countries. DIWA has worked with partners to develop workshops and leadership training programs for women with disabilities to teach them about using the UN Convention to raise awareness. DIWA's other projects include working to increase women's representation in disability organizations and the presence of women with disabilities in women's networks in Zimbabwe.

In the United States, a program focusing on individual empowerment is Reach Out Against Depression (ROAD), a grassroots project based on peer support and community organizing for low-income women with depression. The program includes workshops run by women who are themselves struggling with self-identified depression and poverty and a related program entitled "Feminist Relational Advocacy," designed to address both the material and psychological problems of low-income women who are struggling with depressive symptoms (Goodman et al. 2009: 852). In these programs, a master's student in mental health counseling is paired with a "partner" and helps provide psychological support as well as concrete assistance in defining and meeting goals, finding local resources, and navigating bureaucracies. Advocacy involves accompanying partners at meetings with caseworkers, landlords, and other institutional representatives. In a qualitative study many of the partners said the program helped them develop new tools for problem solving, including being better able to express their needs to those in a position of authority (Goodman et al. 2009: 866). In addition, participants said their advocacy experiences created "a new sense of self-worth" and the ability to make changes in their lives and communities.

In short, while women with disabilities remain politically marginalized in many societies, organizations of women with disabilities are active in many countries and regions around the world. They are helping to raise political awareness, lobby policy makers, and train and mobilize women with disabilities to address the barriers and persistent inequalities they experience.

4. Social Inclusion

Social Isolation

Women and men with disabilities often have different experiences of social exclusion. They have a similar likelihood of living in institutions in the United States, but among those outside of institutions, women with disabilities are more likely than men to be living alone.[14] This is explained largely by their higher likelihood of being widows, which reflects their higher average age.[15]

Both women and men with disabilities in the United States tend to have less social contact than their counterparts without disabilities, with a slightly larger gap for women with disabilities. As shown in Figure 6.5, close to one-fifth (19%) of women with disabilities have attended a meeting of a group or organization in the past 12 months,

---

[14] Among all people with disabilities, 5.5% of women lived in institutions in 2010 compared with 6.1% of men. Among those living in the community, 28% of women with disabilities and 19% of men with disabilities lived alone, while among women and men without disabilities the figures are 12% and 11%, respectively. Based on analysis of the 2010 American Community Survey, conducted by the U.S. Census Bureau.

[15] Among non-widowers there is a greater similarity in the likelihood of living alone (18% and 15% for women and men with disabilities, compared with 9% and 11% for women and men without disabilities).

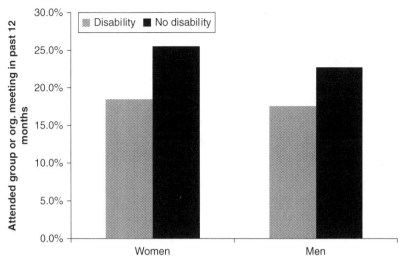

Figure 6.5. Gender, disability, and participation with groups, United States, 2008.

compared with about one-fourth (26%) of women without disabilities. Men are slightly less likely to attend groups meetings overall, and the disability gap is narrower (18% and 23% for men with and without disabilities, respectively). Overall, while disability is associated with greater social isolation among both women and men, the gaps in living alone and attending group meetings appear to be greater for women with disabilities.

Education

Education is a critical element of social, economic, and political inclusion. In many countries girls with disabilities have less access to education than boys with disabilities (Emmett and Alant 2006). This is especially true in poorer countries and in societies with limited recognition of women's rights, where girls with disabilities tend to receive even less education than girls in general. For example, studies have found literacy and education rates of women with disabilities in Syria, Bahrain,

Lebanon, and Turkey that are substantially lower than those of both women in general and of men with disabilities (Nagata 2003: 12; Aybars 2011), while a report from Karnataka State, India, found literacy rates among women with disabilities of 7%, compared with a general literacy rate of 46% (Rao 2004: 2). As one Indian woman stated: "The issues of women with disabilities are the same as other women in India plus more [complex] as they lack access to education, resulting in all the problems linked with illiteracy and poverty, lack of decision making power and lack of available options" (quoted in Rao 2004: 7).

While scholars and policy makers have focused on the relationship between female education and development,[16] few have drawn explicit connections among development, gender inequality, and disability. On this point, Emmett and Alant argue that disability must be included as "an integral part of development, rather than as a separate need competing with other causes and manifestations of poverty" (Emmett and Alant 2006: 446). They maintain that those seeking to eliminate poverty and stimulate sustained development need to address the complex ways disability interacts with gender and race "to create new or more extreme forms of deprivation and oppression" (Emmett and Alant 2006: 459).

Despite a history of neglect, policy makers in developing countries have started to recognize the importance of education for girls with disabilities. For example, in India a government initiative that began in 2003 provides scholarships for people with disabilities to pursue higher education, with 50% of the places reserved for women with disabilities (Rao 2004: 3).

In the United States, women with disabilities have historically received less education than men with disabilities and nondisabled

---

[16] Development scholars have recognized that female education helps reduce fertility, child mortality, and poverty, and improves household incomes and health, all of which help increase well-being in developing nations (Klassen 2000; Subbarao and Raney, 1995).

women (Fine and Asch 1985). However, the educational barriers faced by women with disabilities in the United States have decreased since the 1980s. Two important federal laws – the Individuals with Disabilities Education Act (IDEA) and Title IX of the Education Amendments of 1972 – provide legal protections from gender and disability discrimination and were designed to ensure that schools treat all students fairly and equitably (Blanck et al. 2009).

Efforts to achieve educational equality in the United States have been somewhat successful. Women with disabilities in 2010 were as likely as men with disabilities to have graduated from high school (only one-sixth of those aged 25 or older had not done so, compared with one-eighth of women and men without disabilities). Among all adults, Figure 6.6 shows that women with disabilities were the least likely to have received a college degree (associate, bachelor's, or graduate degree).[17] Both women and men with disabilities were only half as likely as their counterparts without disabilities to have college degrees, and the increased education levels of women with disabilities have not closed the gaps in poverty and employment rates (discussed earlier).

Social Roles

Fine and Asch (1985) argued that women with disabilities were viewed as unable to fulfill traditional adult social roles, such as that of wage earner or homemaker, and if they tried to identify with traditional female sex roles this only reinforced the stereotype of the passive, dependent disabled person. They claimed that the combination

---

[17] The comparison in Figure 6.6 is for people aged 25 or older. When confined to those aged 25–65, women with disabilities are slightly more likely than men with disabilities to have college degrees (21% compared with 18%), while the numbers continue to be about half of those for women and men without disabilities (43% compared with 39%). Based on analysis of the noninstitutional population in the American Community Survey, conducted by U.S. Census Bureau.

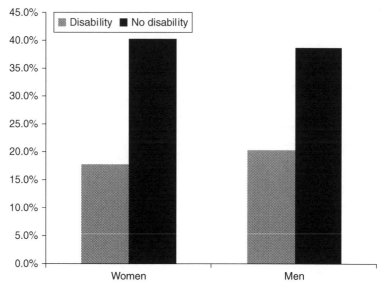

Figure 6.6. Gender, disability, and completion of college, United States, 2010.

of economic, social, and psychological barriers contributed to the "rolelessness" faced by many women with disabilities (Fine and Asch 1985: 12). While this was frequently perceived as a burden, the lack of a clearcut social role allowed some women with disabilities to reject both gender and disability stereotypes and forge their own identities (Fine and Asch 1985: 13, 25).

Fine and Asch argued that men with disabilities, in contrast, had more opportunities to distance themselves from the "disability role" by identifying with the "male" role associated with independence and self-assertion. Other writers, however, point out that men with disabilities may also experience "rolelessness" if their disabilities limit them from performing traditional male roles: "To be a disabled man is to fail to measure up to the general culture's definition of masculinity as strength, physical ability and autonomy" (Morris 1993). For example, men with physical disabilities may be judged (and judge themselves) according to the standards of "hegemonic masculinity" that value work, athleticism, sexual virility and attractiveness, and independence

(Gerschick 1998). Men who cannot live up to these standards may be marginalized and viewed as "failed" men (Gerschick 1998: 189).

A study of men from racial and ethnic minorities who acquired spinal cord injuries by violence found that the "injury and resulting disability violated social understandings of what it means to be a man in their environments," affecting their "sense of safety, sexual encounters, body image and choice of intimate partners" (Ostrander 2008). In response to the denial of gender identity, some men with disabilities engage in "hyper-masculine" behavior, continually trying to prove their masculinity to themselves and others, efforts that are ultimately doomed to failure (Gerschick 1998: 204–205). Others distance themselves from stereotypes and redefine masculinity on their own terms. For example, men with physical disabilities may replace norms of physical strength, athleticism, and self-reliance with the values of mental or emotional strength, interdependence, and cooperation (Gerschick 1998: 206–207).

"Rolelessness" may be a particularly difficult problem for women with disabilities in cultures where a woman's value is determined primarily by her status as a wife and mother. One Indian disability activist has stated: "In a society where the practice of gender inequality has become a convention, disabled women are the most isolated and marginalized" (quoted in Rao 2004: 7). As pointed out in the South African National Disability Strategy (RSA 1997, quoted in Emmett and Alant 2006):

> Disabled women experience the same oppression as non-disabled women, but often without even the status that women traditionally receive as mothers or wives. In addition, disabled women experience more discrimination than other women from being unable to live up to the demanding ideals for womanhood imposed by society.

This sentiment is echoed by an Indian woman with a disability who said that women with disabilities "are not considered to be women who can fulfill the traditional roles of Indian women" (quoted in Rao 2004: 7). Similarly, Irene Feika from Disabled People International stated:

> [Women with disabilities] tend to be left out of the decision-making process. This reality is especially true of women with disabilities in cultures where the role of wife and mother is considered to be the primary role for a female. (Quoted in Rao 2004: 2)

In many regions, in both the developed and developing worlds, women with disabilities are less likely than men with disabilities to be seen as appropriate marriage partners. Consequently, they are more likely to live alone and to be without adequate financial resources. In the Arab context, as in many other cultures, the primary role of women has been seen as wife and mother, and women with disabilities are often viewed as incapable of filling this role (Wehbi and Lakkis 2010: 58).

In addition, the stigma of having a daughter with a disability can be so great within Arab society that parents may hide their daughter's existence for fear of discouraging potential marriage partners for their other children (Wehbi and Lakkis 2010: 58). One exception to this in the Middle East is the treatment of "very mildly retarded women": Nagata argues that "men may accept a young and pretty mildly retarded woman, although women tend to refuse marriage to a mentally retarded man" (Nagata 2003: 13).

In rapidly developing nations such as China, disability can also have a disproportionate impact on women. Lo-Hui et al. (2011), for example, conducted a qualitative study of female migrant workers in China who were seriously injured in industrial accidents. These young women had been raised in rural villages with traditional Chinese cultural values. Although they had migrated to the city and became financially independent, they viewed this arrangement as temporary. They had expected to return to their villages by their mid-twenties in order to marry and have a child. After they were injured, they worried that they would become "a burden for the family" (Lo-Hui et al. 2011: 42). Their families would have to take care of them and would also experience "shame" because of their disabilities. They expressed concern that they would be "looked down upon" by eligible men or their families and would never be able to marry. In contrast, male migrants who were injured could generally expect more support because sons are traditionally considered "permanent" members of their families of origin. Many parents of injured male migrants actively tried to find suitable brides in rural China to "take care" of their sons (Lo-Hui et al. 2011: 43, 45).

While women with disabilities are often viewed as unmarriageable or asexual, they have also been considered sexually deviant or dangerous and are more likely than men with disabilities to face medical interventions to control their fertility. This has been especially true for women with intellectual disabilities. In the United States, Australia, and Canada, for example, historically young women who were considered "mentally defective" or "feeble-minded" were often involuntarily sterilized (Kempton and Kahn 1991; Brady 2001; Beatty et al. 2009).

Girls and women with disabilities are also more likely to experience sexual violence in personal relationships, hospitals, schools, and other institutions (Meekosha 2006b: 765). In poor countries, women with disabilities who are sexually abused often have few if any supports or options (Meekosha 2006b). Abuse sometimes goes unreported because of the shame some families feel about having a daughter with a disability (Emmett and Alant 2006). Girls and women with disabilities who are displaced by war, famine, or natural disasters often have few if any resources to help them survive (Meekosha 2006b). Furthermore, it is important to point out that sexual violence against women often leads to disabling conditions, such as post-traumatic stress disorder, depression, pregnancy-related complications, and HIV-AIDs and other sexually transmitted diseases, such as chlamydia (which a 1990 study found was one of the leading causes of disability among women) (Peters and Opacich 2006).

As noted in a study of a rural community in Lebanon, women with disabilities are often placed in a bind: "On one hand, they are not complete women (or do not adhere to the societally normative definition of womanhood); on the other hand, they are seen as sexual objects that are sometimes translated into being seen as potential victims" (Wehbi and Lakkis 2010: 62). Being seen as a potential victim of sexual assault presented many women with the greatest difficulty in completing their education or finding a job. Educational and job opportunities were limited in this rural community, and the women's families often refused permission for them to work outside their homes or to go to school in other villages because of the perceived danger, as well as the common attitude that women with disabilities are incapable of learning or working outside the home. These attitudes contribute to the low levels of literacy and employment among women with disabilities (Wehbi and Lakkis 2010: 61).

Efforts are starting to be made to address some of the barriers girls and women with disabilities face in rural Lebanon. Social workers associated with the Lebanese Physical Handicapped Union (LPHU) conduct home visits to talk with parents who are reluctant to allow their daughters to work or attend school. The social workers arrange for transportation for the women from their homes to their places of work or study (Wehbi and Lakkis 2010: 64).

Men's roles as warriors during armed conflict affect society's willingness to provide services. The U.S. government, for example, provides disability benefits for injured veterans (Logue and Blanck 2010). Men's wartime roles also affect people's perceptions of disability. In Palestine, for example, disability was traditionally viewed as shameful (Nagata 2003: 14). However, during the Intifada in 1987, retaliation by the Israeli military against Palestinian young men who participated in the uprising caused a sudden, large increase in the number of people with permanent physical disabilities (Nagata 2003: 14). These young men were seen as "heroes" and "martyrs" who had sacrificed their bodies to the cause of national liberation, and disability, which had been a source of stigma, now became a mark of honor and a sign of resistance to oppression (Nagata 2003: 14). This led to the rapid spread of rehabilitation programs in Palestine. The acceptance of services for male war veterans, however, also diverted attention from women who had also been injured during the civil unrest, as well as from people with other types of disability (Nagata 2003: 15).

C. RACE AND ETHNICITY

Racial identity shapes the experience of disability (as discussed in, e.g., Stuart 1992a, 1992b; Alston and Bell 1996; Block et al. 2002; Miller 2002; Connor and Ferri 2005; Bryan 2007; McDonald et al. 2007; Blanchett et al. 2009). While every country has racial and ethnic minorities, the main available sources of information on race, ethnicity, and disability come from comparisons of white non-Hispanic Americans with African-Americans, Hispanics/Latinos, Asians, and Native Americans in the United States, and of white Anglo-Celts with Indigenous people in Australia. Accordingly we focus on the U.S. and Australian evidence.

1. Prevalence of Disability

The likelihood of disability varies by race and ethnicity, as shown by U.S. data in Figure 6.7.[18] The highest rate is among Native Americans, of whom more than one-fifth (22%) have some type of disability. This disparity is caused by greater exposure to health risks, including risks associated with poverty and lack of access to services and "culturally sensitive treatments" (Ni et al. 2011).[19]

---

[18] Based on analysis of the total population (institutional and noninstitutional) in the 2010 American Community Survey, conducted by the U.S. Census Bureau.

[19] A study of four eastern tribes (2011) found gender differences in disability prevalence: Native American women were more likely than men to have arthritis and orthopedic disabilities, while Native American men were more likely than women to

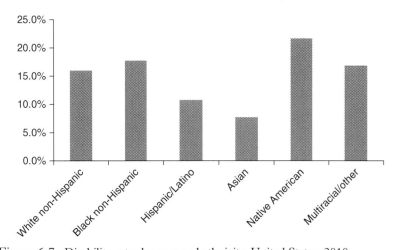

Figure 6.7. Disability rates by race and ethnicity, United States, 2010.

Figure 6.7 also shows a slightly higher prevalence of disability among African-Americans (18%) and a lower prevalence among Hispanics/Latinos (11%) compared with white non-Hispanics (16%).[20] An earlier study of adults aged 65 and older in the United States found that the risk of developing disabilities was substantially higher among African-Americans and Hispanics interviewed in Spanish (although not among Hispanics interviewed in English), which was explained largely by health and socioeconomic differences

experience substance abuse (Ni et al. 2011). Native Americans are also at particular risk for obesity and diabetes (Bryan 2007).

[20] The high incidence of disability among African-Americans is consistent with 2006 data from Nuru-Jeter et al. (2011) and 1994–1995 data from Emmett and Alant (2006: 453) and with data on medical conditions (particularly obesity and diabetes, which are more common among African-Americans than among non-Hispanic whites) (Whitson et al. 2011). The 1994–1995 survey also showed that African-American and Hispanics have a higher incidence of visual impairment after age is adjusted for (Kirchner and Schmeidler 1999). Kelly et al. (2000) found greater physical disorder and sidewalk obstructions in neighborhoods that were mostly African-American, which may influence disparities in the frequency of physical activity.

(Dunlop et al. 2007).[21] The authors concluded that culturally specific programs to increase physical activity and promote weight maintenance may reduce racial and ethnic disparities in disability rates (Dunlop et al. 2007).

Other U.S. studies found that African-Americans and Hispanics are more likely than non-Hispanic whites to have disabilities, and these disparities appear to persist throughout the life cycle (Kelley-Moore and Ferraro 2004; Warner and Brown 2007). A higher rate of disability among African-American children occurs in part because they are more likely than white children to live in poverty (Emmett and Alant 2006: 451).[22]

Racial differences in the prevalence of disability have also been found in Australia. A 1993 study found that more than 80% of Aboriginal people had up to four chronic disabling conditions, the most common being asthma, diabetes, and kidney disease (Kendall and Marshall 2004: 5). They have also been found to have worse overall health and higher incidences of traumatic brain injury, psychological disorders, and diabetes than non-Indigenous Australians (Kendall and Marshall 2004; Davis et al. 2007; Vos et al. 2009).[23]

[21] Other research also found that the higher rate of disability among African-Americans is fully or largely accounted for by socioeconomic factors, health indicators, and social integration (Kelley-Moore et al. 2004; Fuller-Thomson et al. 2008). The high incidence of learning disabilities among African-Americans and Hispanics is also explained by socioeconomic factors (Shifrer et al. 2011).

[22] Blanchett et al. (2009) question, however, the role of poverty, pointing out that a higher risk of special education placement among African-American children may occur because they are less likely to meet the academic and behavioral norms of schools than other children.

[23] The Aboriginal patients with diabetes reported lower diabetes-related quality of life, were diagnosed at younger ages, and tended to die 18 years younger than their Anglo-Celt counterparts (Davis et al. 2007). The large disparities in the incidence of diabetes led the authors of the study to call for "specialized culturally sensitive" programs to encourage groups such as Aboriginal people to obtain diabetes education (Davis et al. 2007: 62).

2. Economic Inclusion

In the United States, working-age people with disabilities have lower employment rates than people without disabilities in all racial and ethnic categories, as shown in Figure 6.8. Among people with disabilities the employment rate is highest for Asians (38%), followed by Hispanics/ Latinos (36%), non-Hispanic whites (35%), and Native Americans (29%), with the lowest employment rate among African-Americans (26%). The employment gaps between people with and without disabilities are highest among white non-Hispanics (76% compared with 35%) and African-Americans (67% compared with 26%). While the disability gaps are similar, the effects may be more serious for African-Americans, since the race and disability gaps combine to give them the lowest employment rate.[24]

Relative employment rates vary by type of disability. Employment rates were found to be similar among African-American, Latino, Asian, and white non-Hispanic men with serious psychiatric disorders (the most stigmatized type of disability, which may overwhelm other characteristics) (Chatterji et al. 2009), while among people with spinal cord injuries, both Hispanics and African-Americans had lower employment rates than white non-Hispanics (Krause et al. 2010: 81).[25]

A study of school-to-work transitions among young adults with disabilities found that both Hispanics and African-Americans were less likely to become employed than their white peers, and those who found jobs were less likely to be working in community settings as opposed to sheltered workshops or other noncompetitive employment (Hasnain and

---

[24] Based on noninstitutional population aged 18-64 in 2010 American Community Survey, U.S. Census Bureau. See Mpofu and Harley (2006) for a discussion of how racial and disability identity can be assets for career counseling of people of color with disabilities.

[25] Krause et al. (2010) also found that while education is the strongest predictor of employment among people with spinal cord injuries, it does not equalize employment outcomes, since whites continue to have higher employment levels than African-Americans at every level of education.

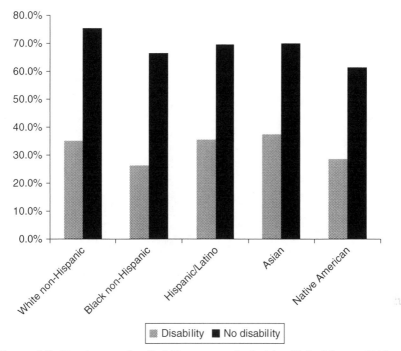

Figure 6.8. Employment by disability, race, and ethnicity, United States, 2010.

Balcazar 2009). This is partly explained by difficulties faced by many low-income African-American and Latino families in gaining information and access to support services to help their children make effective school-to-work transitions (Hasnain and Balcazar 2009: 176).

Poverty rates are higher among people with disabilities in the United States across all racial and ethnic categories, as seen in Figure 6.9.[26] The highest poverty rates are among African-Americans and Native Americans with disabilities (both 33%), the groups that also have the highest disability rates. This may partly reflect a circular relationship, with poverty being both a cause and consequence of disability

[26] Based on adult noninstitutional population in 2010 American Community Survey, U.S. Census Bureau. Consistent with these results, a study of families of individuals with spinal cord injuries found poverty rates of 18.3% among non-Hispanic white families and 42.4% among black/Hispanic families (Dismuke et al. 2011).

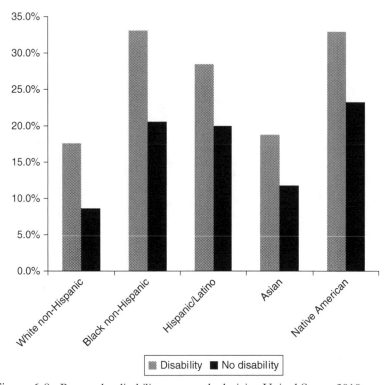

Figure 6.9. Poverty by disability, race, and ethnicity, United States, 2010.

(as discussed in Chapter 2). Similarly, Asians have a low disability rate, and those with disabilities have a low poverty rate (19%). The gaps between the poverty rates of people with and without disabilities are highest for African-Americans (13 points) and Native Americans (10 points). Outside of the United States, a study found that Aboriginal patients with diabetes had significantly lower incomes than comparable Anglo-Celt patients (Davis et al. 2007).

3. Political Inclusion

The political participation gap in the United States between people with and without disabilities appears to be highest among white non-Hispanics. In the 2008 U.S. elections, only 58% of whites with disabilities voted, compared with 67% of whites without disabilities. This nine-point gap exceeded the gap among African-Americans (62% and 66% for people with and without disabilities), and Hispanics (46% and 50%, respectively).[27] The data on other political activities also indicate that disability gaps are concentrated among white non-Hispanics. While white non-Hispanics with disabilities were less likely than those without disabilities to engage in a nonvoting form of political participation in 2008 (24% vs. 28%, respectively), the levels of participation were equal between African-Americans with and without disabilities (23%) and between Hispanics with and without disabilities (12%).[28]

Therefore, while the general political participation of members of racial and ethnic minorities tends to be lower than that of white non-Hispanics in the United States, disability has a smaller effect on their participation. The challenges faced by people with disabilities who are members of minority groups have led to political efforts to improve their situation, including initiatives developed specifically to address the needs of people with disabilities from black and Latino communities.

One example is provided by a Chicago-based program designed to increase awareness of and compliance with the Americans with Disabilities (ADA), focusing on the particular concerns of Latinos, such as inappropriate services for Spanish-speaking children in special education classes, lack of awareness about the ADA in the Latino community, and lack of accessible transportation in minority neighborhoods. This project used a "capacity-building approach" formed around coalitions of Latinos with disabilities, their family members, university personnel, community partner organizations (such as

---

[27] Based on analysis of the 2008 CPS Voter Supplement, conducted by the U.S. Census Bureau. The sample sizes for Asians and Native Americans were too small to calculate reliable numbers.

[28] Based on analysis of the 2008 Civic Engagement Supplement, conducted by the U.S. Census Bureau.

churches), and new community organizations and groups (Balcazar et al. 2001: 53). The project led to an increased level of political involvement among Latinos with disabilities and their families, and three new consumer-led organizations developed as a result (Balcazar et al. 2001: 67). Another example is provided by the National Black Disability Coalition (NBDC), an organization focused on issues having a particularly large impact on African-Americans with disabilities, such as the treatment of prison inmates with developmental and psychiatric disabilities and the overrepresentation of African-American boys in special education classes (see the Web site www.blackdisability.org/). The NBDC provides a wide range of resources, training people to become community advocates and sponsoring the Annual Interfaith Black Disability Conference, which "has a holistic approach to assisting Black faith communities in understanding disability culture and how to include people with disabilities and their families by providing spiritual, physical and advocacy supports."

4. Social Inclusion

Social Isolation

The evidence is mixed regarding whether members of racial and ethnic minority groups in the United States are particularly likely to experience social exclusion. Consistent with their generally high disability rate, African-Americans with disabilities are more likely to live in institutions (8% compared with 6% among non-Hispanic whites, 6% among Native Americans, 5% among Hispanics, and 3% among Asians).[29] As

---

[29] Based on analysis of 2010 American Community Survey, U.S. Census Bureau. While this rate among Native Americans with disabilities is not high, a study of those with spinal cord injuries found that they were the most likely group to be discharged from hospitals into nursing homes rather than returned to community settings, and were three times more likely than whites with spinal cord injuries to experience symptoms of depression (Gary et al. 2011: 277, 279).

with people with disabilities in general, African-Americans with disabilities who live in the community are more likely than people without disabilities to be living alone (25% compared with 15%), but the pattern is similar for non-Hispanic whites (25% compared with 13%).

African-Americans with disabilities are as likely as African-Americans without disabilities to have attended a group or organization meeting in the past 12 months (16% for each), while there is a gap between Hispanics with and without disabilities (8% compared with 10%), but the largest disability gap is among non-Hispanic whites (20% compared with 29%). Therefore, while people with disabilities in general have less social contact than those without disabilities, this disparity does not appear to be larger among African-Americans or Hispanics.

Education

The data are mixed regarding education among people with disabilities who are members of racial and ethnic minorities. Figure 6.10 shows the likelihood of having attained a college degree among those aged 25 or older in the United States. Asians and white non-Hispanics are the most likely to have college degrees in general, but these two groups also have the biggest gaps between people with and without disabilities. People with disabilities in these two groups nonetheless remain more likely to have college degrees than African-Americans, Hispanics, and Native Americans with disabilities. The rates of college attendance among those aged 18–24 show similar patterns, with the highest attendance among Asians and white non-Hispanics, and the disability gaps are largest among these groups.[30]

[30] The percentage of people with and without disabilities attending college are 56% and 72% among Asians, 40% and 56% among white non-Hispanics, 37% and 51% among African-Americans, 37% and 42% among Hispanics, and 24% and 41% among native Americans. Based on analysis of the 2010 American Community Survey, conducted by U.S. Census Bureau.

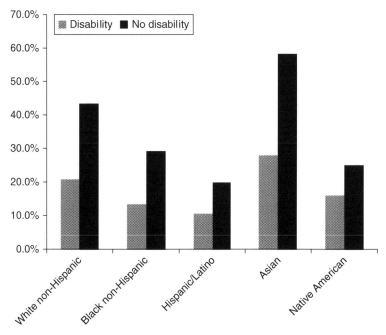

Figure 6.10. College degree by disability, race, and ethnicity, United States, 2010.

In other words, while disability is linked to smaller deficits in educational attainment and attendance for African-Americans, Hispanics, and Native Americans, people with disabilities in these groups still have the lowest levels of educational attainment and attendance, which inhibits their ability to achieve economic, political, and social inclusion. One study of people with spinal cord injuries found that obtaining a college degree was linked to a greater reduction in poverty for African-American and Hispanic families than for non-Hispanic white families, suggesting the greater value of education for minorities with disabilities (Dismuke et al. 2011).

Inclusive and special education programs in the United States are an ongoing topic in policy discussions. Since the 1970s, the U.S. Department of Education has reported the persistent over-representation of minority children – especially African-American boys – in special education programs. Racial disparities are pronounced in the categories of "mental retardation," "emotional disturbance," and "learning disabilities" (Connor and Ferri 2005: 111). Furthermore, African-American children with disabilities appear more likely to be assigned to separate special education programs rather than inclusive programs with general education curricula (Blanchett et al. 2009: 396). This supports an earlier finding that African-American children were more likely than their white peers with the same disability to be in restrictive settings and less likely to be in general education classes (Skiba et al. 2006).

The reasons for the racial disparity in special education programs are complex and "multiply determined" (Skiba et al. 2008: 278). Contributing factors include entrenched poverty in many minority communities, deficient educational facilities and resources in poor school districts with large minority populations, lack of teacher preparation, experience, cultural sensitivity, and supports, as well as possible referral and test bias, and ineffective and overly restrictive special education programs (Skiba et al. 2008: 264). Two studies found that the racial composition of a school's teachers appears to make a difference, with less overrepresentation of African-American children in special education in schools with a higher percentage of African-American teachers (Skiba et al. 2008: 274).

Despite disproportionately high rates of African-American children in special education, evidence suggests that they may be less likely than white children to be identified prior to kindergarten as having an autism spectrum disorder (ASD) or other disabilities, and less likely to receive early interventions that might later reduce the number of their referrals to special education programs (Tincani et al. 2009; Guarino et al. 2010).[31]

---

[31] Some of the particular challenges faced by students from minority groups in special education are illustrated by "Krissy," the focus of a qualitative study. She is a young African-American woman with a learning disability who had to negotiate a

In other countries, children from minority ethnic and racial groups are disproportionately likely to be classified as having learning disabilities or psychosocial impairments. Individuals from minority ethnic or racial groups are more likely to be labeled with these types of disabilities than individuals from majority ethnic or racial groups with the same level of functioning (Lawson 2011: 50). The biases in such classifications are illustrated by the case *DH v. The Czech Republic* (2007), where the European Court of Human Rights held that the disproportionate number of Roma children in special schools for children with "mental handicaps" constituted an indirect form of race discrimination and was an unlawful denial of education (Lawson 2011: 50).

Access to Services and Equipment

Another area where minorities with disabilities appear to face particular obstacles is access to medical services and equipment. African-American veterans face disparities in access to a wide range of services in the Veterans Affairs health care system (Saha et al. 2008). African-Americans with traumatic brain injury tend to receive fewer minutes of therapy per day during inpatient rehabilitation than white patients receive and fewer follow-up services after they are discharged (Arango-Lasprilla et al. 2009: 13). This may contribute to the lower level of life satisfaction for African-Americans compared with whites and Asians one year after experiencing traumatic brain injury (Arango-Lasprilla et al. 2009).

Similarly, a literature review of United States–based studies on racial and ethnic differences among people with spinal cord injury found that patients from minority groups generally had shorter stays

"fragmented identity" in high school; depending on the context, she was "privileged for her race, but penalized for her disability, and vice versa" (Petersen 2006: 730). Consistent with Krissy's experience, several authors have recognized the need for culturally sensitive responses to disability and special education for members of racial and ethnic minorities (e.g., Blanchett et al. 2009; Connor 2006).

in rehabilitation hospitals, more symptoms of depression, higher pain intensity, and greater risk for secondary health complications; they also faced greater barriers to treatment, such as lack of insurance, transportation and financial difficulties than non-Hispanic white patients (Gary et al. 2011: 287). In addition, they had less improvement in functional independence during inpatient rehabilitation and less access to customizable and back-up wheelchairs (Gary et al. 2011: 287). They also faced more environmental barriers after discharge (e.g., inaccessible neighborhoods, lack of transportation), which resulted in a lower level of reported life satisfaction and subjective well-being than among whites with spinal cord injuries in the areas of career, employment, finances, and living arrangements. The findings were mixed, however, regarding racial and ethnic disparities in marital stability. These disparities continued six years after injury (Gary et al. 2011: 287).

Similarly, there were obstacles to care among African-Americans with epilepsy, including limited financial resources, lack of knowledge about epilepsy, poor patient–provider communication, and lack of social support, which contributed to the social stigma felt by these patients (Paschal et al. 2005). Also, despite similar rates of depression, African-Americans may be frequently underdiagnosed and appear significantly less likely to seek, engage, and be retained in professional mental health services than their white counterparts. Cultural differences in the way depressive symptoms are manifested, defined, interpreted, and labeled may in part explain some of these racial differences in help-seeking behaviors (Conner et al. 2009; Bailey et al. 2009).

A study of youth found that members of minority groups were less likely than non-Hispanic white youths to obtain health services for internalized emotional problems (Gudiño et al. 2009). Another study found that older Hispanics reported more difficulty obtaining medical care than older non-Hispanic whites (Rodriguez-Galan and Falcon 2009).

Consistent with the data mentioned earlier on lesser access to customizable and back-up wheelchairs among minority groups with spinal cord injuries, African-American seniors with disabilities are less likely than white seniors with disabilities to have assistive equipment in the home (Rubin and White-Means 2001). While income and other sociodemographic differences explain about half of the gap, racial discrimination in access may also help account for the lower prevalence of home-based assistive devices among African-American senior citizens (Rubin and White-Means 2001). This is supported by a study which demonstrated that African-Americans were less likely than whites to be approved for loans for assistive technology through alternative financing programs; there were, however, promising results from a Pennsylvania program to increase access to assistive technology in minority populations (Carey et al. 2004).

Outside of the United States, despite their high rates of disability, Indigenous Australians were found to be less likely than their non-Indigenous counterparts to receive rehabilitation services (Kendall and Marshall 2004). The reasons for this disparity include aspects of Aboriginal culture (such as attitudes of fatalism and respect for local social hierarchies), the legacy of colonial oppression that leads to distrust of non-Aboriginal institutions and service providers, and stereotypes on the part of non-Aboriginal service providers (such as the belief that Aboriginal people are hostile and unmotivated) (Kendall and Marshall 2004). Kendall and Marshall write that in order to overcome barriers to rehabilitation access, service providers must understand and respect local community structures and include the client's extended family whenever possible. They suggest the adoption of rehabilitation models that focus on community development and participation, which may be more culturally sensitive and effective than current rehabilitation practices (Kendall and Marshall 2004: 12).

In the United Kingdom and Ireland, studies also suggest that people with disabilities from black and ethnic minority backgrounds are particularly disadvantaged and may not have equal access to social services, although there is a lack of reliable statistical evidence on this (Degener 2011: 29).

The evidence in this chapter shows that disability often interacts with gender, race, and ethnicity to create unique disadvantages for women and members of minority groups. These findings show the importance of not regarding disability as a unitary measure, but addressing the complex ways in which it intersects other aspects of identity.

7

Conclusion

Have people with disabilities fully entered the mainstream? Have they overcome the barriers to economic, political, and social inclusion they have historically faced? Inclusion of people with disabilities is obviously a complex and multifaceted topic, and different aspects of inclusion overlap and influence one another. In this final chapter, we examine the progress and prospects for people with disabilities in two complementary ways – first by summarizing the key findings from Chapters 1–6 along with the connections among the different aspects of inclusion as recognized in the implementation of the UN Convention, and second by presenting views from the disability community with a focus on 21 interviews with disability leaders and scholars. The rich interview material reinforces and aids our interpretation of the findings from the other empirical studies; it also deepens our understanding and uncovers new issues on the challenges and opportunities facing people with disabilities.[1]

A. PROGRESS AND PROSPECTS: KEY FINDINGS

1. Prevalence of Disability

Measures of disability have been subject to numerous potential biases and pitfalls (laid out in Chapter 1). In the past decade, however, there has

[1] See Patton (1990) on the uses and strengths of qualitative data and the advantages of triangulation – using multiple methods to compensate for the weaknesses of any one method.

been growing consensus on a set of questions (based on the International Classification of Functioning, Disability, and Health) used to measure impairments and activity limitations. The World Health Organization has conducted two major cross-country surveys, one estimating that 15.6% of adults have disabilities and the other estimating that 19.4% of adults have disabilities. Applied to the 2010 world population, between 785 and 975 million adults have disabilities. Including children brings the latter estimate to slightly more than 1 billion people with disabilities worldwide.

2. Economic Inclusion

People with disabilities face many barriers to economic inclusion. As described in Chapter 2, in comparison with people without disabilities:

- They tend to have lower incomes. In most developed countries their average incomes are only 80–90% of the incomes of people without disabilities. Income levels are lower for those with more severe disabilities.
- They are more likely to live in poverty. Their poverty rates are higher than those of people without disabilities in almost all developed and developing countries.
- They frequently have extra disability-related costs that limit their economic resources, such as for assistive devices, personal services, and health care that often must be paid for by people with disabilities. Studies find extra disability costs averaging 9–49% of average income.
- They may receive disability income and other benefits, which can alleviate economic hardship but also present disincentives for employment.
- Their employment levels are lower in both developed and developing countries. Employment is especially low among those with the most stigmatized mental or cognitive disabilities and those with more severe activity limitations.

Chapter 2 also outlined the following factors behind lower levels of employment among people with disabilities:

- supply-side factors affecting the willingness and ability of people with disabilities to become employed: extra costs of work and extra need for education and training among some people with disabilities, lower levels of education and training on average, disincentives from disability benefit programs, and social stigma; and
- demand-side factors affecting the willingness of employers to hire and retain people with disabilities: employer discrimination and reluctance to hire, inhospitable corporate cultures, and concerns over accommodation costs.

Chapter 2 concluded by describing prospects for increased employment of people with disabilities:

- *Bad news*: lower job growth in occupations where people with disabilities are concentrated, with a large share of that growth in low-paying occupations; along with the
- *Good news*: substantial job growth in occupations where many disabilities are irrelevant; growing importance of computers and new information technologies that have particular benefits for people with disabilities; increased specialization creating more niches for people with disabilities; increased use of telecommuting, as well as part-time and flexible work arrangements; and growing attention to workplace diversity and increased inclusion of disability in diversity programs.

Chapter 3 delved more deeply into several important issues related to employment. The main points and findings are as follows:

- Alternative work arrangements offer particular benefits for many people with disabilities; they are in fact more likely than workers without disabilities to work part time, to be engaged in telecommuting and other home-based employment, and to be temporary workers or self-employed. Employees with disabilities are not more likely in general to have flexible schedules, but this partly reflects occupational patterns, and they are more likely than co-workers in the same occupation to have flexible hours.

- Employees with disabilities tend to have lower average pay, job security, employer-provided benefits, training opportunities, participation in job decisions, job satisfaction, and more negative views of management than employees without disabilities, although limited evidence indicates they may have similar levels of promotion opportunities, work–life balance, and organizational commitment.

- These disparities are not the result of employee choices. They also are not fully explained by differences in abilities and productivity between employees with and without disabilities. It is likely that employer attitudes and discrimination play an important role.

- Results from field research and experimental studies support the personal prejudice and statistical discrimination models of discrimination, indicating that employees with disabilities have worse outcomes due in part to the personal discomfort and uncertainty of employers, supervisors, and co-workers.

- Corporate culture – the attitudes, norms, policies, and practices embedded in an organization – helps shape opportunities and barriers for people with disabilities. Both laboratory studies and field research suggest that employees with disabilities fare better in companies that are responsive to the needs of all employees, where accommodations are less likely to stand out and create resentment.

- The number of employees with disabilities who require accommodations varies widely among studies, from one-eighth to two-thirds of employees. The financial costs of most accommodations are low (less than $500), while less than 5% cost more than $5,000. A majority of managers, co-workers, and accommodated employees report that accommodations improve employee productivity and encourage qualified employees to continue on the job, and many cite other economic benefits.

Chapter 3 ended with a synopsis of policies designed to increase employment of people with disabilities:

- While antidiscrimination statutes provide important protections, they alone do not appear to have increased employment among people with disabilities. There is no solid evidence on the effects of affirmative action or required quotas in enhancing employment rates of persons with disabilities.
- Vocational rehabilitation programs have a high success rate. Other targeted programs such as employer incentives, supported employment, employment agencies, and disability management programs also provide important assistance.
- Self-employment and microfinance often lead to successful outcomes for low-income people in general, although there is no systematic evidence on their effectiveness for people with disabilities specifically.
- Reform of disability income programs may remove many employment disincentives and help people obtain employment supports before being drawn into the disability income system.
- Many prominent companies have adopted policies and practices to improve corporate culture for people with disabilities, including centralized accommodations funds, disability training for managers and co-workers, and disability networks and affinity groups.

3. Political Inclusion

Two broad forms of political inclusion were considered in Chapter 4: civil rights protections and participation in the political process.

Conclusion

Regarding the first, people with disabilities have made substantial progress over the past several decades, with antidiscrimination statutes or constitutional provisions enacted in many countries, encouraged and supported by the UN's 1993 "Standard Rules on the Equalization of Opportunities for Persons with Disabilities" and the 2006 UN Convention. While the enforcement of these acts varies, their enactment is a powerful statement of the growing political inclusion and empowerment of people with disabilities.

Regarding political participation:

- Disability can have both positive and negative effects on the ability and desire to participate in politics. While experiences of discrimination and stigma can lead to fatalism and disengagement among some people with disabilities, such experiences motivate others to become politically active on disability issues.
- Evidence from U.S. surveys indicates that about one-sixth of people with disabilities have been politically active on a disability issue.
- Becoming an activist is a gradual process for many people, often aided by information and identification gained from meeting with disability groups. The process involves (1) recognition of the importance of disability-related problems; (2) a sense of efficacy; (3) identification with others who have disabilities; and (4) the belief that many disability-related problems are caused by social arrangements and require political, rather than purely individual, solutions (consistent with the social model of disability).
- Voter turnout of people with disabilities is lower than that of people without disabilities in the United States and the United Kingdom. People with disabilities are also less likely to engage in other political activities, such as contributing to political campaigns or working with others on community problems.
- The reasons for lower political participation include lower levels of resources (especially income and education), greater isolation

(making recruitment less likely), and a lower likelihood of perceiving that the political system is responsive to people like oneself. This last result may reflect negative messages about the expected participation of people with disabilities, such as the implicit message sent by inaccessible public buildings and polling places.

- The disability gap in political participation appears largest among senior citizens; in fact, young people with disabilities appear to be as active as young people without disabilities, suggesting that the overall gap in political participation may diminish over time as young cohorts age.

- Computer technologies and the Internet are increasingly important tools for political and social participation, providing access to information, networking, and recruitment. However, people with disabilities have less access to computers overall than do people without disabilities.

- Disability does not appear to have strong effects on general political interest and views. Party affiliations and self-ratings on a liberal-to-conservative scale are similar between people with and without disabilities in the United States. Those with disabilities appear, however, to generally favor a greater role for government, particularly in the areas of health care and employment – reflecting the importance of health care and the low employment levels among people with disabilities. They also put a higher priority on civil liberties, perhaps reflecting the experience of being part of a historically marginalized group.

4. Social Inclusion

Chapter 5 considered a number of areas where people with disabilities face barriers to social inclusion. The key points and findings are as follows:

Conclusion

- Stigma and prejudice associated with disability exist around the world. Stigma takes many forms, from simple avoidance to overt discrimination, hostility, and violence. People without disabilities tend to feel most uncomfortable around people with mental and intellectual disabilities. Stigma appears to be more common when there is uncertainty about a disability, and studies have found that improved awareness and information, as well as increased social contact with people with disabilities, can have positive effects on attitudes.

- While the number of people with disabilities living in institutions in the United States has decreased over the past several decades (now representing 6% of all people with disabilities), deinstitutionalization has often not been accompanied by adequate resources and supports. Consequently, many people with mental disabilities have become homeless and have ended up in prison.

- People with disabilities are more likely to be socially isolated than people without disabilities, in part because they are less likely to be married, more likely to live alone, and less likely to report a variety of social activities (socializing, attending a religious service, going to restaurants, shopping, or attending group or organization meetings).

- Inadequate transportation contributes to isolation and is a problem for many people with disabilities. They are twice as likely as people without disabilities in the United States to report transportation problems. Unfortunately, this has not lessened over the 1998–2010 period. Lack of accessible public transportation is common in developing countries, although many countries are working on innovative accessible transportation projects.

- In the United States and many other countries, Centers for Independent Living play an important role in providing resources and social support for people with disabilities living in the community.

People with Disabilities

- Computer and Internet access and use can have particular benefits for people with disabilities, helping to compensate for functional and cognitive limitations and enabling faster return to education, work, higher earnings, and better quality of life. There is, however, a "digital divide": people with disabilities are less likely than those without disabilities to use computers or have Internet access, partly reflecting their lower economic resources. In addition, an audit of Web sites in 20 countries found that only 3 of 100 met the most basic level of accessibility, and most countries do not have accessibility standards for information and communication technology.

- Aside from computers, assistive technology facilitates social inclusion for many people with disabilities, helping them live independently, travel outside the home, and attend social events. However, many people must bear the full cost of assistive technology, and high costs were cited by more than half of people with disabilities in the United States who said there is assistive technology they need but do not have.

- Education appears to have especially beneficial effects for people with disabilities. A U.S. study, for example, found larger wage returns to education for men who experience disability onset after reaching adulthood than for men without disabilities. Low educational levels contribute to high poverty rates among people with disabilities. Despite the benefits of education, people with disabilities are less likely than people without disabilities to have completed primary, secondary, or post-secondary schooling, and these disparities exist in both high- and low-income countries.

- While people with disabilities have often been forced into segregated schools, many developing countries are starting to move toward inclusive education for students with disabilities, while there is general movement in developed countries toward inclusive education.

202

5. Gender, Race, and Ethnicity

Disability-related disparities often vary by gender, race, and ethnicity. The patterns, however, are not simple. The key points and findings from Chapter 6 are as follows:

- Disability rates are especially high among Native Americans and Indigenous Australians. These groups experience especially low employment and high poverty rates.
- In the United States, disability appears to increase the likelihood of poverty particularly for women and African-Americans, supporting the idea of a "double handicap." For another key measure of economic inclusion – employment – disability appears to have a stronger negative effect for men than for women, as well as a stronger negative effect for white non-Hispanics than for members of racial and ethnic minorities. However, since employment levels in general among women and minorities tend to be lower, the end result is that women and members of minority groups with disabilities have the lowest employment rates.
- A similar finding occurs for members of racial and ethnic minorities with respect to voting, other political activities, group involvement, and education: while disability has a smaller effect on members of these groups than on non-Hispanic whites, it nonetheless has a negative effect that contributes to their especially low levels on these measures.
- The story is slightly different for voting, group involvement, and education among women with disabilities. Women in general in the United States tend to have high levels of these measures of inclusion, and disability has especially strong negative effects, bringing down the levels more for women than for men. The end result is that voting, group involvement, and education levels among women with disabilities are similar to those among men with disabilities, but their economic outcomes (employment and poverty levels) are significantly worse.

B. CONNECTIONS AND A HOLISTIC APPROACH IN THE UN CONVENTION

For the sake of clarity, we examined economic, political, and social inclusion in separate chapters, but we recognize that these issues are interrelated and interdependent, and inclusion for people with disabilities has to be approached holistically. It can be difficult to tease out the patterns and connections among economic, political, and social inclusion, but several relationships stand out and require further study.

Looking first at economic inclusion, employment appears to play a special role in increasing political participation among people with disabilities. Several studies have found virtually identical voter turnout between employed working-age people with and without disabilities, while lower voter turnout is concentrated among nonemployed people with disabilities. Employment may raise political participation among people with disabilities by increasing resources and recruitment opportunities (through increased income, communication and technical skills, and social contacts at work) and through psychological effects (such as by increasing efficacy, self-esteem, interest in public issues, and a sense of connection to mainstream society). Relationships and skills developed at work (e.g., the ability to lead meetings, use technology, organize events, and work in teams) also can be applied to political activities.

In addition, employment greatly facilitates social inclusion. Work is a valued social role, and the presence of people with disabilities in the workplace can help combat stereotypes of the people with disabilities as unproductive and helpless. With greater financial resources, people can afford accessible transportation, computers with Internet connections, and assistive technologies that increase their ability to socialize and stay in touch with groups. Social networks at work can also lead to new friends and group connections.

Political inclusion affects economic and social inclusion. The disability rights movement led to the passage of important legislation around the world that has increased economic and social opportunities – for example, accessible workplaces, stores, transportation systems, and educational programs. As with employment, political activism can increase efficacy and self-confidence among people with disabilities and change conceptions and attitudes toward disability by challenging stereotypes of people with disabilities as passive victims.

Social inclusion affects economic and political inclusion in a number of ways. For example, education is a critical factor in employment and political participation. As another example, social networks are sources of information, job referrals, and political recruitment. Similarly, accessible public transportation enables people with disabilities to search for jobs and commute to and from work. Computer and Web accessibility is increasingly important for inclusion: the Internet can help people find jobs, and telecommuting is a viable employment option for some people with disabilities. The Internet also facilitates political involvement by providing information, recruitment opportunities, and cyber communities that help create a shared sense of purpose and efficacy.

The connections among different aspects of inclusion suggest that there are likely multiplier or spillover effects from improvements in any one area. For example, increases in employment and earnings will improve access to social networks, computers, assistive technology, and transportation; these will also improve political participation, which should lead to more policies that improve opportunities and supports for people with disabilities. The connections also imply, however, that improvements in one area may be limited unless simultaneous complementary changes are made in other areas. For example, efforts to improve employment opportunities may not be effective if accessible transportation and personal assistance are not available. This argues for a holistic approach to disability policy and studies, creating strategies in multiple areas that simultaneously address important barriers facing people with disabilities.

The need to address multiple aspects of inclusion was recognized in the UN Convention by the encouragement of national disability strategies among member countries:

> In response to the [Convention] (and in some cases, prior to its adoption), many countries have developed national disability strategies that set out how people with disabilities are to be included in domestic society as fully participating citizens through measures to improve access to education, employment, transport, housing, income, personal support, etc. The [Convention] encouraged the development of these strategies, and set itself as a blueprint for domestic action plans designed to promote and protect the rights of people with disabilities. (Flynn 2011: 1)

The UN Convention provides a substantial amount of guidance to member states in developing disability strategies. These national strategies should be based on more than legislation and should include a range of policies and programs to break down barriers and raise awareness in the general population about the importance of inclusion of people with disabilities. The UN Convention provides many ways to increase the economic, political, and social inclusion of people with disabilities (for a detailed discussion see Rimmerman 2013: 126–148).

Among the important provisions in the UN Convention are the requirements for member countries to (1) include people with disabilities in all aspects of designing and implementing disability strategies; (2) establish focal points within their governments that are responsible for implementing the UN Convention; (3) have independent monitoring of implementation; and (4) collect indicators on the status of people with disabilities.

Flynn (2011) provides detailed accounts of the implementation of disability strategies in 10 countries. The experiences of these countries provide lessons on the "best practices" enabling successful implementation of disability strategies, which include the following:

- strong leadership in government and the disability community (e.g., the leadership by the British Columbia government in partnering with and learning from private organizations) (Flynn 2011: 206–208);
- consultation and participation of people with disabilities, including training in how to conduct participatory research (e.g., the involvement of the Disabled Persons' Assembly in drafting New Zealand's disability strategy) (Flynn 2011: 211–214);
- integration of national disability strategies with implementation of the UN Convention;
- positive obligations and funding for government agencies to address barriers facing people with disabilities (e.g., progress by national ministries was slow in Bolivia until the National Council on Disability obtained financial support for implementing its disability strategy) (Flynn 2011: 238–240);
- transparency and accountability in all aspects of developing and implementing a disability strategy (e.g., in Sweden an electronic tool gathers data online from all counties and municipalities about levels of accessibility and efforts to remove barriers) (Flynn 2011: 247–252);
- ensuring that disability is considered in general in generic public policy development, and not just in disability-specific policies (e.g., "disability proofing" all legislation and policy as they are developed to ensure consistency with the national disability strategy) (Flynn 2011: 256–258);
- independent mechanisms within each country to monitor and evaluate progress in implementing disability strategies (e.g., appointment of an independent reviewer for a wide-ranging assessment of Ontario's accessibility legislation, with public meetings) (Flynn, 2011: 262–265); and
- development of relevant indicators to measure progress toward equality of people with disabilities (e.g., the Life Opportunities Survey in England and Wales) (Flynn 2011: 277–279).

C. PROGRESS AND PROSPECTS: VIEWS FROM THE DISABILITY COMMUNITY

How much progress do people in the disability community feel has been made over the past several decades? How do they view the prospects of people with disabilities in the coming decades? Limited evidence comes from a 2000 U.S. survey which found that a majority of people with disabilities perceived general improvements over the previous 4–10 years, but there are no broad representative surveys that look at perceived progress over a longer time span.[2]

A UK study provides evidence from life history interviews with 50 people with disabilities, including those from older and younger generations (Shah and Priestley 2011). One of the findings was the following:

> There has been a qualitative shift in new ways of thinking about and identifying with disability.... However, there are continuing concerns that families still lack exposure to alternative lay knowledge about everyday life as a disabled child or about disabled adult role models. Young people today still lack access to these resources but, for the minority who do come into contact with them, they can have transformative effects on personal lives and aspirations. (Shah and Priestley, 2011: 179)

The authors describe the positive effects of a number of developments: "Changes in social attitudes, environmental accessibility, new technologies, user-controlled support services and rights-based legislation have all impacted in various ways upon people's experience of family, education, and work. They have also impacted on people's

---

[2] The 2000 U.S. survey found that 63% of people with disabilities felt that things in general for Americans with disabilities had become somewhat or much better over the past 10 years, while a majority felt that conditions had improved over the past 4 years with respect to access to public facilities (77%), quality of life for people with disabilities (65%), media portrayal of people with disabilities (61%), public attitudes toward people with disabilities (59%), and the inclusion of people with disabilities in advertising (55%), and only half felt that access to public transportation (51%) and work opportunities (50%) had improved (NOD/Harris 2000).

personal sense of identity and belonging in British society" (Shah and Priestley 2011: 181). The authors, however, are not optimistic, noting that the cutback of public services in the United Kingdom and the "radical reformulation of financial autonomy in health services and schools" make the future look "far from certain for the next generation of young disabled people" (Shah and Priestley 2011: 183–4).

To explore views on the progress and prospects of people with disabilities, we conducted in-depth interviews with 21 disability leaders and scholars from the United States and the United Kingdom.[3] Our interviewees include heads of disability organizations, people who were instrumental in the passage of the ADA, elected officials with disabilities, current and former heads of government agencies devoted to disability issues, and prominent scholars in disability studies. The interviewees were asked about their own work, the ways the status of people with disabilities has improved or declined in the past few decades, the most important issues and barriers facing people with disabilities today, what strategies can be used to address the barriers, and how optimistic they are that people with disabilities will eventually achieve full equality and inclusion in society.

1. Access to the Built Environment

When asked about changes over the past few decades, a number of the disability leaders described how the physical environment has become more accessible. Lex Frieden stated:

> The environment has changed radically – it hasn't changed a little, it has changed radically in the last 25 years. Thank goodness [young people with disabilities] don't have to grow up calling every

[3] The interviewees and their affiliations are listed in the Appendix. The semi-structured interview protocol is available from the authors. The interviews lasted between 30 and 90 minutes each.

restaurant to find out if they have steps, if they have a bathroom. Thank goodness they don't have to stop drinking 12 hours before they go out to eat with their families to the restaurant so they don't have to use the toilet.... Deaf people now can turn on any TV and watch it. They are not left out.

Similarly, Jaspal Dhani noted that "more people are able to get out" in the United Kingdom, and Jim Dickson gave concrete examples from the United States: "It must have been ... like 12 years ago the last time I was in an elevator which didn't have Braille. It was eight years ago the last time somebody said I couldn't bring my service dog into a restaurant; you know, that used to happen five or six times a year." Jonathan Young said, "I marvel every day when I walk into a restroom and it's accessible.... Maybe companies don't like having to comply with accessibility standards but they do it because it's the rule. As advocates, we can complain that things aren't as accessible as we like, but the fact is there is now an accessibility expectation that has been institutionalized." Representative James Langevin compared the situation before and after the ADA:

> As someone who has lived with a disability both before and after the passage of the ADA in 1990, I can firsthand attest that the living situation for individuals with disabilities has improved immeasurably. Passage of the ADA along with other changes in the law like the Individuals with Disabilities Education Act have really, I think, helped to shatter barriers, opening schools, sidewalks, public transportation, and workplaces for millions. People who used to be relegated to institutions and stigmatized by society now have new opportunities to live independently in their communities and to contribute in their own ways and achieve their own goals and dreams.

2. Technology

There was also general agreement that technology has helped create many opportunities for people with disabilities, consistent with

Conclusion

material presented in Chapter 5. John Kemp said that information and communications technology is "the great equalizer of the future," and Rosemarie Garland-Thomson noted that "technology used to be our enemy and now it's our friend." Darren Jernigan, who drives from a wheelchair, described how computers have helped create accessible vans where "you can just move your thumb and you can drive, or you have a smart home where … you talk to [the computer] and it does it for you, or even wheelchairs with computer displays and speech recognition – technology itself has really brought people with disability much closer to independence." Corinne Kirchner described the benefits of technological advances, saying, "There is now a real market motivation for the computer scientists to try to figure out how you can use mobile devices when you are temporarily in a situation where you can't see or hear, it's dark.… They are trying to solve these problems where the technology can operate under all those kinds of sensory conditions." She also mentioned developments in computer technology to deal with "interruptability situations," which may have particular benefits for people with certain cognitive impairments.

Along with assisting people in activities of daily living, social media such as Facebook can help overcome isolation among people with disabilities, by enabling them to easily keep in touch with family and friends, and make new social, political, and economic connections. Richard Scotch said that the growth of social media is "very promising both in terms of support and also potentially collective action," and Marsha Saxton said that it is "essential" to "incorporate social media into everything that we do … for connection with the disability community." Scotch and others noted that the value of social media may be especially high for the "neurodiversity community of people on the autism spectrum who may relate to each other much better on the Web." Kate Seelman said, "From the standpoint of the [disability rights] movement we have a more integrated global community, especially because we have the power of communication and information technology."

John Kemp described progress and challenges in making information and communication technology more universally accessible:

> The need for embedding accessibility into the core technologies and having developers write accessible code, and not always having to rely on assisted technologies to make up for the failures and the absence of accessible features, is ... kind of getting old school.... It is sort of like where we were in the '60s when the building codes were being developed.... Today we are really talking about this kind of accessible information and communication technology in the same sort of framework.
>
> People following us have to know that this is going to be a very important contribution, because so much information, education, employment, socialization – all of these lifestyle issues – are built around information technologies. And so they have to be accessible to all people.

Despite the benefits of computers, people with disabilities have lower levels of computer use and Internet access than people without disabilities, as shown in Chapter 5, and even those with computers may not be able to access all Web sites. Bobby Silverstein agreed with testimony by Sam Bagenstos on behalf of the Department of Justice that Web accessibility is "the next issue for civil rights of people with disabilities." Kate Seelman expressed concern about low levels of federal funding for technology that enables inclusion of people with disabilities, saying that the two major funding agencies for people with disabilities "are in the basement of their respective agencies," and "it becomes more of a problem as we understand that with proper R&D applications we can invest more and more into empowering our students to do whatever they need to do." Darren Jernigan identified the low level of computer ownership as a key problem, noting that while computers have become cheaper, many people with disabilities – especially those without jobs – cannot afford them. He proposed a major national project to make wireless accessible across the country and give a computer to each person with a disability:

> We used to do big things ... and there are some things that only
> a government can do.... We did the interstate system, the Hoover
> Dam, the transcontinental railroad.... We did big national-scope
> things.... And I think it will be on a smaller level, but to make sure
> that every person with disability had a computer ... [could help]
> take someone with disability off of SSDI and swing them over to
> paying taxes – that swing alone will pay off the debt [and] is a posi-
> tive benefit for everyone.

3. Attitudes

Views about changes in attitudes were complicated. A number of
respondents identified improvements in attitudes toward people with
disabilities as an important development, although others were not certain that attitudes had improved in general. For example, Representative
James Langevin said, "I think attitudes really have changed. In the
past ... if somebody extended assistance, it was a courtesy that was
extended, as opposed to looking at it as a civil right. The passage of
the ADA has changed the mindsets of people in general." Similarly,
Bobby Silverstein said that there has been a "revolution and dramatic
improvements" in the acceptance of people with disabilities in society,
including "architectural, communication, and attitudinal changes that
to me are pretty dramatic," although he added, "That is not to say that
everything is fine; we still have a long way to go." Jonathan Young also
noted improvement: "Look back at some of the things that were said
about people with disabilities in the context of the ADA deliberations.
There was testimony about how people would say, 'We don't want a
person who has cerebral palsy in our restaurant because we don't want
to look at him.' People might think things like that today but people
aren't generally going to say it." Similarly, Jane Dunhamn said, "The
most important is that people with disabilities now move through the
world with very little curiosity response. There seems to be a matter of
fact, visible acceptance of difference in public places."

Other disability leaders gave more qualified responses. Mark Perriello said, "There is absolutely less stigma than there used to be, but that stigma isn't uniform. I think that the experience is different depending on the type of disability. For instance, there is still a lot of stigma around mental health disabilities that we need to overcome." John Kemp agreed, saying that "it is easier for people to … to get their arms around a physical limitation that somebody has … as opposed to an invisible disability and a psychiatric, psychological, or emotional disability which they don't understand. They just can't quite grasp it. I think we do have, very unfortunately, biases that exist in this area."

Richard Scotch focused on attitudes of judges and employers: "You know, civil rights legislation is a good thing but it doesn't necessarily lead to social change. And it's still pretty clear that a lot of the judges don't understand disability and a lot of employers, particularly small employers, don't." Mark Leeds talked about how antigovernment attitudes in the current political climate impede progress for people with disabilities:

> In addition to attitudinal barriers akin to those faced by other minorities and women, we also face architectural and communication barriers – barricades ardently defended by those in the architectural/construction/design field and in the broad spectrum of the communication industry. Efforts to recognize – in practice as well as in words – rights of inclusion for people with disabilities often are met with unwarranted cries of "stifling, intrusive, costly government regulation!" Such cries – applied to many policies – are a staple of the currently popular conservative culture.

Jaspal Dhani said, "The physical environment has improved but in terms of the real lived experiences of certain people, those challenges still remain, the ones around perceptions of disability and who are disabled people," while Corinne Kirchner talked about the continuing "low expectations" for people with disabilities, and Jim Dickson said that the attitudes of the majority of able-bodied people have not changed – "the majority don't think about disability."

Conclusion

The ADA has, however, had profound positive effects on the attitudes of people with disabilities, according to Dickson: "The most important thing about the ADA is the change in attitude. It's the idea that I've got rights, you know, that I don't have to be ashamed or feel guilty." Consistent with this, Bobby Silverstein emphasized that young people with disabilities have higher expectations now, and Kate Seelman said, "We may have a new generation of students with disabilities, if ours are any example, that are not trying to blend in as much." Both Darren Jernigan and Richard Scotch said that they felt there is greater acceptance of people with disabilities among young people. As Jernigan put it, "My kids go to school with people with disabilities in chairs.... There is more exposure around it and I think that, my hope is that, young people growing up with disability are not going to have the stigma." This sentiment was echoed by Andy Imparato: "I'm inspired by young people, so yeah I do think young people are more comfortable with a lot of forms of diversity than the generation before them, and that generation was more comfortable than the generation before them." He added that among young people "there is an idea that having an identity as part of a marginalized group can be exciting, at the same time as it can be scary because it can lead to discrimination."

Andy Imparato, John Kemp, and Richard Scotch drew parallels between attitudes toward people with disabilities and views of gay men and lesbians. As Scotch expressed it:

> We've seen this just profound change in attitudes about gay people over the last 20 years, and why can't we see the same kind of thing happening for disabled people? There are a lot of disabled people – you know, most people have somebody with a disability in their family if they thought about it enough ... the more people who are out there the better it gets.

John Kemp said that "we have a lot to learn and gain from the GLBT [gay, lesbian, bisexual, and transgender] community and we should be embracing, as much as possible, disability power and pride."

The idea that increased exposure leads to greater acceptance was also expressed by Jaspal Dhani: "If you see a disabled person in the community, whether they're getting off or on the bus or going into a local store, it changes your perception; it has to." Several respondents expressed concern, however, that people with disabilities are experiencing a backlash as they become more visible in the community. Rosemarie Garland-Thomson, for example, said:

> Sometimes attitudinal and structural backlashes occur. For example, the idea that disability accommodation is a financial liability rather than a benefit to the social order in general has persisted.... Now we're more present and interacting with able-bodied and other disabled people so that when people display discriminatory attitudes and support discriminatory practices, it is more apparent than when we were all either at home or institutionalized, kept out.

Tom Shakespeare also noted the potential downsides of increased visibility: "For very good reasons people have the right to live in the community and they are much more visible," but sometimes "they are just housed in a very inappropriate place, in a rundown estate, a housing project, where it is full of disadvantaged people and there's a disabled person who looks a bit odd, behaves a bit odd, [who] can easily be the victim of a hate crime, bullying, exploitation." Colin Barnes also expressed concern about hate crimes, saying that they are "a major problem in many countries – which is exacerbated at the current juncture because of the current and ongoing economic crisis" leading to several "ways in which governments are targeting disabled people as scroungers and burdens on the state."

Media depictions of people with disabilities were mentioned as contributing to both positive and negative attitudes. Like Barnes, Tom Shakespeare said that people with disabilities "have been scapegoated as scroungers" in Britain and "media treatment of disabled people is very, very negative at this point." Shakespeare also noted, however, that more disabled people are viewed on television and heard on the radio than in the past, while Darren Jernigan said that people with disabilities are starting to be "mainstreamed into commercials, they are in TV shows now," and Bobby Silverstein pointed out, "If you look at any textbook today there will be people with disabilities, children with disabilities pictured alongside their nondisabled peers." Jonathan Young said that "using people with disabilities for marketing purposes" is an example of "attitudes changing – an embracing of people with disabilities as part of our normal human experience."

Mark Perriello discussed efforts his organization is "making to change hearts and minds" among the American public and to address "misconceptions about what it means to be a person with a disability, who we are as a people." He mentioned a specific campaign featuring a public service announcement (PSA) to be shown during the NASCAR race and in other venues:

> We launched with Comcast the Anti-Bullying PSA, which features three students with disabilities looking at the camera and just saying flat out, "I am not going to be bullied." It is powerful. You know, originally it was running to the tune of about a million dollars across the country and that has skyrocketed up to four million. The team here did a really great job of producing the PSA and it is still getting a lot of traction.

Education clearly contributes to attitudinal change, as well as opening up opportunities for people with disabilities (as discussed in Chapter 5). Many people cited increased access to education and the growth of disability studies as key developments over the past several decades.

4. Education

Improvements in education, and the value of education for other forms of inclusion, were emphasized by several interviewees. As Mark Perriello stated:

> One thing that really has improved – and there is still so much further to go – is education. In many instances, and it is not uniform,

but in many instances people with disabilities have access to a quality education that didn't exist ... 20 or 30 years ago.... And the important thing is that education leads to opportunity, and that means jobs and income and economic security and independent living. And it all starts with education.

Three activists described how they were excluded from mainstream schools when they were young. Ethan Ellis said, "When I was four they wouldn't take me into kindergarten because they didn't have to; I was barred from the public schools because of my disability. Now that doesn't happen, of course.... But being segregated into special ed. classes now offers learning opportunities that are only marginally better than none." Corinne Kirchner echoed this concern when she said that "having a special education system is just exaggerating the separateness" and talked about the need for a universalized policy. Lex Frieden, who was denied admission to a university in the 1970s explicitly because of his disability, said, "A person doesn't get turned down to go to a university now. The universities actually recruit students with disabilities, some of them just like they do other minority students. These are really kind of remarkable changes, and it's happened not only in the United States but in other countries in the world too." Similarly, Colin Barnes, referring to the situation in the United Kingdom, said:

> If you go back to when I was a kid, like most conditions that were considered serious you were institutionalized. Like for schools, my first school was a residential school for the blind and the deaf – now I wasn't blind and I wasn't deaf, I was partially sighted, but it didn't alter the fact that the local education authority believed that this was the only school that was appropriate for someone like me. This was in the 1950s.

David Gray mentioned increased access to higher education: "Access has been enormously affected. You go to most campuses and you can get around ... and that opens up the opportunities to get educated. They have these disability offices so people can go there."

Conclusion

In addition to general educational access, several respondents discussed the growth of the field of disability studies. Rosemarie Garland-Thomson talked about the importance of disability studies and being an academic with a disability:

> The institutionalization … of disability studies has had tremendous effects…. The fact that we are here in these institutions and not locked up somewhere in another kind of an institution is in itself remarkable – that we're just here doing this work and that students with disabilities are here is quite remarkable.

Kate Seelman also remarked on the growth of interest in disability among students, noting, "Our students have just started a university-wide student disability organization. I don't think that would have happened 15 years ago." John Kemp said, "I think there has been a great movement in the way young kids today accept who they are, and a large part of it came from youth with disabilities who petitioned their state governments to have disability history and culture included in the curriculum."

Colin Barnes talked about the impact he has had on students as a professor in disability studies:

> I've had something like 500 students doing disability studies here at Leeds at the post-graduate levels since 1992, when I set up these courses. And thankfully they're now working all over the world. I'd like to think that they all take a little bit of social model thinking with them. That's okay.

Andy Imparato also talked about his role as a mentor for young people with disabilities:

> I've tried to cultivate people coming behind me, and pave the way for them and try to open the doors for them, mentor them. Obviously, mentoring is usually a two-way street, so I get energized by it oftentimes, inspired by young people; but there's probably … forty or fifty young people that I've worked with, over the last twenty years. I feel like I have made an impact on them and some of them are

in pretty important jobs now, and I feel that the most important contribution I can make to the future of the disability movement is cultivating new generations of leaders.

Jane Dunhamn expressed concern that "schools too often see educating students with disabilities as something apart from their core responsibilities.... Black males with disabilities are the most affected by the 'School to Prison Pipeline.' The youth who are most impacted have intellectual, mental health, and learning disabilities."

Other respondents noted that it is important for people with disabilities to be educated in specific areas. For example, Bobby Silverstein emphasized the importance of "independent living training starting for infants, toddlers, pre-schoolers, school-age children, so that ... the next generation will have a sense of self-identification, self-worth, and the ability to live independent lives," while Mark Leeds said that people with disabilities need "to understand that the laws are in recognition of their rights ... and to become knowledgeable about that."

5. Culture and Sports

Several interviewees brought up the importance of participation in cultural and athletic activities. Marsha Saxton talked about changes in attitudes toward participating in sports and dancing among young people with disabilities:

> I interviewed a number of younger people into their 40s.... I was so struck by their saying, "Yeah I'm an athlete, yeah I'm a dancer" with not a hint of defensiveness ... as if they have no knowledge of having ever been excluded from athleticism or dance, and it's so lovely.... There are all these great performances with integrated dance and Paralympics – so many new opportunities for people with disabilities.... I'm struck by the absolute assumption on a part of these younger people that they deserve to be included.

Kate Seelman mentioned a poetry event sponsored by both disability studies in the Rehabilitation Science and Technology Department and the English Department at her university. She discussed an upcoming performance by an African-American hip hop and culture group with disabilities called 4 Wheel City, emphasizing that such activities can play a positive role for young African-Americans with disabilities as well as bring together members of the disability and African-American civil rights movements.

Tom Shakespeare also emphasized the role of culture among people with disabilities:

> I am very interested in this sort of cultural side of things, the arts and creativity of disabled people ... there are more spaces for that. It's more recognized. It is more welcomed. More disabled people are expressing their creativity in collective or individual ways.

He focused specifically on changing views of the cultural contributions they are making:

> In the past when disabled people made creative work, whether it is dancers or comedians or writers, ... [nondisabled people would] say, "Isn't this marvelous, this cripple is doing something. We must be kind and say, 'How lovely.' " There is sort of a charitable response. I'd like to move towards ... an evaluation which is ... of the same rigor as we would apply to any other form of art.

> I would like to see more disabled people achieving the sort of success and quality in their work as nondisabled do. And I see no reason why they can't. And it is true that critics may have to sort of adjust and open their eyes a bit. But I think there is real potential for that.

> I am very excited about that.... I think that disabled people need to be seen as people with something to say, not just learning about the inequities but actually [making] a contribution to the rest of the human experience. I think that's happened and I look forward to that happening, and happening more with more confidence, and with the best possible quality.

6. Employment

The employment rate of people with disabilities remains low around the world, as described in Chapter 2. Most interviewees pointed to the continuing low employment rate as a major problem. Bobby Silverstein said, "We've got a long, long way to go and particularly a long way to go for those with the most significant disabilities." Mark Perriello described the low employment rate as "staggering" and "very stubborn and seemingly impossible to move."

The low employment and earnings rates for people with disabilities appear to be due in part to discrimination, according to the evidence presented in Chapter 3. This was reinforced by David Gray, who has worked with human resource professionals: "They really underestimate the jobs that we can do, and they are almost uniformly afraid that they are going to get [a person with a disability who] is going to sue them, or they are really afraid to interview them because they don't know what's really safe to say." He focused on the potential value of peer associations, social networks, and mentoring for people with disabilities in obtaining jobs and making progress in their careers – such strategies can build confidence and skills, and help decrease employer uncertainty and misconceptions of people with disabilities. He noted, "It would be nice if we had videos for people [with disabilities] to be a little more optimistic about the fact that there is a bunch of us that are working.... It would really be cool if we could do remote job training and they could link up with people who are working and who could become mentors."

The importance of employment was emphasized by many interviewees, such as Andy Imparato: "Employment is always going to be a very important barometer of how we are doing as a society, in terms of really opening doors of opportunity for people with disabilities." He went on to state the need of having many factors aligned, as was discussed in Chapter 3: "In order to get good employment you have to have the right housing, transportation, ... services, infrastructure, the right to access health, higher education, and K-12 education systems." Despite the low employment rate, he is hopeful that "disability is starting to become more sexy, and I think diversity professionals in corporations see ... an interesting diversity thread that they can't really afford to ignore, and that helps to redefine diversity in a way with something in it for everyone." John Kemp echoed this theme: "If a company is still saying 'disability and diversity' they are missing the point. It has to be embedded within. And I now see progressive international companies seeing the proper implementation of disability at the employee level, at the customer level, at the supplier level as being business advantages. And so that's a big driver."

Similarly, Mark Perriello is hopeful that employment opportunities will increase:

> If you were looking back, you know, 20 to 30 years ago there were far fewer opportunities for people with disabilities in the workplace. And I think that is changing. I actually work with a lot of employers here at AAPD [American Association of People with Disabilities] who are actively recruiting from the disability community. They want a diverse workforce and they ... understand that disability is a part of that.

He went on to discuss the impact of federal government leadership, saying that President Obama's executive order requiring 100,000 new hires from the disability community, and the potential implementation of a requirement for federal contractors to set hiring targets for people with disabilities, have the "potential to be a huge, huge game changer for our community. If the private sector sees the federal government leading the way, they will follow suit. That is the history of civil rights."

Several interviewees cautioned, however, against unrealistic expectations for employing all people with disabilities. Colin Barnes argued that it is "naive at best, at worst it is downright mendacious" to claim that it is possible to get all severely disabled people employed, given the "whole range of barriers – cultural, environmental, and institutional – that they face." In several publications (2000, 2004, 2012) he argued that work has to be fundamentally reconceptualized – going beyond paid employment – in order to provide greater inclusion and status for people with impairments. Tom Shakespeare discussed the difficulty of employing all people with disabilities given the restrictions created by some impairments. He focused on the availability of alternative work arrangements (as discussed in Chapter 3):

> When you push some of these issues, you really have to see how complicated it is.... Disabled people can't do all the jobs that non-disabled people do. They can't work the hours that nondisabled people do. So we have to have a welfare or a work system that recognizes [this], just as ... we have to construct a system that doesn't disadvantage women. They are more likely to take career breaks and more likely to work half-time or part time. And I think disability is like that.... I don't want to have a gender-neutral approach, and I don't want to have a disability-neutral approach. You do miss some of the specificity of disabled people's lives, which means they can't do what nondisabled people can do, or at least not always. Some can and some can't. But we can't assume that people can.

Shakespeare's argument against a "disability-neutral approach" is consistent with Chapter 3's discussion of the potential value of alternative work arrangements and, more generally, the value of personalized consideration of the needs of all employees in the workplace.

Jane Dunhamn described the problem faced by people with disabilities who obtain the skills and education for professional careers:

> Professionals with disabilities who need lifelong coordinated services for activities of daily living face a huge problem. Because their salaries are too high for supports, they must pay for them on their own. This cost keeps individuals who should be enjoying a middle- and upper-income status stuck in a low-income status. This population should be entitled to services without penalty in the same way adults who do not reach that level of income receive all services without penalty.

7. Poverty and Inequality

The high poverty rates of people with disabilities are closely connected to their low employment rates but are also influenced by the extra costs of living with a disability, as discussed in Chapter 2. Several disability leaders pointed to the critical problem of poverty, tying it to broader increases in economic inequality. Ethan Ellis said, "There still is no recognition in the disability community that poverty is our major problem" and "until we deal with that issue we will not achieve true equality." He said that the ADA Amendments Act "didn't fix the critical issue – access to the legal process. To file a complaint you have to be able to afford a lawyer. If you don't have a lawyer ... you are going to lose out in the process." Andy Imparato agreed that building financial assets and security has not received sufficient attention in the disability movement:

> I don't think we've prioritized building wealth and ... human capital,
> ... and I think because of that to a large degree we are being supported by a federally driven infrastructure that expects us to be poor
> and expects us to be outside the labor force and punishes us when
> we get too successful.

The recent push for budget cuts in many countries has the potential to increase poverty, according to Colin Barnes:

> Now, what's happening is that we are seeing a restatement of the
> kind of policies which were evident during the Victorian years. And
> we are going to go back, if we are not very careful, to the sort of
> situation where there are vast arrays of poverty in rich states like the
> UK – a situation that is all too common in many poor countries.

The growth of inequality has led to greater disparities among people with disabilities, as described by Richard Scotch: "People in the upper middle class ... who have a lot of social capital and ... parents who advocate for them" are "able to get access to the support services they need, mostly because of ADA and because a lot of schools and employers and transit systems and retailers are kind of a little less clueless than they used to be. So things have improved for them." In contrast, "it's much harder ... for the folks from more working-class backgrounds or from minority communities," only some of whom will get needed education and services. Scotch concluded that "access to an unequal society is not sufficient."

Tom Shakespeare also described how inequality can create vastly different experiences of disability. For some people it is sufficient to "take away discrimination" and "level the playing field" and they will be fine, "but there is a proportion for whom it is not fair, who are not likely to get any job that they are going to live on and who need support [but] don't want to live in an institution." He is concerned that "the inequality between disabled people will become more extreme," particularly in an international context: "In the last 20 years I think the position of disabled people has transformed in high-income countries," while "things are still very, very difficult in low- and middle-income countries.... So I think that in the developing world it is probably a generation behind."

8. Policy and Political Action

The major policy accomplishments over the past few decades were cited by a number of the disability leaders. Colin Barnes discussed the general change in perceptions of disability that accompany these accomplishments:

> Since the 1960s we've had a groundswell of activism amongst disabled people which has changed society's understanding of what disability is – insofar as disability is not just about impairment but also about the environment – not as much as I would like but it certainly has made a difference. Most countries, for example, now recognize that disability is a sociopolitical issue as well as a health issue.... Most countries have got some policies to address the social

dynamics of being a disabled person. How far they are actually implemented is a contentious issue, of course.... There's much rhetoric about addressing disability discrimination and oppression. It is now embedded in policies across much of the world.

Other interviewees echoed this view, discussing the UN Convention's recognition of human rights of persons with disabilities and the value of the growing global community of persons with disabilities.

While overall policy changes in the past several decades are seen as positive, the recent economic crises have put increased stress on government budgets, and several disability leaders voiced strong concern over how budget cuts would affect people with disabilities. Some of the programs subject to cuts are public transportation, health care, and in-home support services such as personal attendant services. Colin Barnes supplemented his previous statement on long-term progress by saying that after the positive accomplishments of the 1990s,

But the situation is deteriorating for all disabled people.... We've had a succession of escalating economic and political crises, particularly over the last decade.... These have fueled long-standing concerns about growing welfare budgets, especially with reference to disabled people, who are presented as one of [the major causes], if not the major cause, of the problem.

To the extent that budget cuts reduce programs that provide valuable support services, they can reduce community participation and employment opportunities. As Jaspal Dhani stated:

So more disabled people are able to get out. But then ... it's not good to have the physical environment if ... support services don't exist because they can't get out, regardless of how the good the environment is.... A whole package comes together and you take out any one of those elements, then I think the whole system collapses.

Consistent with this point, Lex Frieden said that without necessary transportation and assistance, people with disabilities who are living in the community may actually be more isolated than those living in a nursing home. A similar idea is reflected in Andy Imparato's earlier quote about the necessity of having a variety of factors in place to support successful employment outcomes for people with disabilities – cuts in public transportation, for example, reduce the ability of people with disabilities to find jobs to which they can easily commute.

The need for complementary policies that are aligned with each other highlights the importance of focusing on the larger goals of the policies. Jonathan Young, who chairs the presidentially appointed National Council on Disability (NCD), said that the NCD has adopted a "theme of living, learning, and earning," reflecting "what every American wants to do," and added that instead of "talking about housing, transportation and health care as discrete pieces, let's talk about what we are trying to accomplish … and then pull together the things that need to work together to make it happen."

Several disability leaders emphasized the importance of fighting budget cuts in order to preserve important programs serving people with disabilities. Andy Imparato had a slightly different view, saying that many programs could be made more effective for people with disabilities at a lower cost:

> The worst way in my view is just say don't balance the budget on the backs of the disabled people and pretend like the programs that they are cutting are perfect. A better way to respond is say these programs are unnecessarily expensive and here are four ways you could reform these programs that would save money and produce better outcomes for disabled people. I just don't see us doing enough of that.

While budget cuts may save some money now, they can create greater costs in the future. Mark Perriello described this in the context of health care:

> Similar to education, health care often offers the keys to freedom and employment for people with disabilities, and we really need to make sure that whatever programs are out there, that they are not abandoning people with disabilities.... When the funding disappears that

often leads to institutionalization and … the thought is that you will be saving money, but in the long run oftentimes the outlay ends up much more expensive because of the cost of institutionalization.

Jonathan Young noted that budget cuts can "undermine programs enabling people with disabilities to be engaged in the community," which will lead them to go "on the [disability] rolls looking for whatever support they can find rather than live more independently and thus contribute to our tax basis." Bobby Silverstein expressed the idea very simply: "Well, there's pay me now or pay me later. Pay now for independence and economic self-sufficiency or pay later with dependency."

Lex Frieden reflected a similar idea in discussing the issue of costs in policy planning more broadly. Consistent with the ideas of universal design reviewed in Chapter 5 and the value of universalized policy as proposed by Bickenbach and Cieza (2012), he suggested that it will be cheaper in the long run to create more accessible environments:

> I think a lot of the planning that's done by people who actually determine the evolution of society is being done without a clear vision for the role of people with impairments and it's a huge mistake.… We are sort of looking at trying to identify these piecemeal problems and deal with them, and that's the wrong way to solve the systems problem.… It's going to be less expensive if we make the environment and the support networks useful to all people than if we just try to do this customized one-on-one solution.… How can you not afford that?

The policy gains of the past several decades were built on the growth of the disability rights movement, and several people discussed methods to strengthen the political power of the disability community. Jonathan Young said, "I think decision makers on [Capitol] Hill and in the White House don't really view us as a political bloc – they view supporting disability policy as the 'right thing to do.' But why risk being eviscerated in the current budget environment? … Where is the disability community's voice on these big budget issues?" Jim Dickson, who is active in efforts to increase voter turnout of people with disabilities, said he would like to see people with disabilities "become a voting bloc, like sugar beet growers and the Chamber of Commerce." With such recognized political power, Mark Perriello said that you can "walk into the room with an elected official and instead of just asking for something from them, [you are] able to ask from a perspective where they know you bring something hugely significant to the table as well." To this end, he said one of his most important goals at AAPD is "building grassroots strength for the disability community." While AAPD cannot be involved in partisan politics, he envisions an educational program to train people for political involvement, including not only working on campaigns but also "helping people with disabilities learn more about how to run for office successfully ... at the local level and state level, at the federal level, to really put people not just in the right policy positions, but in the decision-making positions."

Direct action has contributed greatly to the political gains of the disability movement, as stated by Jaspal Dhani: "After all here [in the United Kingdom] and I'm guessing equally in America, we would not have achieved legislation if it wasn't for people chaining themselves to stopping buses and so forth." He helped organize a large protest rally and march outside the House of Commons on May 11, 2011, to protest "that it's disabled people who will bear a greater burden of government's planning review" to reduce government spending. He said, "Our view is you need to come from all directions.... I think it requires both, it does require the dialogues around the table as well as the direct action, but my experience ... [is that direct action] has brought about a greater change." In the United States, Mark Perriello agreed that "direct action is such an important piece of making change.... It is ten times easier for [a disability organization] to get something that they want if [government officials] have to walk past a protest that ADAPT has organized.... And so absolutely, 100%, there is a role for ADAPT and I think it is a growing role." John Kemp agreed that organizations like ADAPT that "are not afraid of civil disobedience" are "absolutely essential."

Conclusion

Diversity within the disability movement was discussed by several disability leaders. Jaspal Dhani said, "In the UK I think the disability sector is lousy at promoting the wide diversity issues ... that sector is quite homogeneous." Andy Imparato commented that the same has been true in the United States, but "one of the things that have gotten better – and I'm sure we aren't there yet – is that the leadership of the disability movement is a lot more diverse in every sense of the word." Jonathan Young said, "I don't think we are anywhere near as diverse as we ought to be," and part of the problem may be disability stigma combined with racial and gender stereotypes (as discussed in Chapter 6): "One thing that I have perceived in my experience is that disability has long been a metaphor for weakness, ... [and for] women or African-Americans, who [may be seen as] weak or inferior in certain respects, embracing disability can be perceived as sort of reinforcing those negative stereotypes." Jane Dunhamn stated:

> Institutional racism is particularly damaging to African-Americans with disabilities because, along with quality of life issues, there are issues of exclusion from the greater disability community and from the greater African-American community, leaving African-Americans with disabilities without a place to call home. Historically African-Americans have found safety in the harbor with each other away from whiteness. There is no harbor for African-Americans with disabilities, which leaves them with very few places to rest.

Marsha Saxton also addressed the intersection of race and disability: "I think people of color with disabilities and white allies within the broader disability communities are becoming much more bold in addressing racism, raising issues of exclusion and unconscious racism. This has been called 'micro aggressions,' [which are] basically thoughtless comments, a more 'subtle' degree of racism than blatant exclusion or obvious hatred."

One difficulty in building the political strength of people with disabilities is that many do not identify with the disability community, or identify with only one segment of it. Colin Barnes noted that, despite the injustice of segregating people with disabilities in special schools and institutions, segregation helped create group identity that became the root of disability activism in both the United Kingdom and United States. The decline of institutionalization means that group identity will have to be formed in other ways. Jonathan Young noted that people with disabilities are not naturally in the same households or communities:

> A wheelchair user doesn't naturally give birth to a wheelchair user, to a line of wheelchair users in a way that ... there could be a common cultural heritage.... Even though we use the rhetoric of the civil rights movement, people with disabilities aren't born into communities of color, where there is immediately a foundation for community cohesion.... Maybe you are newly blind and you try to understand what it means to be blind – you're probably not going to call a wheelchair user and say, 'I just became blind, can you help me understand [what it means] to be a person with disability?' No, to the extent you reach out to any other people with disabilities (and are able to reach them) you're probably going to ... reach out to other people who are blind instead ... to navigate a new experience as a blind person.

Several disability leaders described the importance of Centers for Independent Living and the Internet and social media in creating a sense of shared identity and mobilizing people for political action. Jonathan Young said, "We should have more fun as a community and find ways for people physically to be together, or if nothing else be online together. If we cultivated that social bonding, the political power will flow more naturally." Both Jonathan Young and Bobby Silverstein expressed concern about the cohesion of the disability rights movement in the United States today, describing how unity and identity were necessary for passage of the ADA and other disability legislation. But, as Young pointed out, it can be difficult to find "places where the community comes together." Mark Perriello also focused on this issue: "What we are really doing here at AAPD is building connections and building a broader sense of community, so that no matter what the disability we all are part of one movement, one community."

9. Prospects for the Next Few Decades

At the end of our interviews we asked each interviewee, "How optimistic are you about the future for people with disabilities? Do you think they will achieve full equality and inclusion in society, or will they remain marginalized in important ways?" Most people expressed optimism about the future, while also recognizing that continuing progress for people with disabilities is not going to be easy or without challenges. For example, Mark Perriello said:

> I am 100% hopeful about the future of the disability community. When I look around, I see not only AAPD but our partner organizations organizing in ways that they haven't organized in the past. I think that there is a growing recognition and appreciation for the inherent power that people with disabilities have, not only individually but as an entire community, and that more and more people are willing to own that power, and I think that will change things very significantly.
>
> You know, there are definitely challenges ahead. When we look at the ADA there are efforts, ongoing efforts which have been going on for 22 years to dismantle pieces of the ADA, to undermine pieces of the ADA. I think that we will always be fighting those fights, at least in the short term. But I think there is absolutely no stopping this community from moving from a place where we have been marginalized to a place where we are part of the mainstream culture of America, part of the employment culture in this country and really just fully equal. I don't think it will happen overnight, but I think it is the history of America that opportunity expands. And I believe that this decade will be the disability decade.

Representative James Langevin stated:

> I might be the first quadriplegic to serve in the U.S. House, but I most certainly will not be the last. This is one of the most important civil rights issues of the twenty-first century. Having seen the progress our society has made in the last few decades, I really have no doubt that people with disabilities will one day achieve full equality and inclusion in society. It is just going to take time.

Lex Frieden gave a nuanced answer, talking about how standards of inclusion have become higher as earlier goals have been met and conditions have improved:

> Frankly, based on the standard we had in 1985, I think we did see full inclusion in 2005.... So you have to ask that question from a current standard.... We have a whole new set of issues that we're obviously concerned about, and I do think, ... using 2012 as a baseline measure, ... in 20 years we will have succeeded, and if we measure according to the standard we set today, yes we would see full inclusion again; by then we would have redefined the limits of our expectations, and I think it's just sort of an evolutionary [process].... All the new challenges ... are based on a plateau that is way above where we used to look. I mean problems that we see today 25 years ago we would never have the benefit of seeing.

Other people were more qualified in their responses, saying that progress for people with disabilities has been gradual and incremental. John Kemp commented:

> I think we are moving towards acceptance and full equality and inclusion. It is a slow march. It is certainly something I thought would happen faster in my lifetime. But I think we've really built the framework for acceptance and inclusion from a civil rights standpoint, from a systemic standpoint.... But in the broadest sense we are headed in the right direction. It won't be full inclusion in my lifetime, I'm quite sure of that.

Conclusion

Several interviewees mentioned threats to continued progress such as growing inequality, the financial crisis, and regressive government policies. For example, Richard Scotch said:

> We all hoped it would be a kind of transformative thing and it hasn't been, and it's a very incremental process but I think the problems have been exacerbated by the overall increase of inequality in society. I think I am optimistic that some of the positive trends will continue, both changes in the culture and changes in technology and the greater acceptance of some of these legal imperatives.... So I think we will continue to see gradual improvement on a lot of the problems; I don't see a kind of transformative change happening in the foreseeable future though.

Bobby Silverstein reflected the views of several interviewees in both the United States and the United Kingdom who are concerned about the effects of budget cuts:

> I am probably more concerned now than I have been in the past because for many folks with disabilities Medicaid is the key safety net, ... and if the program is [incorporated into block grants for states] and if there are other major changes there, it's going to have very, very serious adverse consequences for people with disabilities, so that makes me very nervous.

Jonathan Young also expressed a cautious view:

> I'm not mechanistically or deterministically optimistic in the sense that I would say we are on a trajectory that necessarily means we are going inevitably in the right direction ... I'm guardedly optimistic. I know that we've made a lot of progress and I think a lot more progress is possible.... But we are not going to get there if we don't do work together to support that progress.

Mark Leeds said that he was "not very" optimistic: "As we have seen with other minority groups (and even with women), true and full equality has not yet been achieved and is unlikely to be achieved for many decades to come.... Until the rank and file of the disability

community take individual and collective interest in understanding –
and preserving – the laws recognizing our rights, those rights will be
eroded rather than advanced."

Tom Shakespeare expressed guarded optimism over the long term,
based on increased exposure of people with disabilities in society:

> More disabled people are enjoying a better quality of life, at least
> in high-income countries. So you have to be optimistic.... I don't
> have a sort of apocalyptic vision.... I am worried about the current
> financial crisis and its impact on disabled people.... But ... in the last
> 20 years I think the position of disabled people has transformed in
> high-income countries.... In Britain we see more disabled people on
> the telly, we hear more disabled people on the radio, we have more
> disabled people in the House of Lords, we have more disabled people
> in Parliament. We are slowly, slowly making disability irrelevant as a
> difference in sort of political life, because there are more and more
> people, doctors and teachers and professors and all the rest of it.

Corinne Kirchner also said that "in terms of the things that policy has
set in motion I would be an optimist over a very long period." Colin
Barnes noted that there will continue to be disparate outcomes for
people with different types of impairment:

> I think certain sections of the disabled community are going to be
> more disadvantaged than others: people with mental health prob-
> lems, people with learning difficulties or what you call intellectually
> disabled people, people who can't conform to societal expectations
> of intelligence and appearance, people with communication dif-
> ficulties too. Without far-reaching economic and cultural change,
> these groups will always be disadvantaged.

His overall prognosis, however, was positive:

> The cat's out of the bag, if you know what I mean. Disabled people
> are not going to sit down and forget it. There is a grassroots move-
> ment in the UK.... These organizations are there, they are growing.
> We have a disability culture, that's not going to fade away. It may be
> a minority issue, but sooner or later things will turn around. I am an

optimist.... It is very difficult to be optimistic at the present time, but sooner or later things will turn around, as they always do.

If you think where we are coming from over the last 60 years in disability, ... from the 1940s, when euthanasia, eugenics, and social hygiene [were] rife among all Western countries – America, Scandinavia, Norway, UK; ... these policies were dominant in the first half of the twentieth century. Since the 1960s they've been over-turned by political activism from below. If we can achieve a society, a global society, which recognizes that disability is an issue of oppres-sion, as we have done with the UN Convention on the Rights of Persons with Disabilities – which has 50 articles covering all aspects of human experience – this is a major achievement. Okay?

If we can do all that in 60 years, then what can we do over the next 60 years?

D. FINAL WORDS

Are people with disabilities entering the mainstream? Have they over-come the economic, political, and social exclusion they have histori-cally faced? The answer to the first question is a qualified yes. People with disabilities have made impressive gains, especially in the adop-tion of policies affirming their equality as citizens and protecting their human rights. The answer to the second question, however, is clearly no: the evidence from hundreds of empirical studies and the views of disability leaders show that people with disabilities still experience a wide range of disparities and have a long way to go to achieve full eco-nomic, political, and social inclusion.

Full inclusion would clearly benefit people with disabilities but would also have broader benefits. Making full use of the talents of peo-ple with disabilities would strengthen the economy, and ensuring that everyone's voice is heard would make democracy stronger and more vibrant. Greater inclusion would also increase social bonds and help create and sustain communities where the full range of human experi-ence is recognized and valued.

Appendix

Interviewees and Affiliations

1. Colin Barnes: Professor of Disability Studies, University of Leeds; founder of the Center for Disability Studies, the Disability Press, and the Disability Archive UK; co-author of *Exploring Disability* (2d ed.) and *The New Politics of Disablement*; author of numerous articles in the field of disability. He is a special-school survivor and a disabled person with a visual impairment.

2. Jaspal Dhani: Chief Executive, United Kingdom Disabled People's Council; freelance trainer and consultant in equality and diversity, including international development; Chairperson of Disability Action in the Borough of Barnet; Trustee of Scope. He is a wheelchair user.

3. Jim Dickson: community organizer focused on bringing the disability community into the electoral process; former Vice President of Organizing and Civic Engagement, American Association of People with Disabilities; played a central role in the effort by the Leadership Conference on Civil and Human Rights to pass the Help America Vote Act; organized a coalition to have President Franklin D. Roosevelt's wheelchair included in his statue at the FDR memorial. He is blind.

4. Jane Dunhamn: founding member and former Chair of the National Black Disability Coalition; member of New Jersey Black Issues Convention; Sub-Committee Chair, New Jersey State Advisory Committee to the U.S. Commission on Civil Rights; co-chair of

the People of Color Caucus for the Society of Disability Studies; recipient of the Exemplary Practice Award in 2009 from the New Jersey Human Relations Council. Ms. Dunhamn is the mother of an adult daughter who has a developmental disability and who lives independently and is employed by the U.S. Department of Labor.

5. Ethan Ellis: President, Next Step; former Executive Director, Alliance for Disabled in Action; former Executive Director, New Jersey Council on Developmental Disabilities; founder and first president, National Association of Protection and Advocacy Services. He is a person born with cerebral palsy.

6. Lex Frieden, Professor of Biomedical Informatics and Professor of Physical Medicine and Rehabilitation, University of Texas Health Center at Houston; former Executive Director and Chair of the presidentially appointed National Council on Disability; past President of Rehabilitation International; past Chairman of the American Association of People with Disabilities; director of the Independent Living Research Utilization Program at TIRR Memorial Hermann Hospital in Houston, Texas; instrumental in conceiving and drafting ADA. He has quadriplegia resulting from a spinal cord injury.

7. Rosemarie Garland-Thomson: Professor of Women's Studies, Emory University; Founder and Presider, American Studies Association Disability Studies Caucus; former fellow at the Radcliffe Institute for Advanced Study at Harvard University; author of *Staring: How We Look* and *Extraordinary Bodies: Figuring Physical Disability in American Culture and Literature*; co-editor of *Re-Presenting Disability: Museums and the Politics of Display* and *Disability Studies: Enabling the Humanities*; editor of *Freakery: Cultural Spectacles of the Extraordinary Body*; author of numerous articles in the disability field. From birth she has had unusual arms and fewer fingers than most people, and identifies as disabled.

8. David Gray: Professor of Occupational Therapy and Neurology, Washington University; Ph.D. in psychology-behavior genetics, University of Minnesota; former director of National Institute of Disability and Rehabilitation Research; former Deputy Director of the National Center for Medical Rehabilitation Research at the National Institutes of Health; active in developing the Participation and Environment components of the International Classification of Functioning, Disability and Health (ICF); author of numerous articles and government reports in the field of disability. He sustained a C 5/6 complete cervical spinal cord injury in 1976 and uses an electric-powered wheelchair for mobility.

9. Andy Imparato: Senior Counsel and Disability Policy Director for the U.S. Senate Health, Education, Labor & Pensions Committee; past President and CEO of the American Association of People with Disabilities; instrumental in the passage of the ADA Amendments Act and other disability legislation. He self-identifies as a person with a disability and has bipolar disorder.

10. Darren Jernigan: Representative of District 60 in the Tennessee General Assembly; Member of the Metro Nashville City Council District 11; Director of Government Affairs, Permobil, Inc. He is a power wheelchair user with quadriplegia.

11. John Kemp: President and CEO of Abilities!; J.D., Washburn University; recipient of the Henry B. Betts Award for disability leadership; co-founder of the American Association of People with Disabilities; serves on State Department's Advisory Committee on Persons with Disabilities, the Medicaid Advisory Commission, and the boards of many disability organizations; former Executive Director of U.S. Business Leadership Network and the United Cerebral Palsy Associations; former member of National Council on Disability. He is a quadruple congenital amputee wearing four prostheses.

12. Corinne Kirchner: Faculty Fellow at the Institute of Social & Economic Research and Policy and Lecturer at the Mailman

School of Public Health at Columbia University; Ph.D. in sociology, Columbia University; former Director of Social Research at the American Foundation for the Blind, which created the Corinne Kirchner Research Award in her honor; former President of the Society for Disability Studies and co-editor, *Disability Studies Quarterly*; author of numerous articles on disability.

13. James Langevin: Member of U.S. House of Representatives for Rhode Island's 2nd District; Co-chair of the Bipartisan Disabilities Caucus; co-sponsor of legislation to improve rehabilitation and quality of life for people with disabilities; master's degree in Public Administration, Harvard University; former member of Rhode Island General Assembly; former Secretary of State of Rhode Island. He is a wheelchair user with quadriplegia.

14. Mark H. Leeds: attorney and former General Counsel and Director of the New York City Mayor's Office for People with Disabilities; first Disability Rights Coordinator at the New York City Board of Education; founding Chair of the Committee on Legal Issues Affecting People with Disabilities at the New York City Bar Association; member of the New York State Bar Association's Executive Committee of the Labor and Employment Law Section and of the Committee on Issues Affecting People with Disabilities; member of the New York City Bar Association's Committee on Civil Rights. He integrated legal blindness and orthopedic disabilities into his life in his late thirties.

15. Mark Perriello: President and CEO of the American Association of People with Disabilities; former White House Priority Placement Director and White House Liaison at the U.S. Department of the Interior; founding Treasurer of Disability PAC; board member of Disability Power & Pride. He has ADHD and a monocular vision.

16. Marsha Saxton: Principal Investigator, World Institute on Disability; teaches disability studies at the University of California, Berkeley; Ph.D., Union Institute; has written widely about women's health issues, genetic technologies, abuse and violence prevention, and

personal assistance services; has been a board member of the Our Bodies, Ourselves Collective and served on the Council for Responsible Genetics and the National Institutes of Health (NIH) Ethical, Legal Social Implications (ELSI) Working Group of the Human Genome Initiative. Her disability is spina bifida.

17. Richard Scotch: Professor of Sociology, Public Policy, and Political Economy at the University of Texas at Dallas; Ph.D. in sociology, Harvard University; past President of the Society for Disability Studies; named a 1999 Switzer Fellow by the National Rehabilitation Association; author, *From Good Will to Civil Rights: Transforming Federal Disability Policy*; co-author, *Disability Protests: Contentious Politics, 1970–99*; co-editor, *Disability and Community*; and author of numerous articles on disability.

18. Katherine D. Seelman: Associate Dean and Professor of Rehabilitation Science and Technology at the School of Health and Rehabilitation Sciences, University of Pittsburgh; Ph.D. in public policy (emphasis on science and technology policy), New York University; former Director of the U.S. National Institute of Disability and Rehabilitation Research; member of the editorial committee for WHO's first *World Report on Disability*; co-editor of *Handbook of Disability Studies*; and author of numerous chapters and articles in the field of disability. She has severe hearing loss and recently enjoyed a trip to New York with her hearing dog, Steen. She teaches graduate disability studies and health ethics using an assistive listening system and microphones installed in the infrastructure of the classroom.

19. Tom Shakespeare: has worked for Universities of Sunderland, Leeds, and Newcastle, United Kingdom, and the World Health Organization; Ph.D. in sociology, Cambridge University; author of *Disability Rights and Wrongs* and *The Sexual Politics of Disability*; co-editor of *Arguing About Disability*; author of numerous articles in the field of disability; contributor to the WHO's *World Report on Disability*; participant in disability movement and disability arts.

He was born with restricted growth and developed spinal cord injury at the age of 42.

20. Bobby Silverstein: principal in the law firm of Powers Pyles Sutter & Verville, PC; J.D., Georgetown University; director of the Center for the Study and Advancement of Disability Policy; former Staff Director and Chief Counsel for the Subcommittee on Disability Policy of the Senate Committee on Labor and Human Resources, plus other staff positions in the U.S. Senate and House of Representatives; instrumental in the passage of ADA.

21. Jonathan Young: Chair of the National Council on Disability; Partner and General Counsel at FoxKiser; co-founder and former Chair of the Committee on Disability Power & Pride; former Associate Director of the White House Office of Public Liaison; Ph.D. in history, University of North Carolina–Chapel Hill; J.D., Yale Law School; author of *Equality of Opportunity: The Making of the Americans with Disabilities Act*. He is partially paralyzed from spinal cord injury.

Bibliography

Acemoglu, D., & Angrist, J. D. (2001). Consequences of employment protection? The case of the Americans with Disabilities Act. *Journal of Political Economy* 109(5), 915–957.

Aldred, R., & Woodcock, J. (2008). Transport: Challenging disabling environments. *Local Environment* 13(6), 485–496.

Ali, M., Schur, L., & Blanck, P. (2011). What types of jobs do people with disabilities want? *Journal of Occupational Rehabilitation* 21(2), 199–210.

Alston, R. J., & Bell, T. J. (1996). Racial identity and African Americans with disabilities: Theoretical and practical considerations. *Journal of Rehabilitation* 62(2), 11.

Altman, B. M. (2001). Disability definitions, models, classification schemes, and applications. *Handbook of Disability Studies*, 97–122.

Altman, B. M., & Bernstein, A. B. (2008). *Disability and health in the United States, 2001–2005*. Department of Health and Human Services, Centers for Disease Control and Prevention, National Center for Health Statistics.

Altman, B. M., & Gulley, S. P. (2009). Convergence and divergence: Differences in disability prevalence estimates in the United States and Canada based on four health survey instruments. *Social Science & Medicine* 69(4), 543–552.

Altman, B. M., Rasch, E. K., & Madans, J. H. (2006). Disability measurement matrix: A tool for the coordination of measurement purpose and instrument development. *Research in Social Science and Disability* 4, 263–284.

Anspach, R. (1979). From stigma to identity politics: Political activism among the physically disabled and former mental patients. *Social Science and Medicine* 13A, 765–773.

Antonak, R. F., & Livneh, H. (1988). *The measurement of attitudes toward people with disabilities: Methods, psychometrics and scales*. Springfield, IL: Charles C. Thomas.

Bibliography

Appelbaum, E., Bailey, T., Berg, P., & Kalleberg, A. (2005). Organizations and the intersection of work and family: A comparative perspective. In P. Thompson, S. Ackroyd, P. Tolbert, & R. Batt (Eds.), *The Oxford handbook of work & organization* (pp. 52–73). New York: Oxford University Press.

Arango-Lasprilla, J. C., Ketchum, J. M., Gary, K., Hart, T., Corrigan, J., Forster, L., et al. (2009). Race/ethnicity differences in satisfaction with life among persons with traumatic brain injury. *NeuroRehabilitation* 24(1), 5–14.

Aranovich, G., Bhattacharya, J., Garber, A. M., & MaCurdy, T. E. (2009). *Coping with chronic disease? Chronic disease and disability in elderly American population, 1982–1999.* Paper No. 14811. Cambridge, MA: National Bureau of Economic Research Working Papers.

Aristotle (1962). In Barker E. (Ed.), *The politics of Aristotle.* New York: Oxford University Press.

Arnold, N. L., & Ipsen, C. (2005). Self-employment policies: Changes through the decades. *Journal of Disability Policy Studies* 16(2), 115–122.

Autor, D. H. (2011). *The unsustainable rise of the disability rolls in the United States: Causes, consequences, and policy options.* Paper no. 17697. Cambridge, MA: National Bureau of Economic Research.

Autor, D. H., & Duggan, M. G. (2003). The rise in the disability rolls and the decline in unemployment. *Quarterly Journal of Economics* 118(1), 157–205.

Aybars, A. I. (2011). Women with disability in Turkey and France. In D. Schiek & A. Lawson (Eds.), *European Union non-discrimination law and intersectionality* (pp. 79–96). Burlington, VT: Ashgate.

Bailey, D. (1991). Guidelines for authors. *Journal of Early Intervention* 15(1), 118–119.

Bailey, R. K., Blackmon, H., & Stevens, F. (2009). Major depressive disorder in the African American population. *Journal of the National Medical Association* 101(11), 1084–1089.

Baker, M., Stabile, M., & Deri, C. (2001). *What do self-reported, objective, measures of health measure?* Paper No. 8419. Cambridge, MA: National Bureau of Economic Research Working Papers.

Balcazar, D. F. E., Keys, C. B., & Suarez-Balcazar, Y. (2001). Empowering Latinos with disabilities to address issues of independent living and disability rights. *Journal of Prevention & Intervention in the Community* 21(2), 53–70.

Baldwin, M. L. (1997). Gender differences in Social Security disability decisions. *Journal of Disability Policy Studies* 8(1–2), 25–49.

Baldwin, M., & Choe, C. (2010). *New estimates of disability-related wage discrimination with controls for job demands* Paper No. 2010–14. Luxembourg: CEPS/INSTEAD.

Bibliography

Baldwin, M. L., & Johnson, W. G. (1995). Labor market discrimination against women with disabilities. *Industrial Relations* 34(4), 555–577.

(2006). A critical review of studies of discrimination against workers with disabilities. In W. M. Rodgers (Ed.), *Handbook on the economics of discrimination* (pp. 119–160). Northampton, MA: Edward Elgar.

Baldwin, M. L., & Schumacher, E. J. (2002). A note on job mobility among workers with disabilities. *Industrial Relations* 41(3), 430–441.

Ball, P., Monaco, G., Schmeling, J., Schartz, H., & Blanck, P. (2005). Disability as diversity in Fortune 100 companies. *Behavioral Sciences & the Law* 23(1), 97–121.

Ballou, J., & Markesich, J. (2009). Counting working-age people with disabilities: Survey data collection methods. In A. J. Houtenville, D. C. Stapleton, R. R. Weathers II, & R. V. Burkhauser (Eds.), *Counting working-age people with disabilities: What current data tell us and options for improvement* (pp. 265–297). Kalamazoo, MI: W. E. Upjohn Institute for Employment Research.

Banks, J., Kapteyn, A., Smith, J. P., & van Soest, A. H. O. (2004). *International comparisons of work disability.* Paper No. 36. Tilburg: Tilburg University, Center for Economic Research.

Banks, J., Kapteyn, A., Smith, J. P., & van Soest, A. (2005). *Work disability is a pain in the *****, especially in England, the Netherlands, and the United States.* Paper No. 11558. Cambridge, MA: National Bureau of Economic Research Working Papers.

Barnartt, S. (2010a). *Disability as a fluid state.* Bingley, UK: Emerald Group Publishing.

(2010b). The globalization of disability protests, 1970–2005: Pushing the limits of cross-cultural research? *Comparative Sociology* 9(2), 222–240.

Barnartt, S. N., & Scotch, R. K. (2001). *Disability protests: Contentious politics, 1970–1999.* Washington, DC: Gallaudet University Press.

Barnes, C. (1992). *Disabling imagery and the media: An exploration of the principles for media representations of disabled people.* London: British Council of Organizations of Disabled People.

(2000). A working social model? Disability, work and disability politics in the 21st century. *Critical Social Policy* 24(4), 441–458.

(2004). Disability, the organisation of work and the need for change. In B. Marin, C. Prinz, and M. Queisser (Eds.), *Transforming welfare policies: Towards work and equal opportunities, European Centre Vienna* (pp. 133–139). Burlington, VT: Ashgate.

(2012). Re-thinking disability, work and welfare. *Sociology Compass* 6(6), 458–471.

247

Bibliography

Barnes, C., & Mercer, G. (2005). Disability, work, and welfare. *Work, Employment & Society* 19(3), 527.

(2010). *Exploring disability* (2d ed.). Cambridge: Polity Press.

Bates, P. (2002). *Working for inclusion*. London: Sainsbury Centre for Mental Health.

Bates, P., & Davis, F. A. (2004). Social capital, social inclusion and services for people with learning disabilities. *Disability & Society* 19(3), 195–207.

Beatty, C., Fothergill, S., Houston, D., Powell, R., & Sissons, P. (2009). A gendered theory of employment, unemployment, and sickness. *Environment and Planning C: Government and Policy* 27(6), 958–974.

Beegle, K., & Stock, W. A. (2003). The labor market effects of disability discrimination laws. *Journal of Human Resources* 38(4), 806–859.

Bell, D., & Heitmueller, A. (2009). The disability discrimination act in the UK: Helping or hindering employment among the disabled? *Journal of Health Economics* 28(2), 465–480.

Benitez-Silva, H., Buchinsky, M., Chan, H. M., Cheidvasser, S., & Rust, J. (2004). How large is the bias in self-reported disability? *Journal of Applied Econometrics* 19(6), 649–670.

Benitez-Silva, H., Disney, R., & Jimenez-Martin, S. (2010). Disability, capacity for work and the business cycle: An international perspective. *Economic Policy* 63, 483.

Bennett, J. A. (2009). Disability and labor market outcomes in the United States: Exploring the linkage between disability, education, and labor market earnings (ProQuest, Ann Arbor, MI). *Masters Abstracts International* 47 (05), 2586–2586.

Berkowitz, M., O'Leary, P. K., Kruse, D. L., & Harvey, C. (1998). *Spinal cord injury: An analysis of medical and social costs*. New York: Demos Medical.

Berube, M. (2009). Citizenship and disability. In R. Baird, S. Rosenbaum, & S.K. Toombs, *Disability: The social, political, and ethical debate* (pp. 205–216). Amherst, NY: Prometheus Books.

Bickenbach, J. E., & Cieza, A. (2012). The prospects for universal disability law and policy. *Journal of Accessibility and Design for All* 1(1), 23–37.

Bhambhani, M. (2006). Marriage and disabled women in India. In G. Albrecht, J. Bickenbach, D. Mitchell, W. Schalick, & S. Snyder (Eds.), *Encyclopedia of disability* (pp. 939–943). Thousand Oaks, CA: Sage.

Blanchett, W. J., Klingner, J. K., & Harry, B. (2009). The intersection of race, culture, language, and disability: Implications for urban education. *Urban Education* 44(4), 389–409.

Blanck, P. (2001). Civil war pensions and disability. *Ohio State Law Journal* 62, 109–249.

Bibliography

(2004). Americans with disabilities and their civil rights: Past, present, and future. *University of Pittsburgh Law Review* 66, 687–719.

(2012). *Digital democracy: Towards a right to web access for people with cognitive disabilities.* Boulder: University of Colorado, Coleman Institute for Cognitive Disabilities.

Blanck, P., Goldstein, B., & Myhill, W. (2013). *Legal rights of persons with disabilities: An analysis of federal law* (2d ed.). Horsham, PA: LRP Publications.

Blanck, P., Hill, E., Siegal, C., & Waterstone, M. (2009). *Disability civil rights law and policy* (2d ed.). Eagan, MN: Thomson/West.

Blanck, P., Sandler, L., Schmeling, J., & Schartz, H. (2000). The emerging workforce of entrepreneurs with disabilities: Preliminary study of entrepreneurship in Iowa. *Iowa Law Review* 85(5), 1583–1644.

Blanck, P., Schartz, H. A., & Schartz, K. M. (2002). Labor force participation and income of individuals with disabilities in sheltered and competitive employment: Cross-sectional and longitudinal analyses of seven states during the 1980s and 1990s. *William and Mary Law Review* 44, 1029–1108.

Blanck, P., & Steele, P. (1998). *The emerging role of the staffing industry in the employment of persons with disabilities: A case report on Manpower Inc.* Iowa City: University of Iowa, Law, Health Policy, and Disability Center.

Blaska, J. (1993). The power of language: Speak and write using "person first." In M. Nagler (Ed.), *Perspectives on disability* (pp. 25–32). Palo Alto, CA: Health Markets Research.

Blázquez Cuesta, M., & Malo Ocaña, M. A. (2005). Educational mismatch and labour mobility of people with disabilities: The Spanish case. *Revista de Economía Laboral* 2(1), 31–55.

Block, P., Balcazar, F., & Keys, C. (2002). Race, poverty and disability: Three strikes and you're out! Or are you? *Social Policy* 33(1), 34–38.

Bogdan, R. (2009). Freak shows. In S. Burch (Ed.), *Encyclopedia of American disability history* (pp. 381–383). New York: Facts on File, Inc.

Bond, J. T., Galinsky, E., Kim, S., & Bownfield, E. (2005). *2005 national study of employers.* New York: Families and Work Institute.

Bonwich, E. (1985). Sex role attitudes and role reorganization in spinal cord injured women. In M. J. Deegan & N. A. Brooks (Eds.), *Women and disability, the double handicap* (pp. 56–67). New Brunswick, NJ: Transaction Books.

Bound, J., & Burkhauser, R. V. (1999). Economic analysis of transfer programs targeted on people with disabilities. In O. Ashenfelter & D. Card (Eds.), *Handbook of labor economics, vol. 3C* (pp. 3417–3528). Amsterdam: Elsevier Science / Oxford: North-Holland.

Bibliography

Bound, J., & Waidmann, T. (2002). Accounting for recent declines in employment rates among working-aged men and women with disabilities. *Journal of Human Resources* 37(2), 231–250.

Boyle, M. A. (1997). Social barriers to successful reentry into mainstream organizational culture: Perceptions of people with disabilities. *Human Resource Development Quarterly* 8(3), 259–268.

Braddock, D., & Parish, S. (2001). An institutional history of disability. In G. Albrecht, K. Seelman, and M. Bury (Eds.), *Handbook of disability studies* (pp. 11–68). Thousand Oaks, CA: Sage.

Brady, S. M. (2001). Sterilization of girls and women with intellectual disabilities. *Violence Against Women* 7(4), 432–461.

Braithwaite, J., & Mont, D. (2009). Disability and poverty: A survey of World Bank poverty assessments and implications. *European Journal of Disability Research* 3, 219–232.

Brault, M. W. (2012). *Americans with disabilities, 2010.* Report No. P70–131. Washington, DC: U.S. Census Bureau.

Brazenor, R. (2002). Disabilities and labour market earnings in Australia. *Australian Journal of Labour Economics* 5(3), 319–334.

Brown, S. C. (2006). Accessibility. In G. Albrecht, J. Bickenbach, D. Mitchell, W. Schalick, & S. Snyder (Eds.), *Encyclopedia of disability* (pp. 9–13). Thousand Oaks, CA: Sage.

Bruyère, S. (2000). *Disability employment policies and practices in private and federal sector organizations.* Ithaca, NY: Cornell University, Program on Employment and Disability.

Bryan, W. V. (2007). *Multicultural aspects of disabilities: A guide to understanding and assisting minorities in the rehabilitation process.* Springfield, IL: Charles C. Thomas.

Bryen, D. N., Potts, B. B., & Carey, A. C. (2007). So you want to work? What employers say about job skills, recruitment and hiring employees who rely on AAC. *Augmentative and Alternative Communication* 23(2), 126–139.

Burch, S. (Ed.) (2009). *Encyclopedia of American disability history.* New York: Facts on File, Inc.

Burchardt, T. (2003a). *Being and becoming: Social exclusion and the onset of disability.* London: London School of Economics and Political Science, Centre for Analysis of Social Exclusion.

(2003b). The risks of disability and poverty: Breaking the chains [I rischi di disabilita e poverta: rompere le catene]. *Sociologia e Politiche Sociali* 6(2), 125–145.

Burke, R. (1999). Disability and women's work experiences: An exploratory study. *International Journal of Sociology and Social Policy* 19(2), 21–33.

Bibliography

Burkhauser, R. V. (1999). The importance of accommodation on the timing of disability insurance applications: Results from the survey of disability and work and the health and retirement study. *Journal of Human Resources* 34(3), 589–611.

——— (2002). Self-reported work-limitation data: What they can and cannot tell us. *Demography* 39(3), 541–555.

Burkhauser, R. V., Butler, J. S., & Kim, Y. W. (1995). The importance of employer accommodation on the job duration of workers with disabilities: A hazard model approach. *Labour Economics* 2(2), 109–130.

Burkhauser, R. V., Houtenville, A. J., & Tennant, J. R. (Forthcoming). Using the ACS and CPS-BMS to track prevalence and the employment of working-age people with disabilities: A case of throwing the baby out with the bathwater? *Journal of Disability Policy Studies.*

Burkhauser, R. V., Rovba, L., & Weathers, R. R. (2009). Counting working-age people with disabilities: Household income. In A. J. Houtenville, D. C. Stapleton, R. R. Weathers, & R. V. Burkhauser (Eds.), *Counting working-age people with disabilities: What current data tell us and options for improvement* (pp. 145–192). Kalamazoo, MI: W. E. Upjohn Institute for Employment Research.

Burkhauser, R. V., Schmeiser, M. D., & Weathers II, R. R. (2012). The importance of anti-discrimination and workers' compensation laws on the provision of workplace accommodations following the onset of a disability. *Industrial and Labor Relations Review* 65(1), 161–180.

Butler, R. J., Baldwin, M. L., & Johnson, W. G. (2006). The effects of occupational injuries after returns to work: Work absences and losses of on-the-job productivity. *Journal of Risk and Insurance* 73(2), 309–334.

Cambois, E., Robine, J., & Ormiche, I. (2007). Did the prevalence of disability in France really fall sharply in the 1990s? A discussion of questions asked in the French health survey. *Population: English Edition* 62(2), 315–337.

Campolieti, M. (2004). Disability insurance benefits and labor supply: Some additional evidence. *Journal of Labor Economics* 22(4), 863–889.

Campolieti, M., & Krashinsky, H. (2006). Disabled workers and wage losses: Some evidence from workers with occupational injuries. *Industrial and Labor Relations Review* 60(1), 120–138.

Carey, A. C. (2009). *On the margins of citizenship: Intellectual disability and civil rights in twentieth-century America.* Philadelphia: Temple University Press.

Carey, A. C., DelSordo, V., & Goldman, A. (2004). Assistive technology for all. *Journal of Disability Policy Studies* 14(4), 194–203.

Carlson, E., & Coffey, G. (2010). 10-plus years after the Olmstead ruling. *National Senior Citizens Law Center. September.* thescanfoundation.org/sites/thescanfoundation.org/files/nsclc_olmstead.pdf.

Bibliography

Carpenter, C. S. (2006). The effects of employment protection for obese people. *Industrial Relations* 45(3), 393–415.

Case, A., Lee, D., & Paxson, C. (2008). The income gradient in children's health: A comment on Currie, Shields and Wheatley Price. *Journal of Health Economics* 27(3): 801–807.

Case, A., Lubotsky, D., & Paxson, C. (2002). Economic status and health in childhood: The origins of the gradient. *American Economic Review* 92(5), 1308–1334.

CEDEFOP. (2010). *Skills supply and demand in Europe: Medium-term forecast up to 2020*. Luxembourg: European Centre for the Development of Vocational Training, Publications Office of the European Union.

Charles, K. K., & Stephens, M., Jr. (2004). Job displacement, disability, and divorce. *Journal of Labor Economics* 22(2), 489–522.

Charlton, J. I. (1998). *Nothing about us without us: Disability oppression and empowerment* Berkeley, CA: University of California Press.

Chatterji, P., Alegria, M., & Takeuchi, D. (2009). Racial/ethnic differences in the effects of psychiatric disorders on employment. *Atlantic Economic Journal* 37(3), 243–257.

Chemers, M. (2006). Freak show. In G. Albrecht, J. Bickenbach, D. Mitchell, W. Schalick, & S. Snyder (Eds.), *The encyclopedia of disability* (pp. 741–743). Thousand Oaks, CA: Sage.

Chen, S., & der Klaauw, W. von (2006). *The work disincentive effects of the disability insurance program in the 1990s*. Washington, DC: Center for Economic Studies, U.S. Census Bureau.

Cherney, J. L. (2009). Temporarily able-bodied. In S. Burch (Ed.), *Encyclopedia of American disability history* (pp. 893–894). New York: Facts on File, Inc.

Chung, K. (2006). Accessible Internet. In G. Albrecht, J. Bickenbach, D. Mitchell, W. Schalick, & S. Snyder (Eds.), *Encyclopedia of disability* (pp. 16–19). Thousand Oaks, CA: Sage.

Cimera, R. E. (2010a). National cost efficiency of supported employees with intellectual disabilities: 2002 to 2007. *American Journal of Intellectual and Developmental Disabilities* 115(1), 19–29.

(2010b). The national cost-efficiency of supported employees with intellectual disabilities: The worker's perspective. *Journal of Vocational Rehabilitation* 33(2), 123–131.

(2011a). Does being in sheltered workshops improve the employment outcomes of supported employees with intellectual disabilities? *Journal of Vocational Rehabilitation* 35(1), 21–27.

(2011b). Supported versus sheltered employment: Cumulative costs, hours worked, and wages earned. *Journal of Vocational Rehabilitation* 35(2), 85–92.

Bibliography

Clark, L., & Marsh, S. (2002). *Patriarchy in the UK: The Language of Disability.* Leeds: University of Leeds, Centre for Disability Studies.

Clarke, H., Sanders, D., Stewart, M., & Whiteley, P. (2006). Taking the bloom off new Labour's rose: Party choice and voter turnout in Britain, 2005. *Journal of Elections, Public Opinions, and Parties* 16(1), 3–36.

Cohen, A. L. (2006). Social capital through workplace connections: Opportunities for workers with intellectual disabilities. *Dissertation Abstracts International, A: The Humanities and Social Sciences* 66(12), 45–47.

Cohen, D. (2006). Disabled veterans. In G. Albrecht, J. Bickenbach, D. Mitchell, W. Schalick, & S. Snyder (Eds.), *The encyclopedia of disability* (pp. 495–499). Thousand Oaks, CA: Sage.

Colella, A. (2001). Coworker distributive fairness judgments of the workplace accommodation of employees with disabilities. *Academy of Management Review*, 100–116.

(1996). Organizational socialization of newcomers with disabilities: A framework for future research. In G. R. Ferris (Ed.), *Research in personnel and human resources management*, vol. 14 (pp. 351–417) Greenwich, CT: JAI Press.

Colella, A., DeNisi, A. S., & Varma, A. (1998). The impact of ratee's disability on performance judgments and choice as partner: The role of disability–job fit stereotypes and interdependence of rewards. *Journal of Applied Psychology* 83(1), 102.

Collins, P. H. (1998). Intersections of race, class, gender, and nation: Some implications for black family studies. *Journal of Comparative Family Studies* 29(1): 27–36.

Conner Kyaien O., Lee Brenda, & Mayers, V. (2009). Attitudes and beliefs about mental health among African American older adults suffering from depression. *Journal of Aging Studies* 24(4), 266.

Connor, D. J. (2006). Michael's story: "I get into so much trouble just by walking": Narrative knowing and life at the intersections of learning disability, race, and class. *Equity & Excellence in Education* 39(2), 154–165.

Connor, D. J., & Ferri, B. A. (2005). Integration and inclusion – a troubling nexus: Race, disability, and special education. *Journal of African American History* 90(1), 107–127.

Conway, M. M. (1991). *Political participation in the United States* (2d ed.). Washington, DC: CQ Press.

Cook, G. (2012). The Autism Advantage. New York Times, November 29 (http://www.nytimes.com/2012/12/02/magazine/the-autism-advantage.html), accessed January 20, 2013.

Cooney, G., Jahoda, A., Gumley, A., & Knott, F. (2006). Young people with intellectual disabilities attending mainstream and segregated schooling: Perceived stigma, social comparison and future aspirations. *Journal of Intellectual Disability Research* 50(6), 432–444.

Corporate Leadership Council. (2000). *Work-life balance policies in support of innovative cultures.* Paper No. 070240550. Arlington, VA: Corporate Leadership Council.

(2003). *Maintaining a work-life balance in the professional services industry.* Paper No. CLC118WIWT. Arlington, VA: Corporate Leadership Council.

Council of Economic Advisors. (2011). *Economic report of the president.* Washington, DC: U.S. Government Printing Office.

Cowen, T. (2011). An Economic and Rational Choice Approach to the Autism Spectrum and Human Neurodiversity. GMU Working Paper in Economics No. 11–58. Available at SSRN: http://ssrn.com/abstract=1975809 or http://dx.doi.org/10.2139/ssrn.1975809.

Crenshaw, K. (1991). Mapping the margins: Intersectionality, identity politics, and violence against women of color. *Stanford Law Review* 43(6), 1241–1299.

CUD. *Center for universal design, North Carolina State University.* www.ncsu.edu/project/design-projects/udi/ (accessed May 30, 2012).

(2006). *Universal design in housing.* Raleigh: North Carolina State University, Center for Universal Design.

Cullinan, J., Gannon, B., & Lyons, S. (2011). Estimating the extra cost of living for people with disabilities. *Health Economics* 20(5), 582–599.

Currie, A., Shields, M. A., & Price, S. W. (2007). The child health/family income gradient: Evidence from England. *Journal of Health Economics* 26(2), 213–232.

Currie, J., Stabile, M., Manivong, P., & Roos, L. L. (2010). Child health and young adult outcomes. *Journal of Human Resources, 45*(3), 517–548.

Currie, J., & Stabile, M. (2006). Child mental health and human capital accumulation: The case of ADHD. *Journal of Health Economics* 25(6), 1094–1118.

Cutler, D. M., Landrum, M. B., & Stewart, K. A. (2009). How do the better educated do it? Socioeconomic status and the ability to cope with underlying impairment. In D. A. Wise (Ed.), *Developments in the economics of aging* (pp. 203–248). A National Bureau of Economic Research Conference Report. Chicago: University of Chicago Press.

Davis, T. M. E., McAullay, D., Davis, W. A., & Bruce, D. G. (2007). Characteristics and outcome of type 2 diabetes in urban aboriginal people: The Fremantle diabetes study. *Internal Medicine Journal* 37(1), 59–63.

Dean, D., Pepper, J., Schmidt, R., & Stern, S. (2011). *The effects of vocational rehabilitation for people with mental illness.* Richmond, VA: University of Richmond.

Bibliography

Deegan, M. J., & Brooks, N. A. (Eds.). (1985). *Women and disability: The double handicap*. New Brunswick, NJ: Transaction.

Degener, T. (2005). Disability discrimination law: A global comparative approach. In A. Lawson & C. Gooding (Eds.), *Disability rights in Europe: From theory to practice* (pp. 87–106). Oxford: Hart.

(2011). Intersections between disability, race, and gender in discrimination law. In D. Schiek & A. Lawson (Eds.), *European Union non-discrimination law and intersectionality* (pp. 29–46). Burlington, VT: Ashgate.

Degener, T., & Quinn, G. (2002). A survey of international, comparative and regional disability law reform. In M. L. Breslin & S. Yee (Eds.), *Disability rights law and policy: International and national perspectives* (pp. 129). Ardsley, NY: Transnational.

Dejong, G. (1983). Defining and implementing the independent living concept. In N. Crewe and I. Zola (Eds.), *Independent living for disabled people* (pp. 4–27). San Francisco: Jossey-Bass.

Delbosc, A., & Currie, G. (2011). Transport problems that matter: Social and psychological links to transport disadvantage. *Journal of Transport Geography* 19(1), 170–178.

DeLeire, T. (2000). The wage and employment effects of the Americans with Disabilities Act. *Journal of Human Resources* 35(4), 693–715.

(2001). Changes in wage discrimination against people with disabilities: 1984–93. *Journal of Human Resources* 36(1), 144–158.

Dewson, S., Williams, C., Aston, J., Carta, E., Willison, R., & Martin, R. (2010). *Organisations' responses to the Disability Discrimination Act*. Paper No. 685. London: Department for Work and Pensions.

DH v. the Czech Republic, App. No. 57325/00 (European Court of Human Rights 2007).

Dibben, P., James, P., Cunningham, I., & Smythe, D. (2002). Employers and employees with disabilities in the UK: An economically beneficial relationship? *International Journal of Social Economics*, 29(6), 453–467.

Dijkers, M. P., Abela, M. B., Gans, B. M., & Gordon, W. A. (1995). The aftermath of spinal cord injury. In S. Stover, J. DeLisa & G. Whiteneck (Eds.), *Spinal cord injury: Clinical outcomes from the model systems*. Gaithersburg, MD: Aspen Publishers.

Dismuke, C. E., Krause, J. S., & Terza, J. V. (2011). Racial disparities in poverty status among families of individuals with spinal cord injury. *Poverty and Public Policy*, 3(1): 105–115.

DIWA (2010). *Disabled women in Africa: 2010 annual report*. Bulawayo, Zimbabwe: Disabled Women in Africa (DIWA).

Bibliography

Dixon, K. A., Kruse, D., & Van Horn, C. E. (2003). *Restricted access: A survey of employers about people with disabilities and lowering barriers to work*. New Brunswick, NJ: Rutgers University, John J. Heldrich Center for Workforce Development.

Dobransky, K., & Hargittai, E. (2006). The disability divide in Internet access and use. *Information Communication and Society* 9(3), 313.

Domzal, C., Houtenville, A., & Sharma, R. (2008). *Survey of employer perspectives on the employment of people with disabilities*. McLean, VA: CESSI.

Donohue III, J. J., Stein, M. A., Griffin Jr, C. L., & Becker, S. (2011). Assessing Post-ADA employment: Some econometric evidence and policy considerations. *Journal of Empirical Legal Studies* 8(3), 477–503.

Dowler, D. L., Solovieva, T. I., & Walls, R. T. (2011). Personal assistance services in the workplace: A literature review. *Disability and Health Journal* 4, 208.

Dowse, L. (2001). Contesting practices, challenging codes: Self advocacy, disability politics and the social model. *Disability & Society* 16(1), 123–141.

Dunlop, D. D., Song, J., Manheim, L. M., Daviglus, M. L., & Chang, R. W. (2007). Racial/ethnic differences in the development of disability among older adults. *American Journal of Public Health* 97(12), 2209–2215.

Ebersold, S. (2011). *Inclusive education for young disabled people in Europe: Trends, issues, and challenges*. Leeds: University of Leeds, Centre for Disability Studies, Academic Network of European Disability Experts.

Emerson, E., Madden, R., Robertson, J., Graham, H., Hatton, C., & Llewellyn, G. (2009). *Intellectual and physical disability, social mobility, social inclusion & health*. Lancaster: Lancaster University, Centre for Disability Research.

Emmett, T., & Alant, E. (2006). Women and disability: Exploring the interface of multiple disadvantage. *Development Southern Africa* 23(4), 445–460.

Engstrom, P., Hagglund, P., & Johansson, P. (2012). *Early interventions and disability insurance: Experience from a field experiment*. Paper No. 6553. Bonn: Institute for the Study of Labor.

Famulari, M. (1992). The effects of a disability on labor market performance: The case of epilepsy. *Southern Economic Journal* 58(4), 1072–1087.

Farber, S., & Paez, A. (2010). Employment status and commute distance of Canadians with disabilities. *Transportation* 37(6), 931–952.

Filmer, D. (2008). Disability, poverty, and schooling in developing countries: Results from 14 household surveys. *World Bank Economic Review* 22(1), 141–163.

Fine, M. & Asch, A. (1985). Disabled women: Sexism without the pedestal. In M.J. Deegan & N. Brooks, *Women and disability: The double handicap* (pp. 6–22) New Brunswick, N.J.: Transaction Books.

Bibliography

Fine, M., & Asch, A. (1988). *Women with disabilities: Essays in psychology, culture, and politics.* Philadelphia: Temple University Press.

Fisher, K., & Jing, L. (2008). Chinese disability independent living policy. *Disability & Society* 23(2), 171–185.

Fitzsimons, N. (2009). *Combating violence & abuse of people with disabilities.* Baltimore: Brookes.

Flynn, E. (2011). *From rhetoric to action: Implementing the UN convention on the rights of persons with disabilities.* Cambridge, England: Cambridge University Press.

Frazis, H., Gittleman, M., Horrigan, M., & Joyce, M. (1998). Results from the 1995 survey of employer-provided training. *Monthly Labor Review* 121, 3.

Fremstad, S. (2009). *Half in ten: Why taking disability into account is essential to reducing income poverty and expanding economic inclusion.* Washington, DC: Center for Economic and Policy Research.

Fuller-Thomson, E., Nuru-Jeter, A., Minkler, M., & Guralnik, J. M. (2010). Black-white disparities in disability among older Americans. *Journal of Aging & Health* 22(5), 677–698.

Gannon, B., & Nolan, B. (2007). The impact of disability transitions on social inclusion. *Social Science & Medicine* 64(7), 1425–1437.

GAO (2009). *Voters with disabilities: More polling places had no potential impediments than in 2000, but challenges remain.* Paper No. 09–685. Washington, DC: Government Accountability Office.

Gary, K. W., Arango-Lasprilla, J. C., & Stevens, L. F. (2009). Do racial/ethnic differences exist in post-injury outcomes after TBI? A comprehensive review of the literature. *Brain Injury* 23(10), 775–789.

Gary, K. W., Nicholls, E., Shamburger, A., Stevens, L. F., & Arango-Lasprilla, J. (2011). Do racial and ethnic minority patients fare worse after SCI? A critical review of the literature. *NeuroRehabilitation* 29(3), 275–293.

Gastil, J. (2000). The political beliefs and orientations of people with disabilities. *Social Science Quarterly.* 81(2), 588–603.

Gayle, A., & Palmer, D. (2005). The activism of persons with disabilities in Jamaica: An evaluation of the impact. *Social and Economic Studies* 54(4), 122–142.

Gerschick, T. (1998). Sisyphus in a wheelchair: Men with physical disabilities confront gender domination. In J. O'Brien & J. Howard (Eds.), *Everyday inequalities* (pp. 189–211). Malden, MA: Blackwell.

Giles, L. C., Cameron, I. D., & Crotty, M. (2003). Disability in older Australians: Projections for 2006–2031. *Medical Journal of Australia* 179(3), 130–134.

Goffman, E. (1963). *Stigma: Notes on the management of spoiled identity.* New York: Touchstone Books.

Bibliography

Goldin, C. D., & Katz, L. F. (2008). *The race between education and technology.* Cambridge, MA: Harvard University Press.

Goodman, L., Glenn, C., Bohleg, A., Banyard, V., & Borges, A. (2009). Feminist relational advocacy: Processes and outcomes from the perspective of low income women. *Counseling Psychologist* 37(6), 848–876.

Grammenos, S. (2010). *Indicators of disability equality in Europe, ANED 2010 task 4.* Leeds: University of Leeds, Centre for Disability Studies, Academic Network of European Disability Experts.

Gray, D., & Cook, A. (2006). Assistive technology. In G. Albrecht, J. Bickenbach, D. Mitchell, W. Schalick, & S. Snyder (Eds.), *Encyclopedia of disability* (pp. 128–134). Thousand Oaks, CA: Sage.

Grutter v. Bollinger, 539 U.S. 306 (U.S. Supreme Court 2003).

Guarino, C. M., Buddin, R., Pham, C., & Cho, M. (2010). Demographic factors associated with the early identification of children with special needs. *Topics in Early Childhood Special Education* 30(3), 162–175.

GUDC. (2012) *Global universal design commission.* www.globaluniversaldesign.org (accessed May 30, 2012).

Gudiño, O. G., Lau, A. S., Yeh, M., McCabe, K. M., & Hough, R. L. (2009). Understanding racial/ethnic disparities in youth mental health services: Do disparities vary by problem type? *Journal of Emotional and Behavioral Disorders* 17(1), 3–16.

Hagner, D., & Davies, T. (2002). "Doing my own thing": Supported self-employment for individuals with cognitive disabilities. *Journal of Vocational Rehabilitation* 17(2), 65–74.

Hahn, H. (1985). Toward a politics of disability: Definitions, disciplines, and policies. *Social Science Journal* 22(4): 87–105.

 (1986). Disability and the urban environment: A perspective on Los Angeles. *Environment and Planning D: Society and Space* 4(3), 273–288.

 (1988). The politics of physical differences: Disability and discrimination. *Journal of Social Issues* 44(1), 39–47.

Hale, T. W. (2008). Development of the new disability questions for the CPS and what they can tell us about the employment status of people with disabilities. *Journal of Legal Economics* 14(3), 101–110.

Hall, S. A. (2009). The social inclusion of people with disabilities: A qualitative meta-analysis. *Journal of Ethnographic & Qualitative Research* 3(3), 12.

Hamlin, T., & Simeonsson, R. (2006). Education and disability. In G. Albrecht, J. Bickenbach, D. Mitchell, W. Schalick, & S. Snyder (Eds.), *The encyclopedia of disability* (pp. 565–572). Thousand Oaks, CA: Sage.

Bibliography

Hanna, W., & Rogovsky, E. (1993). On the situation of African-American women with physical disabilities. In M. Nagler (Ed.), *Perspectives on disability* (pp. 149–160). Palo Alto, CA: Health Markets Research.

Harris, C. (2003). *Self-employment of disabled people in developing countries.* www. disabilityworld.org/11–12_03/employment/selfemployment.shtml (accessed May 30, 2012).

Hasler, F. (2006). Independent living. In G. Albrecht, J. Bickenbach, D. Mitchell, W. Schalick, & S. Snyder (Eds.), *Encyclopedia of disability* (pp. 930–935). Thousand Oaks, CA: Sage.

Hasnain, R., & Balcazar, F. (2009). Predicting community- versus facility-based employment for transition-aged young adults with disabilities: The role of race, ethnicity, and support systems. *Journal of Vocational Rehabilitation* 31(3), 175–188.

Hastings, J., & Thomas, H. (2005). Accessing the nation: Disability, political inclusion and built form. *Urban Studies* 42(3), 527.

Hayashi, R., & Okuhira, M. (2001). The disability rights movement in Japan: Past, present and future. *Disability & Society* 16(6), 855–869.

Hays, J., & Kirby, S. (2012). *ADA amendments breathe new life into disability claims.* mobile.www.law.com/jsp/nylj/PubArticleNY.jsp?id=1202551343734&ADA_Amendments_Breathe_New_Life_Into_Disability_Claims (accessed May 30, 2012).

Heady, C. (2002). Sickness and disability. In M. Barnes et al. (Eds.), *Poverty and social exclusion in Europe* (pp. 101–122). Northampton, MA: Edward Elgar.

Hendershot, G. (2005). *Statistical analyses based on the national health interview survey on disability: A bibliography and summary of findings.* Minneapolis: University of Minnesota, Research and Training Center on Community Living.

Hernandez, B., McDonald, K., Lepera, N., Shahna, M., Wang, T. A., & Levy, J. M. (2009). Moving beyond misperceptions: The provision of workplace accommodations. *Journal of Social Work in Disability & Rehabilitation* 8(3–4), 189–204.

Heshmati, A., & Engström, L.G. (2001). Estimating the effects of vocational rehabilitation programs in Sweden. In M. Lechner and P. Friedhelm (Eds.), *Econometric evaluation of labour market policies* (pp. 183–210). Heidelberg: Physica, Zentrum fur Europäische Wirtshaftsforschung.

Hockenberry, J. (2004). Public transit. In R. O'Brien (Ed.), *Voices from the edge* (pp. 137–153). New York: Oxford University Press.

Holland, D. (2008). The current status of disability activism and non-governmental organizations in post-communist Europe: Preliminary findings based on reports from the field. *Disability & Society* 23(6), 543–555.

Bibliography

Hollenbeck, K., & Huang, W. (2006). *Net impact and benefit-cost estimates of the workforce development system in Washington state.* Paper No. 06–020. Kalamazoo, MI: W. E. Upjohn Institute for Employment Research.

Hollenbeck, K., & Kimmel, J. (2008). Differences in the returns to education for males by disability status and age of disability onset. *Southern Economic Journal* 74(3), 707–724.

Hollenweger, J. (2006a). International education. In G. Albrecht, J. Bickenbach, D. Mitchell, W. Schalick, & S. Snyder (Eds.), *The encyclopedia of disability* (pp. 556–561). Thousand Oaks, CA: Sage.

(2006b). Primary and secondary education. In G. Albrecht, J. Bickenbach, D. Mitchell, W. Schalick, & S. Snyder (Eds.), *The encyclopedia of disability* (pp. 562–565). Thousand Oaks, CA: Sage.

Honeycutt, T. C. (2010). *The effects of the Americans with Disabilities Act on the health coverage and post-secondary education of people with disabilities.* Unpublished dissertation. Rutgers University and University of Medicine and Dentistry of New Jersey, New Brunswick.

Hotchkiss, J. L. (2003). *The labor market experience of workers with disabilities: The ADA and beyond.* Kalamazoo, MI: W. E. Upjohn Institute for Employment Research.

(2004a). Growing part-time employment among workers with disabilities: Marginalization or opportunity? *Federal Reserve Bank of Atlanta Economic Review* 89(3), 25–40.

(2004b). A closer look at the employment impact of the Americans with Disabilities Act. *Journal of Human Resources* 39(4), 887–911.

Houtenville, A. J., & Burkhauser, R. V. (2004). *Did the employment of people with disabilities decline in the 1990s, and was the ADA responsible? A replication and robustness check of Acemoglu and Angrist (2001) – research brief.* Ithaca, NY: Cornell University, Employment and Disability Institute.

Houtenville, A. J., Stapleton, D. C., Weathers, R. R., & Burkhauser, R. V. (Eds.) (2009). *Counting working-age people with disabilities: What current data tell us and options for improvement.* Kalamazoo, MI: W. E. Upjohn Institute for Employment Research.

Hudson, G. (2006). History of disability: Early modern West. In G. Albrect (Ed.), *Encyclopedia of disability* (pp. 855–858). Thousand Oaks, CA: Sage.

Human Rights Watch (2003). *Ill-equipped: U.S. prisons and offenders with mental illness.* New York: Human Rights Watch.

(2009). *Mental illness, human rights, and U.S. prisons: Human Rights Watch statement for the record, Senate Judiciary Committee, Subcommittee on Human Rights and the Law.* New York: Human Rights Watch.

Bibliography

Institute of Medicine (2007). *The future of disability in America*. Washington, DC: National Academies Press.

ITAA (2003). *Report of the ITAA blue ribbon panel on IT diversity*. Washington, DC: Information Technology Association of America.

Jaeger, P. T. (2006). Telecommunications policy and individuals with disabilities: Issues of accessibility and social inclusion in the policy and research agenda. *Telecommunications Policy* 30(2), 112–124.

Jennings, M. K. (1999). Political responses to pain and loss: Presidential address, American Political Science Association, 1998. *American Political Science Review*, 1–13.

Jolls, C. (2004). Identifying the effects of the Americans with Disabilities Act using state-law variation: Preliminary evidence on educational participation effects. *American Economic Review* 94(2), 447–453.

Jolls, C., & Prescott, J. J. (2004). *Disaggregating employment protection: The case of disability discrimination*. Paper No. 10740. Cambridge, MA: National Bureau of Economic Research Working Paper Series.

Jones, M. K. (2006). Is there employment discrimination against the disabled? *Economics Letters* 92(1), 32–37.

(2007). Does part-time employment provide a way of accommodating a disability? *Manchester School* 75(6), 695–716.

(2008). Disability and the labour market: A review of the empirical evidence. *Journal of Economic Studies* 35(5–6), 405–424.

(2009). The employment effect of the Disability Discrimination Act: Evidence from the health survey for England. *LABOUR: Review of Labour Economics & Industrial Relations* 23(2), 349–369.

Jones, M. K., & Jones, J. (2008). The labour market impact of the UK Disability Discrimination Act: Evidence from the repeal of the small firm exemption. *Bulletin of Economic Research* 60(3), 289–306.

Jones, M. K., & Latreille, P. L. (2010). Disability and earnings: Are employer characteristics important? *Economics Letters* 106(3), 191–194.

Jones, M. K., Latreille, P. L., & Sloane, P. J. (2006a). Disability, gender and the labour market in wales. *Regional Studies* 40(8), 823–845.

(2006b). Disability, gender, and the British labour market. *Oxford Economic Papers* 58(3), 407–449.

(2007). Disability and work: A review of the British evidence. *Estudios de Economía Aplicada* 25(2), 473–497.

Jones, M. K., & Sloane, P. J. (2010). Disability and skill mismatch. *Economic Record* 86, 101–114.

Kailes, J. (1985). Watch your language, please. *Journal of Rehabilitation* 51(1), 68–69.

261

Bibliography

Kapteyn, A., Smith, J. P., & van Soest, A. (2007). Vignettes and self-reports of work disability in the United States and the Netherlands. *American Economic Review* 97(1), 461–473.

(2009). *Work disability, work, and justification bias in Europe and the U.S.* Paper No. 15245. Cambridge, MA: National Bureau of Economic Research Working Papers.

Kaye, H. S., Jans, L. H., & Jones, E. C. (2011). Why don't employers hire and retain workers with disabilities? *Journal of Occupational Rehabilitation 21(4): 526–536.*

Kaye, H. S. (2000). *Computer and Internet use among people with disabilities.* Paper No. 13. Washington, DC.: U.S. Department of Education, National Institute on Disability and Rehabilitation.

(2010). The impact of the 2007–09 recession on workers with disabilities. *Monthly Labor Review* 133(10), 19–30.

Kayess, R., & French, P. (2008). Out of darkness into light? Introducing the Convention on the Rights of Persons with Disabilities. *Human Rights Law Review* 8(1), 1–34.

Keeley, H., Redley, M., Holland, A., & Clare, I. (2008). Participation in the 2005 general election by adults with intellectual disabilities. *Journal of Intellectual Disability Research* 52(3), 175–181.

Kelly, C. M., Schootman, M., Baker, E. A., Barnidge, E. K., & Lemes, A. (2007). The association of sidewalk walkability and physical disorder with area-level race and poverty. *Journal of Epidemiology & Community Health* 61(11), 978–983.

Kelley-Moore, J. A., & Ferraro, K. F. (2004). The black/white disability gap: Persistent inequality in later life? *Journals of Gerontology, Series B: Psychological Sciences and Social Sciences* 59(1), S34.

Kempton, W., & Kahn, E. (1991). Sexuality and people with intellectual disabilities: A historical perspective. *Sexuality and Disability* 9(2), 93–111.

Kendall, E., & Marshall, C. A. (2004). Factors that prevent equitable access to rehabilitation for Aboriginal Australians with disabilities: The need for culturally safe rehabilitation. *Rehabilitation Psychology* 49(1), 5.

Kersh, J. (2011). Attitudes about people with intellectual disabilities: Current status and new directions. *International Review of Research in Developmental Disabilities,* 41: 199–231.

Kessler/NOD/Harris (2010). *The ADA, 20 years later.* New York: Harris Interactive. Sponsored by Kessler Foundation and National Organization on Disability.

Kidd, M. P., Sloane, P. J., & Ferko, I. (2000). Disability and the labour market: An analysis of British males. *Journal of Health Economics* 19(6), 961–981.

Bibliography

Kim, E. (2006). History of disability: Korea. In G. Albrecht, J. Bickenbach, D. Mitchell, W. Schalick, & S. Snyder (Eds.), *The encyclopedia of disability* (pp. 858–864). Thousand Oaks, CA: Sage.

Kirchner, C. (1996). Looking under the street lamp: Inappropriate uses of measures just because they are there. *Journal of Disability Policy Studies* 7(1), 77–90.

(2003). *Yes, people with disabilities probably are in your sample: Methodological issues and strategies for including them effectively.* Paper presented at the American Association for Public Opinion Research annual meeting, Nashville, TN.

Kirchner, C., & Schmeidler, E. (1999). Life chances and ways of life: Statistics on race, ethnicity, and visual impairment. *Journal of Visual Impairment & Blindness* 93(5), 319.

Kjellberg, A. (2002). Being a citizen. *Disability & Society* 17(2), 187–203.

Klassen, S. (2000). Does gender inequality reduce growth and development? Evidence from cross country regressions. *Collaborative Research Center* 386 (Conference Paper 212).

Klaus, L. A. (1997). Work-life programs help reduce employee absenteeism. *Quality Progress* 30(11): 13.

Klein, D., Schmeling, J., & Blanck, P. (2005). Emerging technologies and corporate culture at Microsoft: A methodological note. *Behavioral Sciences & the Law* 23(1), 65–96.

Klijs, B., Mackenbach, J. P., & Kunst, A. E. (2011). Future disability projections could be improved by connecting to the theory of a dynamic equilibrium. *Journal of Clinical Epidemiology* 64(4), 436–443.

Knowling, R. (2003). *Keynote speech.* National IT Workforce Convocation, Arlington, VA.

Konrad, A. M., & Mangel, R. (2000). The impact of work-life programs on firm productivity. *Strategic Management Journal* 21(12), 1225–1237.

Korte, G (2012). Study Shows Voters with Disabilities Face Access Barriers. *USA Today*, August 9, page 4.

Krause, J. S., Saunders, L., & Staten, D. (2010). Race-ethnicity, education, and employment after spinal cord injury. *Rehabilitation Counseling Bulletin* 53(2), 78–86.

Kreider, B. (1999). Latent work disability and reporting bias. *Journal of Human Resources* 34(4), 734–769.

Kreider, B., & Pepper, J. V. (2007). Disability and employment: Reevaluating the evidence in light of reporting errors. *Journal of the American Statistical Association* 102(478), 432–441.

Bibliography

Kroll, T., Keer, D., Placek, P., Cyril, J., & Hendershot, G. (2006). *Towards best practices for surveying people with disabilities*. Hauppage, NY: Nova Science.

Krueger, A., & Kruse, D. (1995). *Labor market effects of spinal cord injuries in the dawn of the computer age*. Paper No. 5302. Cambridge, MA: National Bureau of Economic Research Working Papers.

Kruse, D., & Schur, L. (2002). *Non-standard work arrangements and disability*. Urbana-Champaign: University of Illinois, Disability Research Institute.

   (2003). Employment of people with disabilities following the ADA. *Industrial Relations* 42(1), 31–66.

Kruse, D., Schur, L., Han, K., & Kim, A. (2011). *Employer demand for alternative workers and work arrangements*. Syracuse, NY: Syracuse University, Burton Blatt Institute.

Kruse, D., Schur, L., & Ali, M. (2010). Disability and occupational projections. *Monthly Labor Review* 133(10): 31–78.

Kulkarni, M., & Lengnick-Hall, M. L. (2011). Socialization of people with disabilities in the workplace. *Human Resource Management* 50(4), 521–540.

Lamp, S. (2006). Public transportation. In G. Albrecht, J. Bickenbach, D. Mitchell, W. Schalick, & S. Snyder (Eds.), *Encyclopedia of disability* (pp. 1320–1322). Thousand Oaks, CA: Sage.

Lawson, A. (2011). Disadvantage at the intersection of race and disability: Key challenges for EU Non-Discrimination Law. In D. Schiek & A. Lawson (Eds.), *European Union Non-Discrimination Law and intersectionality: Investigating the triangle of racial, gender and disability discrimination* (pp. 47–62). Burlington, VT: Ashgate.

Lechner, M., & Vazquez-Alvarez, R. (2011). The effect of disability on labour market outcomes in Germany. *Applied Economics* 43(4–6), 389–412.

Lengnick-Hall, M. L., Gaunt, P. M., & Kulkarni, M. (2008). Overlooked and underutilized: People with disabilities are an untapped human resource. *Human Resource Management* 47(2), 255–273.

Lijphart, A. (1997). Unequal participation: Democracy's unresolved dilemma. *American Political Science Review* 91(1): 1–14.

Livermore, G. A., Goodman, N., & Wright, D. (2007). Social Security disability beneficiaries: Characteristics, work activity, and use of services. *Journal of Vocational Rehabilitation* 27(2), 85–93.

LoBianca, A. (1998). *Are the costs too high? Political participation among disabled Americans*. Lexington: University of Kentucky, Department of Political Science.

Logue, L. M., & Blanck, P. D. (2010). *Race, ethnicity, and disability: Veterans and benefits in post–Civil War America*. Cambridge: Cambridge University Press.

Bibliography

Lo-Hui, K. Y. L., Luo, L., & Yang, X. (2011). Psychosocial adjustment of women with work-related disabilities in rural China. *Review of Disability Studies: An International Journal* 7(1), 34–40.

Longmore, P. K. (2009). Disability rights movement. In S. Burch (Ed.), *Encyclopedia of American disability history* (pp. 280–285). New York: Facts on File, Inc.

Lustig, D. C., & Strauser, D. (2004). Employee benefits for individuals with disabilities: The effect of race and gender. *Journal of Rehabilitation* 70(2), 38–46.

Lynch, R. T., Thuli, K., & Groombridge, L. (1994). Person-first disability language: A pilot analysis of public perceptions. *Journal of Rehabilitation* 60(2), 18–22.

MacInnes, M. D. (2011). Altar-bound? The effect of disability on the hazard of entry into a first marriage. *International Journal of Sociology* 41(1), 87–103.

Madans, J. H., Loeb, M. E., & Altman, B. M. (2011). Measuring disability and monitoring the UN Convention on the Rights of Persons with Disabilities: The work of the Washington Group on Disability Statistics. *BMC Public Health* 11, 1–8.

Malo, M. A., & Pagan, R. (2007). Existe la doble discriminación salarial por sexo y discapacidad en españa? Un analisis empirico con datos del panel de hogares (with English summary.). *Moneda y Credito* (225), 7–42.

Manus, G. I. (1975). Is your language disabling? *Journal of Rehabilitation* 41(5), 35.

Marti, M. W., & Blanck, P. (2000). Attitudes, behavior, and the ADA. In P. Blanck (Ed.), *Employment, disability, and the Americans with Disabilities Act: Issues in law, public policy, and research* (pp. 356–384). Evanston, IL: Northwestern University Press.

Martin, L. G., Schoeni, R. F., & Andreski, P. M. (2010). Trends in health of older adults in the United States: Past, present, future. *Demography* 47, S17–40.

Mashaw, J. L., Reno, V. P., Burkhauser, R. V., & Berkowitz, R. (Eds.) (1996). *Disability, work and cash benefits.* Kalamazoo, MI: W. E. Upjohn Institute for Employment Research.

Mathers, C. D., & Loncar, D. (2006). Projections of global mortality and burden of disease from 2002 to 2030. *PLoS Med* 3(11), e442.

McAfee, J. K., & McNaughton, D. (1997a). Transitional outcomes – job satisfaction of workers with disabilities, part one: General job satisfaction. *Journal of Vocational Rehabilitation* 8(2), 135–142.

(1997b). Transitional outcomes: Job satisfaction of workers with disabilities, part two: Satisfaction with promotions, pay, co-workers, supervision, and work conditions. *Journal of Vocational Rehabilitation* 8(3), 243–251.

Bibliography

McDonald, K. E., Keys, C. B., & Balcazar, F. E. (2007). Disability, race/ethnicity and gender: Themes of cultural oppression, acts of individual resistance. *American Journal of Community Psychology* 39(1), 145–161.

McPhedran, S. (2011). Disability and community life: Does regional living enhance social participation? *Journal of Disability Policy Studies* 22(1), 40–54.

Meekosha, H. (2002). Virtual activists? Women and the making of identities of disability. *Hypatia* 17(3), 67–88.

(2006a). What the hell are you? An intercategorical analysis of race, ethnicity, gender and disability in the Australian body politic. *Scandinavian Journal of Disability Research* 8(2–3), 161–176.

(2006b). Gender, international. In G. Albrecht, J. Bickenbach, D. Mitchell, W. Schalick, & S. Snyder (Eds.), *Encyclopedia of disability* (pp. 764–769). Thousand Oaks, CA: Sage.

Miesenberger, K., Klaus, J., Zagler, W., & Karshmer, A. (2012). Computers helping people with special needs. 13th international conference, ICCHP, Vienna, Austria.

Miller, A. H., Gurin, P., Gurin, G., & Malanchuk, O. (1981). Group consciousness and political participation. *American Journal of Political Science 25(3):* 494–511.

Miller, S. D. (2002). Disability and the black community. *Journal of Health & Social Policy* 16(1/2), 5–220.

Milner, P., & Kelly, B. (2009). Community participation and inclusion: People with disabilities defining their place. *Disability & Society* 24(1), 47–62.

Mitra, S. (2008). The recent decline in the employment of persons with disabilities in South Africa, 1998–2006. *South African Journal of Economics* 76(3), 480–492.

(2009). Temporary and partial disability programs in nine countries: What can the United States learn from other countries? *Journal of Disability Policy Studies* 20(1), 14–27.

Mitra, S., Findley, P., & Sambamoorthi, U. (2008). *Healthcare expenditures of living with a disability: Total expenditures, out of pocket expenses and burden, 1996–2004.* New York: Fordham University, Department of Economics Discussion Paper Series.

Mitra, S., & Kruse, D. (2011a). *The disability gap in job loss rates: Evidence from the 2010 current population survey.* New York: Fordham University, Department of Economics.

(2011b). *Disability and worker displacement.* New York: Fordham University, Department of Economics.

Mitra, S., Posarac, A., & Vick, B. C. (2011). *Disability and poverty in developing countries: A snapshot from the World Health Survey. Paper 1109.* World Bank Social Protection Working Paper Series.

Bibliography

Mont, D. (2004). *Disability employment policy.* Paper No. 0413. Washington, DC: World Bank Social Protection Discussion Paper Series.

Montana RRTC. (2001). *First national study of people with disabilities who are self-employed.* Paper No. 8. Missoula, MT: Research and Training Center on Rural Rehabilitation Services.

Moon, N. W., & Baker, P. M. A. (2012). Assessing stakeholder perceptions of workplace accommodations barriers: Results from a policy research instrument. *Journal of Disability Policy Studies* 23(2): 94–109.

Morris, A., & Abelló, D. (2005). *Disability support pension new customer focus groups.* Sydney: Social Policy Research Centre.

Morris, J. (1993). Feminism and disability. *Feminist Review 43(Autumn),* 57–70.

Morrison, R. L., & Nolan, T. (2009). I get by with a little help from my friends … at work. *Kōtuitui: New Zealand Journal of Social Sciences Online* 4(1), 41–54.

Moulta-Ali, Umar (2012). *Primer on Disability Benefits: Social Security Disability Insurance (SSDI) and Supplemental Security Income (SSI).* 7–5700, RL32279. Washington, DC: U.S. Congressional Research Service.

Mpofu, E., & Harley, D. A. (2006). Racial and disability identity: Implications for the career counseling of African Americans with disabilities. *Rehabilitation Counseling Bulletin* 50(1), 14–23.

Mudrick, N. (1988). Disabled women and public policies for income support. In M. Fine & A. Asch (Eds.), *Women with disabilities: Essays in psychology, culture, and politics* (pp. 245–268). Philadelphia: Temple University Press.

Muzzatti, B. (2008). Attitudes towards disability: Beliefs, emotive reactions, and behaviors by non disabled persons [Gli atteggiamenti verso la disabilita: Credenze, reazioni emotive e comportamenti delle persone non disabili]. *Giornale Italiano di Psicologia* 35(2), 313–333.

Nagata, K. K. (2003). Gender and disability in the Arab region: The challenges in the new millennium. *Asia Pacific Disability Rehabilitation Journal* 14(1), 10–17.

National Council on Disability (2007). *Empowerment for Americans with disabilities: Breaking barriers to careers and full employment.* Washington, DC: National Council on Disability.

NBDC. (2012) *National Black Disability Coalition.* www.blackdisability.org/ (accessed May 30, 2012).

Ni, C., Wilkins-Turner, F., Liebert, D., Ellien, V., & Harrington, C. (2011). Native Americans with disabilities: A comparison of male and female eastern tribal members. *Review of Disability Studies: An International Journal* 7(1), 48–59.

Nielsen, K. (2012). *A disability history of the United States.* Boston: Beacon Press.

Bibliography

NOD (2003). *Workplace diversity programs enhance employment of people with disabilities, survey finds.* Washington, DC: National Organization on Disability.

NOD/Harris (1998). *1998 National Organization on Disability/Harris survey of Americans with disabilities.* New York: Harris Interactive.

(2000). *2000 National Organization on Disability/Harris survey of Americans with disabilities.* New York: Harris Interactive.

(2004). *2004 National Organization on Disability/Harris survey of Americans with disabilities.* New York: Harris Interactive.

Novak, J. A., & Rogan, P. M. (2010). Social integration in employment settings: Application of intergroup contact theory. *Intellectual and Developmental Disabilities* 48(1), 31–51.

Nowicki, E. A., & Sandieson, R. (2002). A meta-analysis of school-age children's attitudes towards persons with physical or intellectual disabilities. *International Journal of Disability, Development and Education* 49(3), 243–265.

Nuru-Jeter, A., Thorpe, R., & Fuller-Thomson, E. (2011). Black-white differences in self-reported disability outcomes in the U.S.: Early childhood to older adulthood. *Public Health Reports* 126(6), 834–843.

OECD (2003). *Transforming disability into ability: Policies to promote work and income security for disabled people.* Paris: Organisation for Economic Co-operation and Development.

(2010). *Sickness, disability, and work: Breaking the barriers.* Paris: Organisation for Economic Co-operation and Development.

Office of Disability Employment Policy (2005). *Entrepreneurship: A flexible route to economic independence for people with disabilities.* www.dol.gov/odep/pubs/misc/entrepre.htm (accessed May 30, 2012).

Oguzoglu, U. (2012). *Dynamics of disability and work in Canada.* Paper No. 6603. Bonn: IZA Discussion Paper Series.

Oliver, M. (1990). *The politics of disablement.* Basingstoke: MacMillan.

(2004). The social model in action: If I had a hammer. In C. Barnes & G. Mercer (Eds.), *Implementing the social model of disability: Theory and research* (pp. 18–31). Leeds: Disability Press.

Oliver, M., & Barnes, C. (2010). Disability studies, disabled people and the struggle for inclusion. *British Journal of Sociology of Education* 31(5), 547–560.

Olkin, R. (2002). Could you hold the door for me? Including disability in diversity. *Cultural Diversity and Ethnic Minority Psychology* 8(2), 130.

Ostrander, R. N. (2008). When identities collide: Masculinity, disability and race. *Disability & Society* 23(6), 585–597.

Padden, C., & Humphries, T. L. (2006). *Inside Deaf culture.* Cambridge, MA: Harvard University Press.

Bibliography

Pagan, R., & Malo, M. A. (2009). Job satisfaction and disability: Lower expectations about jobs or a matter of health? *Spanish Economic Review* 11(1), 51–74.

Paludi, M. A., DeSouza, E., & Dodd, D. (2010). Disability discrimination. In M. A. Paludi, C. A. Paludi, & E. DeSouza (Eds.), *Praeger handbook on understanding and preventing workplace discrimination* (pp. 17–44). Santa Barbara, CA: Praeger.

Parish, S. L., Grinstein-Weiss, M., Yeong, H. Y., Rose, R. A., & Rimmerman, A. (2010). Assets and income: Disability-based disparities in the United States. *Social Work Research* 34(2), 71–82.

Parish, S. L., Rose, R. A., & Andrews, M. E. (2009). Income poverty and material hardship among U.S. women with disabilities. *Social Service Review* 83(1), 33–52.

Paschal, A. M., Ablah, E., Wetta-Hall, R., Molgaard, C. A., & Liow, K. (2005). Stigma and safe havens: A medical sociological perspective on African-American female epilepsy patients. *Epilepsy & Behavior* 7(1), 106–115.

Patton, M. (1990). *Qualitative evaluation and research methods* (2d edition). Newbury Park, CA: Sage Publications.

Perry, E. L., Hendricks, W., & Broadbent, E. (2000). An exploration of access and treatment discrimination and job satisfaction among college graduates with and without physical disabilities. *Human Relations* 53(7), 923–955.

Perske, R. (1988). *Circle of friends: People with disabilities and their friends enrich the lives of one another.* Coppell, TX: Abingdon Press.

Peters, K. E., & Opacich, K. (2006). Gender. In G. Albrecht, J. Bickenbach, D. Mitchell, W. Schalick, & S. Snyder (Eds.), *Encyclopedia of disability* (pp. 760–764). Thousand Oaks, CA: Sage.

Petersen, A. (2006). An African-American woman with disabilities: The intersection of gender, race and disability. *Disability & Society* 21(7), 721–734.

Phillips, M. J. (1985). "Try harder": The experience of disability and the dilemma of normalization. *Social Science Journal,* 22(4): 45–57.

Polidano, C., and Hong, H. (2012). Labour Market Impacts from Disability Onset. Melbourne Institute Working Paper No. 22. Available at SSRN: http://ssrn.com/abstract=2166603.

Power, D., & Power, M. (2010). The Internet and government disability policy development in the United Kingdom. Paper presented at the In *Internet, Politics, Policy 2010: An Impact Assessment* conference Oxford: University of Oxford.

Presser, H. B., & Altman, B. (2002). Work shifts and disability: A national view. *Monthly Labor Review* 125(9), 11–24.

Bibliography

Price, J. (2011). *The seeds of a movement: Disabled women and their struggle to organize.* Toronto: Association for Women's Rights in Development.

Priestley, M., & Roulstone, A. (2009). *Targeting and mainstreaming disability in the 2008–2010 national reform programmes for growth and jobs.* Leeds: University of Leeds, Centre for Disability Studies, Academic Network of European Disability Experts.

Priestley, M., & Shah, S. (2011). *Disability and social change: Private lives and public policies.* Portland, OR: Policy Press.

Prince, M. J. (2007). *The electoral participation of persons with special needs.* Ottawa: Elections Canada.

Pruett, S. R., Swett, E. A., Chan, F., Rosenthal, D. A., & Lee, G. K. (2008). Empirical evidence supporting the effectiveness of vocational rehabilitation. *Journal of Rehabilitation* 74(2), 56–63.

Putnam, R. D. (2001). *Bowling alone: The collapse and revival of American community.* New York: Simon & Schuster.

Quarmby, K. (2011). *Scapegoat: Why we are failing disabled people?* London: Portobello Books.

Ramirez, S. A. (2000). Diversity and the boardroom. *Stanford Journal of Law, Business and Finance* 6(1), 85–133

Rankhumise, E. M. (2010). The advancement of people with disabilities in the private sector: A case of South Africa. *Problems and Perspectives in Management* 8(2), 4–8.

Rao, I. (2004). *Equity to women with disabilities in India.* Bangalore: CBR Network. (v1.dpi.org/lang-en/resources/details.php?page=90), accessed January 20, 2013.

Ravaud, J. F., Madiot, B., & Ville, I. (1992). Discrimination towards disabled people seeking employment. *Social Science & Medicine* 35(8), 951–958.

Ren, L. R., Paetzold, R. L., & Colella, A. (2008). A meta-analysis of experimental studies on the effects of disability on human resource judgments. *Human Resource Management Review* 18(3), 191–203.

Renaud, S. (2002). Rethinking the union membership/job satisfaction relationship: Some empirical evidence in Canada. *International Journal of Manpower* 23(2), 137–150.

Reville, R. T., & Schoeni, R. F. (2003). The fraction of disability caused at work. *Social Security Bulletin* 65(4), 31–37.

Rigg, J. A. (2005). *Labour market disadvantage amongst disabled people: A longitudinal perspective.* London: London School of Economics, Centre for Analysis of Social Exclusion, CASE Papers.

Bibliography

Rimmerman, A. (2013). *Social inclusion of people with disabilities: National and international perspectives.* Cambridge, England: Cambridge University Press.

Rimmerman, A., & Herr, S. S. (2004). The power of the powerless: A study on the Israeli disability strike of 1999. *Journal of Disability Policy Studies* 15(1), 12–18.

Rizzo, D. C. (2002). With a little help from my friends: Supported self-employment for people with severe disabilities. *Journal of Vocational Rehabilitation* 17(2), 97–105.

Robert, P. M., & Harlan, S. L. (2006). Mechanisms of disability discrimination in large bureaucratic organizations: Ascriptive inequalities in the workplace. *Sociological Quarterly* 47(4), 599–630.

Rodriguez-Galan, M., & Falcón, L. M. (2009). Perceived problems with access to medical care and depression among older Puerto Ricans, dominicans, other Hispanics, and a comparison group of non-Hispanic whites. *Journal of Aging & Health* 21(3), 501–518.

Rubin, R. M., & White-Means, S. (2001). Race, disability and assistive devices: Sociodemographics or discrimination. *International Journal of Social Economics* 28(10–11), 927–941.

Saha, S., Freeman, M., Toure, J., Tippens, K. M., Weeks, C., & Ibrahim, S. (2008). Racial and ethnic disparities in the VA health care system: A systematic review. *Journal of General Internal Medicine* 23(5), 654–671.

Salzer, M., Kaplan, K., & Atay, J. (2006). State psychiatric hospital census after the 1999 Olmstead decision: Evidence of decelerating deinstitutionalization. *Psychiatric Services* 57(10), 1501–1504.

Sandler, L. A., & Blanck, P. (2005). The quest to make accessibility a corporate article of faith at Microsoft: Case study of corporate culture and human resource dimensions. *Behavioral Sciences & the Law* 23(1), 39–64.

Saunders, P. (2007). The costs of disability and the incidence of poverty. *Australian Journal of Social Issues* 42(4), 461–480.

Schartz, H., Hendricks, D. J., & Blanck, P. (2006). Workplace accommodations: Evidence based outcomes. *Work* 27, 345–354.

Schartz, H. A., Schartz, K. M., Hendricks, D., & Blanck, P. (2005). Workplace accommodations: Empirical study of current employees. *Mississippi Law Journal* 75, 917.

Scherbaum, C. A., Scherbaum, K. L., & Popovich, P. M. (2005). Predicting job-related expectancies and affective reactions to employees with disabilities from previous work experience. *Journal of Applied Social Psychology* 35(5), 889–904.

Bibliography

Schiek, D., & Lawson, A. (Eds.) (2011). *European Union non-discrimination law and intersectionality: Investigating the triangle of racial, gender and disability discrimination.* Burlington, VT: Ashgate.

Schneider, A., & Ingram, H. (1993). Social construction of target populations: Implications for politics and policy. *American Political Science Review* 87(2), 334–347.

Schoeni, R. F., Freedman, V. A., & Martin, L. G. (2008). Why is late-life disability declining? *Milbank Quarterly* 86(1), 47–89.

Schriner, K., Ochs, L. A., & Shields, T. G. (1997). The last suffrage movement: Voting rights for persons with cognitive and emotional disabilities. *Publius: The Journal of Federalism* 27(3), 75–96.

Schulze, M. (2010). *Understanding the UN Convention on the Rights of Persons with Disabilities.* New York: Handicap International.

Schur, L. (1998). Disability and the psychology of political participation. *Journal of Disability Policy Studies* 9(2), 3.

   (2002a). Dead-end jobs or a path to economic well-being? The consequences of non-standard work for people with disabilities. *Behavioral Sciences & the Law* 20, 601–620.

   (2002b). The difference a job makes: The effects of employment among people with disabilities. *Journal of Economic Issues* 36(2), 339–347.

   (2003a). Contending with the "double handicap": Political activism among women with disabilities. *Women and Politics* 25(1/2), 31–62.

   (2003b). Barriers or opportunities? The causes of contingent and part-time work among people with disabilities. *Industrial Relations* 42(4), 589–622.

   (2003c). Employment and the creation of an active citizenry. *British Journal of Industrial Relations* 41(4), 751–771.

   (2004). Is there still a "double handicap"? Economic, social and political disparities experienced by women with disabilities. In B. Smith & B. Hutchison (Eds.), *Gendering disability* (pp. 253–271). New Brunswick, NJ: Rutgers University Press.

Schur, L., & Adya, M. (2012). Sidelined or mainstreamed? Political participation and attitudes of people with disabilities in the United States. *Social Science Quarterly*, published on-line July 2012 (http://onlinelibrary.wiley.com/doi/10.1111/j.1540-6237.2012.00885.x/abstract), access January 20, 2013.

Schur, L., Kim, A., Han, K., Kruse, D., Adya, M., & Blanck, P. (2011). *Disability at work: Job characteristics, preferences, and attitudes of people with disabilities.* New Brunswick, NJ: Rutgers University, School of Management and Labor Relations.

Bibliography

Schur, L. A., & Kruse, D. L. (2000). What determines voter turnout? Lessons from citizens with disabilities. *Social Science Quarterly* 81(2), 571–587.

Schur, L., & Kruse, D. (2012). Disabiity and Election Policies and Practices. Paper presented at Measures of Elections conference, M.I.T., Cambridge, MA, June 2012.

Schur, L., Kruse, D., & Blanck, P. (2005). Corporate culture and the employment of persons with disabilities. *Behavioral Sciences & the Law* 23(1), 3–20.

Schur, L., Kruse, D., Blasi, J., & Blanck, P. (2009). Is disability disabling in all workplaces? Workplace disparities and corporate culture. *Industrial Relations* 48(3), 381–410.

Schur, L., Nishi, L., Adya, M., Kruse, D., Bruyere, S., & Blanck, P. (2013). Accommodating workers with and without disabilities. *Human Resource Management*, forthcoming 2013.

Schur, L., Shields, T., Kruse, D., & Schriner, K. (2002). Enabling democracy: Disability and voter turnout. *Political Research Quarterly* 55(1), 167–190.

Schur, L., Shields, T., & Schriner, K. (2003). Can I make a difference? Efficacy, employment, and disability. *Political Psychology* 24(1), 119–149.

(2005). Generational cohorts, group membership, and political participation by people with disabilities. *Political Research Quarterly* 58(3), 487–496.

Scior, K. (2011). Public awareness, attitudes and beliefs regarding intellectual disability: A systematic review. *Research in Developmental Disabilities* 32(6), 2164–2182.

Scotch, R. K. (1988). Disability as the basis for a social movement: Advocacy and the politics of definition. *Journal of Social Issues* 44(1), 159–172.

(2001). *From good will to civil rights: Transforming federal disability policy* Philadelphia: Temple University Press.

Scotch, R. K., & Schriner, K. (1997). Disability as human variation: Implications for policy. *Annals of the American Academy of Political and Social Science* 549(1), 148–159.

Scott, R., and Crooks, A. (2005). *Polls apart 4: Campaigning for accessible democracy*. London: Scope.

Shah, S., & Priestley, M. (2011). *Disability and social change: Private lives and public policies*. Bristol, UK: Policy Press.

Shakespeare, T. (1993). Disabled people's self-organization. *Disability and Society* 8, 249–264.

(2006). *Disability rights and wrongs*. New York: Taylor & Francis.

Shapiro, J. (1993). *No pity: People with disabilities forging a new civil rights movement*. New York: Three Rivers Press.

273

Bibliography

Sharma, U., & Deppeler, J. (2005). Integrated education in India: Challenges and prospects. *Disability Studies Quarterly* : 25(1) (dsq-sds.org/article/view/524/701), accessed January 20, 2013.

She, P., & Livermore, G. A. (2007). Material hardship, poverty, and disability among working-age adults. *Social Science Quarterly* 88(4), 970–989.

(2009). Long-term poverty and disability among working-age adults. *Journal of Disability Policy Studies* 19(4), 244–256.

Shepard, T., Clifton, E., & Kruse, D. (1996). Flexible work hours and productivity: Some evidence from the pharmaceutical industry. *Industrial Relations: A Journal of Economy and Society* 35(1), 123–139.

Shields, T. G., Schriner, K. F., & Schriner, K. (1998). The disability voice in American politics. *Journal of Disability Policy Studies* 9(2), 33.

Shields, T. G., Schriner, K., Schriner, K., & Ochs, L. (2000). Disenfranchised: People with disabilities in American electoral politics. In B. Altman & S. Barnartt (Eds.), *Expanding the scope of social science research on disability* (pp. 177–203). Bingley, UK: Emerald Group Publishing.

Shier, M., Graham, J. R., & Jones, M. E. (2009). Barriers to employment as experienced by disabled people: A qualitative analysis in Calgary and Regina, Canada. *Disability & Society* 24(1), 63–75.

Shifrer, D., Muller, C., & Callahan, R. (2011). Disproportionality and learning disabilities: Parsing apart race, socioeconomic status, and language. *Journal of Learning Disabilities* 44(3), 246–257.

Skiba, R. J., Simmons, A. B., Ritter, S., Gibb, A. C., Rausch, M. K., Cuadrado, J., et al. (2008). Achieving equity in special education: History, status, and current challenges. *Exceptional Children* 74(3), 264–288.

Skiba, R., Simmons, A., Ritter, S., Kohler, K., Henderson, M., & Wu, T. (2006). The context of minority disproportionality: Practitioner perspectives on special education referral. *Teachers College Record* 108(7), 1424–1459.

Snyder, L. A., Carmichael, J. S., Blackwell, L. V., Cleveland, J. N., & Thornton, G. C., III. (2010). Perceptions of discrimination and justice among employees with disabilities. *Employee Responsibilities and Rights Journal* 22(1), 5–19.

Soffer, M., Tal-Katz, P., & Rimmerman, A. (2011). Sub minimum wage for persons with severe disabilities: Comparative perspectives. *Journal of Comparative Policy Analysis: Research and Practice* 13(3), 265–286.

Solovieva, T., Dowler, D., & Walls, R. (2011). Employer benefits from making workplace accommodations. *Disability and Health Journal* 4(1), 39–45.

South–North Dialogue. (2006). *Global survey on government action on the implementation of the standard rules on the equalization of opportunities for persons with disabilities.* Amman: South-North Center for Dialogue and Development.

Bibliography

Spithoven, A. H. G. M. (2001). Lean production and disability. *International Journal of Social Economics* 28(9), 725–741.

Stapleton, D. C., Goodman, N., & Houtenville, A. J. (2003). Have changes in the nature of work or the labor market reduced employment prospects of workers with disabilities? In D. C. Stapleton & R. V. Burkhauser (Eds.), *The decline in employment of people with disabilities: A policy puzzle* (pp. 125–179). Kalamazoo, MI: W. E. Upjohn Institute for Employment Research.

Stapleton, D., Protik, A., & Stone, C. (2008). *Review of international evidence on the cost of disability.* Washington, DC: Mathematica Policy Research, Department for Work and Pensions.

Stapleton, D., Wittenburg, D., & Maag, E. (2005). *A difficult cycle: The effect of labor market changes on the employment and program participation of people with disabilities.* Washington, DC: Mathematica Policy Research.

Stapleton, D. C., Wittenburg, D. C., & Thornton, C. (2009). Counting working-age people with disabilities: Program participants. In A. J. Houtenville, D. C. Stapleton, R. R. Weathers II, & R. V. Burkhauser (Eds.), *Counting working-age people with disabilities: What current data tell us and options for improvement* (pp. 299–351). Kalamazoo, MI: W. E. Upjohn Institute for Employment Research.

Stefanescu, R., Dumitriu, R., & Nistor, C. (2012). Policies to encourage the employment of people with disabilities: Case of Romania. Available at SSRN: http://ssrn.com/abstract=2043703 or http://dx.doi.org/10.2139/ssrn.2043703.

Stock, W. A., & Beegle, K. (2004). Employment protections for older workers: Do disability discrimination laws matter? *Contemporary Economic Policy* 22(1), 111–126.

Stoddard, S., Jans, L., Ripple, J., & Kraus, L. (1998). *Chartbook on work and disability in the United States, 1998.* Berkeley, CA: InfoUse and National Institute on Disability and Rehabilitation Research.

Stoker, L., & Jennings, M. K. (1995). Life-cycle transitions and political participation: The case of marriage. *American Political Science Review 89(2),* 421–433.

Stone, D. L., & Colella, A. (1996). A model of factors affecting the treatment of disabled individuals in organizations. *Academy of Management Review* 21(2), 352–401.

Story, M., Mueller, J., & Mace, R. (1998). *The universal design file: Designing for people of all ages and abilities. Raeligh:* North Carolina State University, Center for Universal Design.

Stuart, O. (1992a). Race and disability: Just a double oppression? *Disability, Handicap and Society* 7(2), 177–188.

Bibliography

(1992b). Race and disability: What type of double disadvantage? *Disability, Handicap and Society* 8(3), 249–264.

Sturm, R., Ringel, J. S., & Andreyeva, T. (2004). Increasing obesity rates and disability trends. *Health Affairs* 23(2), 199–205.

Subbarao, K., & Raney, L. (1995). Social gains from female education: A cross-national study. *Economic Development and Cultural Change* 44(1), 105–128.

Tahmincioglu, E. (2003). By telecommuting, the disabled get a key to the office, and a job. *New York Times,* July 20.

Thompson, D., Fisher, K., Purcal, C., Deeming, C., & Sawrikar, P. (2011). *Community attitudes to people with disability: Scoping project.* Paper No. 39. Kensington: University of New South Wales, Disability Studies and Research Centre.

Tincani, M., Travers, J., & Boutot, A. (2009). Race, culture, and autism spectrum disorder: Understanding the role of diversity in successful educational interventions. *Research & Practice for Persons with Severe Disabilities* 34(3), 81–90.

Todorov, A., & Kirchner, C. (2000). Bias in proxies' reports of disability: Data from the national health interview survey on disability. *American Journal of Public Health* 90(8), 1248–1253.

Tokaji, D. P., & Colker, R. (2007). Absentee voting by people with disabilities: Promoting access and integrity. *McGeorge Law Review* 38, 1015.

Townsley, R. (2009). *The implementation of policies supporting independent living for disabled people in Europe: Synthesis report.* Leeds: University of Leeds, Centre for Disability Studies, Academic Network of European Disability Experts.

Trani, J. F., & Loeb, M. (2012). Poverty and disability: A vicious circle? Evidence from Afghanistan and Zambia. Journal of International Development, 24(S1): S19–S52.

Trent, J. (2006). Freak show. In G. Albrecht, J. Bickenbach, D. Mitchell, W. Schalick & S. Snyder (Eds.), *The encyclopedia of disability* (pp. 741–743). Thousand Oaks, CA: Sage.

Tucker, Foster K. (2009). Achieving progress towards reasonable accommodation on Article 29 of the United Nations Convention on the Rights of Persons with Disabilities. www.article29.org/english.htm (accessed August 28, 2012).

Twamley, E. W., Jeste, D. V., & Lehman, A. F. (2003). Vocational rehabilitation in schizophrenia and other psychotic disorders: A literature review and meta-analysis of randomized controlled trials. *Journal of Nervous and Mental Disease* 191(8), 515.

U.S. Commission on Civil Rights. (1983). *Accommodating the spectrum of individual abilities.* Washington, DC: Clearinghouse.

Bibliography

U.S. Department of Commerce (2011). *Exploring the digital nation: Computer and Internet use at home.* Washington, DC: U.S. Department of Commerce.

Uppal, S. (2005). Disability, workplace characteristics and job satisfaction. *International Journal of Manpower* 26(4), 336–349.

Van Brakel, W. H. (2006). Measuring health-related stigma: A literature review. *Psychology, Health & Medicine* 11(3), 307–334.

van Soest, A., Andreyeva, T., Kapteyn, A., & Smith, J. P. (2011). *Self reported disability and reference groups.* Paper No. 17153. Cambridge, MA: National Bureau of Economic Research Working Papers.

Vaughn, C. E. (2009). *People-first language: An unholy crusade.* nfb.org/images/nfb/ publications/bm/bn09/bm0903/bm090309.htm. (accessed May 30, 2012).

Verba, S., Schlozman, K. L., & Brady, H. E. (1995). *Voice and equality: Civic voluntarism in American politics.* Cambridge, MA: Harvard University Press.

Vicente, M. R., & López, A. J. (2010). A multidimensional analysis of the disability digital divide: Some evidence for Internet use. *Information Society* 26(1), 48–64.

Vos, T., Barker, B., Begg, S., Stanley, L., & Lopez, A. D. (2009). Burden of disease and injury in aboriginal and torres strait islander peoples: The indigenous health gap. *International Journal of Epidemiology* 38(2), 470–477.

Ward, A., Baker, P. M. A., & Moon, N. W. (2009). Ensuring the enfranchisement of people with disabilities. *Journal of Disability Policy Studies* 20(2), 79–92.

Warner, D. F., & Brown, T. H. (2011). Understanding how race/ethnicity and gender define age-trajectories of disability: An intersectionality approach. *Social Science & Medicine* 72(8), 1236–1248.

Wehbi, S., & El-Lahib, Y. (2008). Sit (or stand) and be counted! Campaigning for the voting rights of people with disabilities in Lebanon. *Disability Studies Quarterly* 28(2) (dsq-sds.org/article/view/98/98), accessed January 20, 2013.

Wehbi, S., & Lakkis, S. (2010). Women with disabilities in Lebanon: From marginalization to resistance. *Affilia* 25(1), 56–67.

Westerholm, R., Radak, L., Keys, C., & Henry, D. (2006a). Stigma. In G. Albrecht, J. Bickenbach, D. Mitchell, W. Schalick, & S. Snyder (Eds.), *Encyclopedia of disability* (pp. 1502–1507). Thousand Oaks, CA: Sage.

   (2006b). Stigma, international. In G. Albrecht, J. Bickenbach, D. Mitchell, W. Schalick, & S. Snyder (Eds.), *Encyclopedia of disability* (pp. 1507–1510). Thousand Oaks, CA: Sage.

WHO/World Bank (2011). *World report on disability.* Geneva: World Health Organization and World Bank.

Whitson, H. E., Hastings, S. N., Landerman, L. R., Fillenbaum, G. G., Cohen, H. J., & Johnson, K. S. (2011). Black-white disparity in disability: The role of medical conditions. *Journal of the American Geriatrics Society* 59(5), 844–850.

Wilgosh, L. R., & Skaret, D. (1987). Employer attitudes toward hiring individuals with disabilities: A review of the recent literature. *Canadian Journal of Rehabilitation* 1(2), 89–98.

Wilkinson-Meyers, L., Brown, P., McNeill, R., Patston, P., Dylan, S., & Baker, R. (2010). Estimating the additional cost of disability: Beyond budget standards. *Social Science & Medicine* 71(10), 1882–1889.

Wilson, D. J. (2009). Ed Roberts. In S. Burch (Ed.), *Encyclopedia of American disability history* (pp. 782–784). New York: Facts on File, Inc.

Wise, D. A. (Ed.) (Forthcoming). *Social security and retirement around the world: Historical trends in mortality and health, employment, and disability insurance participation and reforms.* Chicago: University of Chicago Press.

Wood, R. G., Avellar, S., & Goesling, B. (2007). *The effects of marriage on health: A synthesis of recent research evidence.* Princeton, NJ: Mathematica Policy Research.

Work Incentives Support Center. (2004). *Self-employment and the benefits planning process.* Paper No. 17. Ithaca, NY: Cornell University, Employment and Disability Institute.

Yelin, E. H., & Trupin, L. (2003). Disability and the characteristics of employment. *Monthly Labor Review* 126(5), 20–31.

Young, J. (2012). Disability and politics. In D. Coates (Ed.), *The Oxford companion to American politics* (pp. 269–280). Oxford: Oxford University Press.

Yuker, H. (Ed.) (1988). *Attitudes toward persons with disabilities.* New York: Springer.

Yuker, H. E. (1994). Variables that influence attitudes toward people with disabilities: Conclusions from the data. *Journal of Social Behavior & Personality* 9(5), 3–22.

Zaidi, A., & Burchardt, T. (2005). Comparing incomes when needs differ: Equalization for the extra costs of disability in the U.K. *Review of Income and Wealth* 51(1), 89–114.

Zola, I. K. (1989). Toward the necessary universalizing of a disability policy. *Milbank Quarterly* 67(2), 401–428.

 (1993). Self, identity and the naming question: Reflections on the language of disability. *Social Science & Medicine* 36(2), 167–173.

Zwerling, C., Whitten, P. S., Sprince, N. L., Davis, C. S., Wallace, R. B., & Heeringa, S. G. (2003). Workplace accommodations for people with disabilities: National health interview survey disability supplement, 1994–1995. *Journal of Occupational and Environmental Medicine* 45(5), 517.

Index

Index

Index

Index

Index

Index

Index

Index

Index

Index